CW01081717

800 Great Places to Stay

in Britain

The Best of British Holidays

Full range of family accommodation

Pubs & Inns

Wi-Fi Directory

2012

On the Coastal Path at Polperro, Cornwall, see Cutkive Wood Holiday Lodges, page 219

The Long Cross Hotel & Victorian Gardens, Port Isaac, Cornwall, page 16

www.holidayguides.com

Contents

England

Board

Self-Catering

Wales

Scotland

Ireland

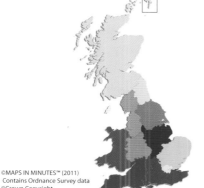

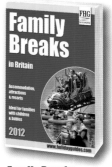
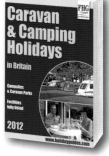

Boscastle, Bude

Cornwall

The Old Coach House

Relax in a 300 year old former coach house now tastefully equipped to meet the needs of the new millennium with all rooms en suite, colour TVs, refreshment trays and central heating. Good cooking. This picturesque village is a haven for walkers with its dramatic coastal scenery, a photographer's dream, and an ideal base to tour both the north and south coasts.

The area is famed for its sandy beaches and surfing whilst King Arthur's Tintagel is only three miles away.
Come and enjoy a friendly holiday with people who care. Large garden and patio area.
- *Bed and Breakfast from £35-£39pp*
- *Non-smoking*
- *Accessible for disabled guests.*

SB

Wi-Fi

**Geoff and Jackie Horwell, The Old Coach House,
Tintagel Road, Boscastle PL35 0AS
Tel: 01840 250398 • Fax: 01840 250346
e-mail: stay@old-coach.co.uk • www.old-coach.co.uk**

Highbre Crest, Whitstone, Holsworthy,
Near Bude EX22 6UF • www.highbrecrest.co.uk
email: lindacole285@btinternet.com

SB

Stunning views to coasts and moors make this very spacious house a special destination for your holiday. With the added bonus of peace, tranquillity and delicious breakfasts, how can you resist paying us a visit? We are well situated for the coast and moors in Devon and Cornwall, including The Eden Project. Two double and one twin room - all en suite. Lounge with full size snooker table, dining room and comfortable large conservatory with spectacular coastal views. Garden for guests' use. Car parking space. Non-smoking establishment. Children over 12 welcome. Bed and Breakfast from £32. Open all year.

Mrs Cole • 01288 341002

Bude

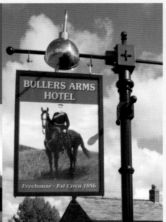

Falmouth

SB

Wi-Fi

The Westcott

Falmouth has always been a stylish resort.
At The Westcott we maintain the tradition of comfort
and service, with the added warm, friendly welcome
you can only find at a family-run Guesthouse.
There are 9 guest bedrooms at the Westcott. Five
doubles, two twins, one single, and one which can be
changed from a 6ft super kingsize to a twin as required.

All of the rooms have an en-suite bathroom with either a shower
cubicle or a bath. In addition for those with a shower only
there is a separate bathroom.
Our nearest beach is only 2 minutes' walk away and there are
so many other activities and visits you can enjoy on our
doorstep. We are proud of the 4 star grading we have
achieved through hard work by all the family. As we like to say,
you will arrive as a guest but leave as a friend.

Gyllyngvase Hill, Falmouth, Cornwall TR11 4DN
westcotthotel@btinternet.com
www.westcotthotelfalmouth.co.uk
Mark & Sally Humphreys • Tel: 01326 311309

Heritage House

1 Clifton Terrace, Falmouth TR11 3QG
Tel: 01326 317834 • 07938 715195
e-mail: heritagehouse@tinyonline.co.uk • www.heritagehousefalmouth.co.uk

A relaxed, friendly, homely atmosphere awaits at our comfortable, family-run guest
house, centrally located for town, beaches and the University. We offer elegant en suite
and standard room accommodation, all bedrooms having been recently refurbished; TV,
hairdryer, free tea, coffee and bicuits, filtered water and complimentary toiletries.
We also offer free wifi internet access for those who wish to bring a laptop.

Bed and Full English/
vegetarian/special diet breakfast
from £29pppn.
Reduced rates for longer stays

• Accommodation includes single, twin, double
and family bedrooms.

• On-street parking available with no restrictions.

• Open all year (except Christmas)

• Resident Proprietor: Lynn Grimes

• Recommended on ⊙⊙ tripadvisor.co.uk

Fowey

Mawgan Porth

SB
Wi-Fi

Blue Bay
HOTEL, RESTAURANT & LODGES

**Trenance, Mawgan Porth,
Cornwall TR8 4DA
Tel: 01637 860324
e-mail: hotel@bluebaycornwall.co.uk
www.bluebaycornwall.co.uk**

Blue Bay offers two different styles of accommodation across two different sites, beautifully situated in a tranquil location between Padstow and Newquay, overlooking Mawgan Porth beach.

Blue Bay Lodges
Five individually designed Cornish lodges, open all year round. The lodges are located in the heart of Mawgan Porth, overlooking the Vale of Lanherne and beach. All fully equipped (sleep 4-8) with own balcony or patio area. Linen, towels, electricity incl. Laundry room. Dogs welcome.

Blue Bay Hotel
Located in Trenance on the cliff tops overlooking Mawgan Porth beach, the hotel has two garden rooms, two family suites, one family room and one double room, all en suite. Twin and single rooms available.

**Hotel prices
from £38pppn
Lodge prices from
£50 per Lodge per night.**

Newquay

Polperro, Port Isaac

St Mawes

Wi-Fi

Renowned for its wonderful coastline, the longest in the UK, Cornwall has everything to
offer for lovers of watersports, whether sailing, surfing, windsurfing, water-skiing, scuba
diving or simply enjoying a family holiday on the beach. In busy fishing towns like Looe
and Padstow, and traditional villages such as Polperro, there are plenty of inns and
restaurants where you can sample the fresh catch. The best-known centre for the arts is St
Ives, with the Tate St Ives, and artists and galleries are also to be found in Fowey, St Agnes
and Penzance. In summer, when the seaside towns are at their busiest, visit the Rame
Peninsula in the south east of the county for a quieter break, or take a trip to the Isles of
Scilly for a traditional and relaxing stay. Exotic gardens are a major attraction, whether long-
established, like Trebah, Mount Edgcumbe and the Lost Gardens of Heligan, or the modern
biomes of the Eden Project. The magnificent coast is ideal for birdwatchers, artists and
photographers, golfers of every standard will find a wide choice of courses, while on
Bodmin Moor, one of Cornwall's 12 Areas of Outstanding Natural Beauty, there is abundant
evidence of a prehistoric past.

The FHG Directory of Website Addresses
on pages 531-541 is a useful quick reference guide for
holiday accommodation with e-mail and/or website details

Dalswinton House

St. Mawgan-in-Pydar, Cornwall TR8 4EZ. Tel: 01637 860385
www.dalswinton.com • dalswintonhouse@btconnect.com

HOLIDAYS FOR DOGS AND THEIR OWNERS

Overlooking the village of St Mawgan, Dalswinton House stands in 10 acres of gardens and meadowland midway between Padstow and Newquay with distant views to the sea at dog-friendly Mawgan Porth.

- Dogs free of charge and allowed everywhere except the restaurant
- 8 acre meadow for dog exercise. Nearby local walks. Beach 1.5 miles
- Heated outdoor pool (May-Sep). Off street car parking
- All rooms en suite with tea/coffee fac., digital TV and clock radios
- Wifi access in public rooms and all bedrooms (except the lodge)
- Residents' bar and restaurant serving breakfast and dinner
- Bed and breakfast from £46 per person per night
- Weekly rates available and special offers in Mar/Apr/May/Oct
- Self-catering lodge sleeps 3 adults
- Easy access to Padstow, Eden Project, Newquay Airport & Coastal Path

Regret no children under 16
Maximum 3 dogs per room at proprietor's discretion

Bampton

Devon

Think of Devon, and wild moorland springs to mind, but this is a county of contrasts, with the wild moors of the Exmoor National Park to the north fringed by dramatic cliffs and combes, golden beaches and picturesque harbours, and busy market towns and sleepy villages near the coast. The award-winning resort of Woolacombe has everything to offer for a traditional family holiday, while Ilfracombe, originally a Victorian resort, provides all kinds of family entertainment including an annual Victorian festival. An experience not to be missed is the cliff railway between the pretty little port of Lynmouth and its twin village of Lynton high on the cliff, with a backdrop of dramatic gorges or combes.

Axminster

SB
Wi-Fi

Fairwater Head Hotel
3 Star Accommodation at Sensible Prices

 ★★★ *77%*

Located in the tranquil Devon countryside and close to
Lyme Regis, this beautiful Edwardian Country House Hotel
has all you need for a peaceful and relaxing holiday.

Dogs Most Welcome and Free of Charge
Countryside location with panoramic views • AA Rosette Restaurant

The Fairwater Head Hotel
Hawkchurch, Near Axminster, Devon EX13 5TX
Tel: 01297 678349 • Fax: 01297 678459
e-mail: stay@fairwaterheadhotel.co.uk
www.fairwaterheadhotel.co.uk

SB

SB

Lower Yelland Farm Guest House

Situated half way between Barnstaple and Bideford, this delightfully modernised 17thC farmhouse accommodation is part of a working farm. The farm is centrally located for easy access to the many attractions of North Devon, its beautiful beaches, varied walks and sports facilities including golf, surfing, fishing, riding etc. Its proximity to both Exmoor and Dartmoor makes this location perfect for those who wish to explore. Instow with its sandy beach, pubs and restaurants is a just mile away. It lies adjacent to the Tarka Trail, part of the South West Coastal Footpath, and RSPB bird sanctuary.

enjoyEngland.com
★★★★
FARMHOUSE

The bed and breakfast accommodation comprises 2 twin/super king-size and one room with four-poster bed, 2 double rooms and 2 single rooms; all rooms en suite, with TV and tea/coffee making facilities. Breakfast includes eggs from our free-range chickens, home-made bread, jams and marmalade. The delightful sitting room has a large selection of books for those who want to relax and browse.

Winner Golden Achievement Award of Excellence for Devon Retreat of the Year

Please visit our website for further details
www.loweryellandfarm.co.uk

**Lower Yelland Farm Guest House, Fremington, Barnstaple EX31 3EN
Tel: 01271 860101 • e-mail: peterday@loweryellandfarm.co.uk**

West Titchberry Farm

Situated on the rugged North Devon coast, West Titchberry is a traditionally run working stock farm, half a mile from Hartland Point.

The South West Coastal Path crosses the farm making it an ideal base for walkers. Pick ups and kit transfers available. Long term parking on site

Tel & Fax: 01237 441287

The three guest rooms comprise an en suite family room; one double and one twin room, with wash basins. Bathroom/toilet and separate shower room on the same floor, plus a downstairs toilet. All bedrooms have colour TV, radio, hairdryer, tea/coffee making facilities. Outside, guests may take advantage of a sheltered walled garden. Sorry, no pets.
Hartland village is 3 miles away, Clovelly 6 miles, Bideford and Westward Ho! 16 miles and Bude 18 miles.
- *B&B from £25–£30pppn (based on 2 sharing)*
- *3 Course Evening meal £15*
- *Children welcome at reduced rates for under 11s*
- *Open all year except Christmas*

Mrs Yvonne Heard, West Titchberry Farm, Hartland Point, Near Bideford EX39 6AU

Bideford

SB

Wi-Fi

Riversford Hotel
and Riverview Restaurant

Limers Lane, Bideford, Devon EX39 2RG

The Riversford is a beautifully located hotel overlooking the River Torridge in peaceful North Devon. Enjoying fabulous, seasonal views all year round, the hotel offers warmth and friendliness to guests.

Bideford is only a five minute drive away and The Riversford is ideally located for many attractions including Westward Ho!, Appledore, shopping centres, Arlington Court and Rosemoor Gardens.

There are fifteen en suite rooms, most overlooking the river. Four-poster rooms and suites are also available.

Beautiful, well maintained gardens are to the front, with a patio area for morning coffees, Devonshire cream teas and lunches.

The Riverview Restaurant (open to non-residents) opens every lunchtime and evening.

We have an extensive à la carte menu and specialise in local seafood dishes; all food is cooked to order. Cosy bar. Private car park at rear.

Tel: 01237 474239

e-mail: Riversford@aol.com • www.Riversford.co.uk

Lake House Cottages and B&B

Lake Villa, Bradworthy, Devon EX22 7SQ
Brochure: Peter & Lesley Lewin on 01409 241962
e-mail: lesley@lakevilla.co.uk • www.lakevilla.co.uk

SB

Wi-Fi

Peter and Lesley extend a warm welcome to B&B guests in their period home, with two extremely well appointed en suite bedrooms, a double and a twin. The rooms have tea/coffee making facilities and TV/DVD and share a sunny balcony overlooking the gardens.

Situated on a private landing they are ideal for a family or friends holidaying together. Outside there are one acre of gardens, tennis, a six acre meadow, two lakes and coarse fishing.

Breakfasts (incl. vegetarian) use locally sourced quality ingredients. Packed lunches available upon request and dogs are welcome by arrangement.

SELF-CATERING COTTAGES ALSO AVAILABLE

Hayne Farm

Cheriton Fitzpaine Crediton EX17 4HR

Occupied by members of the same family since the 17th century, Hayne Farm is sited in a quiet lane with its own extensive gardens, summer house, small wood and duck pond. It is the ideal setting for a relaxing break or holiday.

Many charming features include an oak beamed fireplace, and lounge with easy chairs and television. Three bedrooms, two with double beds and a third en suite family room. All have tea and coffee making facilities. Children are welcome and cot, high chair and baby sitting can be provided. No smoking or pets.

There are many places to see in the area including National Trust houses and gardens. Exmoor and Dartmoor are within easy driving time as are the north and south Devon coasts. The cathedral city of Exeter is a 30 minute drive away and provides shopping and entertainment.

Full cooked breakfasts are provided for guests, and local pubs are within easy reach for evening meals. Packed lunches are available on request.

Bed & Breakfast from £28.00, reductions for children.

Mrs M Reed • Tel: 01363 866392

Dartmoor

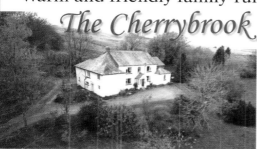

Dartmouth, Dawlish

In the centre of the county lies Dartmoor, with its vast open spaces, granite tors and spectacular moorland, rich in wildlife and ideal for walking, pony trekking and cycling. The Channel coast to the south, with its gentle climate and scenery, is an attractive destination at any time of year. The long stretches of beautiful sandy beaches, pebble and shingle are intersected by river estuaries which provide shelter for migrating birds and other wildlife, and there are fascinating towns full of history to visit.

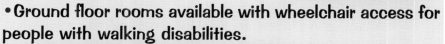

Standing in four acres of mature subtropical gardens, overlooking two miles of sandy beach, yet within easy reach of Dartmoor and Exeter, Devoncourt provides an ideal base for a family holiday.

BEDROOMS: The accommodation is in 54 single, double or family rooms, all with private bathroom, colour TV, tea and coffee making facilities and telephone.

LEISURE: Swimming pool, sauna, steam room, whirlpool spa, solarium and fitness centre, snooker room, hair and beauty salon. For those who prefer to be out of doors there is a tennis court, croquet lawn, attractive outdoor heated pool, 18 hole putting green and golf practice area, all within the grounds. Wi-Fi throughout.

DINING: Brasserie 16 operate the attractive lounge bar and restaurant overlooking the fabulous gardens, with fantastic sea views from the large picture windows. Children's menus and vegetarian options available.

DEVONCOURT HOTEL
Douglas Avenue, Exmouth,
Devon EX8 2EX
Tel: 01395 272277
Fax: 01395 269315
e-mail: enquiries@devoncourt.com
www.devoncourthotel.com

SB

A most attractively situated working farm. The house is a very old traditional Devon farmhouse located just three miles east of Honiton and enjoying a superb outlook across the Otter Valley. Enjoy a stroll down by the River Otter which runs through the farmland. Try a spot of trout fishing. Children will love to make friends with Peter the horse. Lovely seaside resorts 12 miles, swimming pool, adventure parks and garden nearby. Traditional English breakfast, colour TV, washbasin, heating, tea/coffee facilities in all rooms.

Bed and Breakfast from £25 • Reductions for children.

Mrs June Tucker, Yard Farm, Upottery, Honiton EX14 9QP • • 01404 861680

The Foxhunters Inn

West Down, Near Ilfracombe EX34 8NU

- *300 year-old coaching Inn conveniently situated for beaches and country walks.*
- *Serving good local food.*
- *En suite accommodation.*
- *Pets allowed in bar areas and beer garden, may stay in accommodation by prior arrangement.*

Water bowls provided.

Tel: 01271 863757 • Fax: 01271 879313
www.foxhuntersinn.co.uk

Pittaford Farm Bed & Breakfast

Pittaford is a beautiful Devonshire 17th century farmhouse set in peaceful countryside on a family farm 1½ miles from the pretty village of Slapton, 2 miles from the coast and beaches. Guests have their own cosy sitting room with TV, DVD, books and games, and log fire for chilly evenings.

Wi-Fi One double and one twin en suite bedrooms with tea/coffee making facilities, hairdryer and TV; views over the garden to the fields and meadows.

Child's bed and cot available. Pets by prior arrangement.
£32 - £38 per person per night including breakfast.

Pittaford Farm B&B • Slapton • Kingsbridge • Devon TQ7 2QG • Tel: 01548 580357
Mob 07585 375069 • e-mail: pittafordbandb@live.co.uk • www.pittafordbandb.co.uk

Lifton, Lynton/Lynmouth

The North Cliff Hotel, standing in its own grounds, has some of the finest views of the North Devon coastline. It is in a peaceful position some 500 feet above sea level overlooking Lynmouth Bay, and a 200 metre walk to Lynton. With car parking facilities on the forecourt, the hotel is an ideal base for exploring the coastline and Exmoor National Park, whether it is your annual holiday or off-season break.

The rooms boast some of the best sea views in Lynton; bedrooms are individually decorated and are en suite. All bedrooms have colour television and facilities for making your favourite beverage.

We can accommodate family gatherings or walking parties as there are 7 doubles, 2 twins, 1 single and 4 family rooms (which can be used as twins or doubles).

We have a licensed bar available for a drink after a hard day of walking or an aperitif before dinner in our restaurant, which has magnificent sea and coastal views.

Children of all ages and pets are very welcome.

Local activities include walking, riding, tennis, and putting. The famous water-powered Cliff Railway linking Lynton and Lynmouth passes within a few feet of the hotel and is accessed via the stepped garden.

SB

Wi-Fi

North Cliff Hotel

North Walk, Lynton, North Devon EX35 6HJ

Tel: 01598 752357
e-mail: holidays@northcliffhotel.co.uk
www.northcliffhotel.co.uk

Blue Ball Inn
formerly The Exmoor Sandpiper Inn

is a romantic Coaching Inn dating in part back to the 13th century, with low ceilings, blackened beams, stone fireplaces and a timeless atmosphere of unspoilt old world charm. Offering visitors great food and drink, a warm welcome and a high standard of accommodation.

The inn is set in an imposing position on a hilltop on Exmoor in North Devon, a few hundred yards from the sea, and high above the twin villages of Lynmouth and Lynton, in an area of oustanding beauty.

The spectacular scenery and endless views attract visitors and hikers from all over the world.

We have 16 en suite bedrooms, comfortable sofas in the bar and lounge areas, and five fireplaces, including a 13th century inglenook. Our extensive menus include local produce wherever possible, such as locally reared meat, amd locally caught game and fish, like Lynmouth Bay lobster; specials are featured daily. We also have a great choice of good wines, available by the bottle or the glass, and a selection of locally brewed beers, some produced specially for us.

Stay with us to relax, or to follow one of the seven circular walks through stunning countryside that start from the Inn. Horse riding for experienced riders or complete novices can be

arranged. Plenty of parking. Dogs (no charge), children and walkers are very welcome!

Blue Ball Inn formerly The Exmoor Sandpiper Inn
Countisbury, Lynmouth, Devon EX35 6NE
01598 741263
www.BlueBallinn.com • www.exmoorsandpiper.com

Callisham Farm B&B

Rustic charm in rural Devon countryside

Esme Wills and her family extend a warm welcome to their guests all year round. Feel at home in one of the three comfortable en suite bedrooms, with tea/coffee tray, clock radio and TV. Relax in the warm and cosy guests' lounge. A superb English breakfast is the perfect beginning to the day; vegetarian and special diets catered for on request. Terms from £60 double room. With easy access to rolling moorland, Callisham is a perfect base for riding, fishing, golf, and touring the beautiful coasts of Devon and Cornwall. In the nearby village of Meavy, the Royal Oak offers a selection of real ales and fine food; other pubs within a mile and a half; Plymouth 12 miles.

www.callisham.co.uk • esme@callisham.co.uk
Meavy, Near Yelverton PL20 6PS • Tel/Fax: 01822 853901

Great Sloncombe Farm

Moretonhampstead Devon TQ13 8QF
Tel: 01647 440595

Share the magic of Dartmoor all year round while staying in our lovely 13th century farmhouse full of interesting historical features. A working mixed farm set amongst peaceful meadows and woodland abundant in wild flowers and animals, including badgers, foxes, deer and buzzards. A welcoming and informal place to relax and explore the moors and Devon countryside. Comfortable double and twin rooms with en suite facilities, TV, central heating and coffee/tea making facilities. Delicious Devonshire breakfasts with new baked bread.

Open all year~No smoking~Farm Stay UK
e-mail: hmerchant@sloncombe.freeserve.co.uk • www.greatsloncombefarm.co.uk

symbols 🐎 SB ♿ ♈ Wi-Fi

🐕	Pets Welcome	🐎	Children Welcome
SB	Short Breaks	♿	Suitable for Disabled Guests
♈	Licensed	Wi-Fi	Wi-Fi available

Okehampton

Salcombe, Seaton

Sidmouth

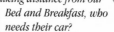

Pinn Barton, Peak Hill, Sidmouth EX10 0NN

SB

Peace, comfort and a warm welcome where we offer the little extras that attract guests back time and time again. Two miles from Sidmouth seafront. Lovely coastal walks and views from the farm. Warm and comfortable en suite bedrooms with TV, fridge, beverage trays and access at all times.

**Open all year • No smoking
Children welcome**

One twin, one double and
one family room available.

Terms from £32 to £36 per person.

**Mrs Betty S. Sage
Tel & Fax: 01395 514004
e-mail: betty@pinnbartonfarm.co.uk
www.pinnbartonfarm.co.uk**

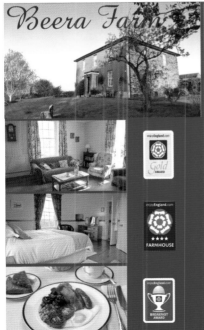

Beera Farm

Hilary Tucker
Beera Farm, Milton Abbot,
Tavistock PL19 8PL

Tel: 01822 870216•Mobile: 07974 957966

SB

Wi-Fi

Area of Outstanding Natural Beauty
- Delicious food served by trained chef. Special diets can be catered for.
- All rooms with en suite facilities (power shower), digital TV, hairdryer, toiletries etc.
- Children welcome - travel cot, bedding, highchair and children's meals can be provided.
- Lounge with cosy log fire in winter.
- Breakfast room with separate tables and views of garden and countryside.
- Free wireless broadband available.

**www.beera-farm.co.uk
hilary@beera-farm.co.uk**

Torquay

Aveland House

Aveland Road, Babbacombe,
Torquay, Devon, TQ1 3PT
Tel: +44 (0)1803 326622

e-mail avelandhouse@aol.com
www.avelandhouse.co.uk

Quietly situated close to Cary Park and St Marychurch Village, just a short walk to Babbacombe sea front, beaches, shops, restaurants, theatres and attractions. Ideal location for holidays and short breaks.

AA Friendliest Landlady Finalist 2010/2011

- Licensed
- All rooms en-suite
- Special diets catered for
- Sign language OCSL

- Free wi-fi internet access
- Car Park and Garden
- Non Smoking
- All major credit cards accepted

Rates from £36 B&B per person per night

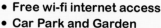

SB

The Glenorleigh

26 Cleveland Road
Torquay, Devon TQ2 5BE
Tel: 01803 292135
Fax: 01803 213717

As featured on BBC Holiday programme

David & Pam Skelly

AA ★★★★

Situated in a quiet residential area, Glenorleigh is 10 minutes' walk from both the sea front and the town centre. • Delightful en suite rooms, with your comfort in mind. • Digital flat screen TVs and free Wi-Fi internet access. • Good home cooking, both English and Continental, plenty of choice, with vegetarian options available daily. • Bar leading onto terrace overlooking Mediterranean-style garden with feature palms and heated swimming pool.

• Brochures and menus available on request • Discounts for children and Senior Citizens. • B&B £30–£40; Dinner £16.

e-mail: glenorleighhotel@btinternet.com
www.glenorleigh.co.uk

Totnes

Bournemouth

Dorset

In Dorset on the south coast, there are resorts to suit everyone, from traditional, busy Bournemouth with 10 kilometres of sandy beach and a wide choice of entertainment, shopping and dining, to the quieter seaside towns of Seatown, Mudeford and Barton-on-Sea, and Charmouth with its shingle beach. Lulworth Cove is one of several picturesque little harbours. In 2012 attention will be focussed on Weymouth, the venue for the Olympic and Paralympic sailing events, and one of several very popular sailing centres along the coast. Fossil hunters of all age groups are attracted by the spectacular cliffs of the Jurassic Coast, a World Heritage Site, and walkers can enjoy the wonderful views from the South West Coast Path at the top.

Bournemouth, Bridport

Bridport, Charmouth

Dorchester

Pubs & Inns

See the Supplement on pages 483-530

Sherborne

SB

Alms House Farm

This charming old farmhouse was a monastery during the 16th century, restored in 1849 and is now a Listed building. A family-run working dairy farm, overlooking the Blackmoor Vale. Accommodation is in three comfortable en suite rooms with colour TV and tea/coffee making facilities. Diningroom with inglenook fireplace, lounge with colour TV, for guests' use at all times. Also garden and lawn. Plenty of reading material and local information provided for this ideal touring area.

Bed and Breakfast from £30. Excellent evening meals in all local inns nearby. Situated six miles from Sherborne with its beautiful Abbey and Castle.

SAE for further details.

Mrs Jenny Mayo
**Hermitage, Holnest, Sherborne, Dorset DT9 6HA
Tel and Fax: 01963 210296**

- 21 individually decorated bedrooms
- Superb food using fresh local produce
- Overlooking Studland Bay
- Private path to beaches

- Pets welcome & beautiful walks
- 2 all-weather Tennis Courts
- Golf Course & Riding Stables nearby

Manor House Hotel
STUDLAND BAY DORSET

* * *

Old fashioned charm & service

3, 5 & 7 day Bargain Breaks

" Welcome to one of the most beautiful places in England. I can't take the credit for the glorious views and the beaches. But I am proud to provide a comfortable and relaxing hotel with good food and attentive but informal service, to give you the break you deserve. '

Andrew Purkis

Manor House Hotel, Studland, Dorset BH19 3AU • T– 01929 450288
• www.themanorhousehotel.com • E-mail: info@themanorhousehotel.com

SB

Wi-Fi

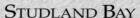

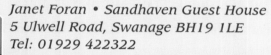

Arlingham, Corse Lawn

Gloucestershire

Chipping Campden

Gloucester, Stow-on-the-Wold

SB

QUALITY ALL GROUND FLOOR ACCOMMODATION.
"Kilmorie" is Grade II Listed (c1848) within
conservation area in a lovely part of
Gloucestershire. Only three miles
from Hartpury College and 10
miles from Malvern's Three
Counties Showground. Mostly
en suite double, twin, family or
single bedrooms, all having tea
tray, colour digital TV, radio.
Very comfortable guests' lounge,
traditional home cooking is served in
the separate diningroom overlooking large
garden. Perhaps walk waymarked farmland footpaths
which start here.
We have ponies and "free range" hens. Rural yet perfectly
situated to visit Cotswolds, Royal Forest of Dean, Wye Valley and
Malvern Hills. Gloucester and Tewkesbury seven miles. Children over five years welcome.
Ample parking. Cycle storage. From £27 per night.

Tel: 01452 840224

S.J. Barnfield, **"Kilmorie Smallholding"**
Gloucester Road, Corse, Staunton, Gloucester GL19 3RQ
e-mail: sheila-barnfield@supanet.com; Mobile 07966 532377

SB

THE *Old Stocks*
Hotel, Restaurant & Bar
The Square,
Stow-on-the-Wold GL54 1AF

Ideal base for touring this beautiful area.
Tasteful guest rooms in keeping with
the hotel's old world character, yet with
modern amenities. 3-terraced patio garden with smoking area.

Mouth-watering menus offering a
wide range of choices.
Special bargain breaks also available.

AA
★★
SMALL HOTEL

★★
SMALL HOTEL

Tel: 01451 830666 • Fax: 01451 870014
e-mail: fhg@oldstockshotel.co.uk
www.oldstockshotel.co.uk

Stow-on-the-Wold, Stroud

Just to the north of Bath, Gloucestershire forms the major part of the Cotswolds Area of Outstanding Natural Beauty, with gently rolling hills, sleepy villages and market towns full of character and wonderful local food to sample, altogether ideal for a relaxing break whatever the season. There are gardens to visit, country pubs, antiques, craft and farm shops, cathedrals and castles, as well as all kinds of outdoor activities, from horse riding and 4x4 off-road driving to all the watersports on offer at the Cotswold Water Park, in the south east corner of the county. Canoeing, kayaking, climbing and abseiling are all available in the Wye Valley, while the dedicated cycle routes in the Forest of Dean are ideal for families. There's a vast network of underground caves just waiting to be explored, or walk above ground on the local paths or long distance trails.

Somerset

On Devon/Somerset borders, 230 acre family-run farm with cattle, sheep, poultry and horses. Ideal for walking, touring Exmoor, Quantocks, both coasts and many National Trust properties. Pleasant farmhouse, tastefully modernised but with olde worlde charm, inglenook fireplaces and antique furniture, set in large gardens with lawns and flower beds in peaceful, scenic countryside. Two family bedrooms with private facilities and tea/coffee making. Large lounge, separate dining room offering guests every comfort. Noted for relaxed, friendly atmosphere and good home-cooking.

Bed and Breakfast from £28; Dinner £14 per person.
Reductions for children.

Tel: 01398 361296
lowerwestcott@aol.com
www.lowerwestcottfarm.co.uk

Mrs Ann Heard, Lower Westcott Farm, Ashbrittle, Wellington Somerset TA21 0HZ

SB

The Old Red House

Welcome to our romantic Victorian "Gingerbread" house which is colourful, comfortable and warm; full of unexpected touches and intriguing little curiosities. The leaded and stained glass windows are now double glazed to ensure a peaceful night's stay.
All rooms have colour TV with Freeview, complimentary beverages, radio alarm clock, hairdryer and en suite shower.
Easy access to city centre, via road or river paths. The English breakfast and buffet will keep you going all day. We have private parking. Non-smoking.

Wi-Fi

Theresa Elly, The Old Red House,
37 Newbridge Road, Bath BA1 3HE
01225 330464
e-mail: theoldredhousebath@onebillinternet.co.uk
www.theoldredhousebath.co.uk

SB

Toghill House Farm

Freezing Hill, Wick, Near Bath BS30 5RT

Situated just four miles north of Bath and within a few miles of Lacock, Castle Combe, Tetbury and the Cotswolds.

Stay at Toghill in one of our tastefully decorated rooms offering a high level of comfort. Combine this with a traditional English breakfast and you will soon understand why many guests return time after time. All rooms have en suite bathroom, television and tea/coffee making facilities. Ample car parking.

Self Catering also available in luxury converted 17th century cottages.

Tel: 01225 891261 • Fax: 01225 892128 • www.toghillhousefarm.co.uk

Leigh Farm
Bed & Breakfast and Self-Catering Accommodation

Leigh Farm is a working beef and sheep farm, situated at Pensford and close to Bath and Bristol. Bristol International Airport 10 miles approx.

Bed and Breakfast is offered in this 200 year-old comfy, warm farmhouse, with open log fire in the comfortable guest lounge in winter months. Central heating, TV. Accommodation comprises double en suite and family room with private bathroom; extra bedrooms in self-catering units when available, serviced on B&B basis. Access at all times.

Self Catering Accommodation available in four family bungalows and one bungalow suitable for couples. The open-plan bungalows are very sturdily constructed, with either one or two bedrooms, sleeping 2-4 persons.Regret no smoking, no pets.

**For brochure contact: Josephine Smart,
Leigh Farm, Pensford, Near Bristol BS39 4BA
Tel & Fax: 01761 490281 • www.leighfarmholidays.co.uk**

Bridgwater

SB
Wi-Fi

THE Hood Arms

A famous 17th century coaching Inn. Situated on the A39 at the foot of the Quantock Hills, close to the spectacular fossil beach at Kilve, a paradise for walkers, mountain bikers, dogs, sporting parties or simply relaxing.

Twelve en suite bedrooms include stylish four-posters. Stag Lodge in the courtyard garden has two luxury bedrooms and sitting room.

The beamed restaurant offers a relaxed dining experience whilst providing delicious locally sourced food. A full à la carte menu, chef's specials and bar snacks are available 7 days a week.

The bar is full of character and boasts an impressive array of real ales.

A warm welcome awaits locals and traveller alike. Dogs welcome.

Please look at our website for more details and prices.

Kilve Beach

The Hood Arms, Kilve, Bridgwater, Somerset TA5 1EA

01278 741210 • Fax: 01278 741477
e-mail: info@thehoodarms.com
www.thehoodarms.com

SB

Wi-Fi

Dulverton, Exmoor National Park (Dulverton)

Marsh Bridge Cottage

This superb accommodation has been made possible by the refurbishment of this Victorian former gamekeeper's cottage on the banks of the River Barle. The friendly welcome, lovely rooms, delicious (optional) evening meals using local produce, and clotted cream sweets are hard to resist! Open all year, and in autumn the trees that line the river either side of Marsh Bridge turn to a beautiful golden backdrop. Just off the B3223 Dulverton to Exford road, it is easy to find and, once discovered, rarely forgotten. From outside the front door footpaths lead in both directions alongside the river. Fishing available. Terms from £30pp B&B or £49.50pp DB&B.

Mrs Carole Nurcombe, Marsh Bridge Cottage, Dulverton TA22 9QG

01398 323197 • www.marshbridgedulverton.co.uk

e-mail: stay@marshbridgedulverton.co.uk

SB

Bruneton House
Brompton Regis
Exmoor National Park
TA22 9NN

Built around 1625 for a wealthy landowner, Bruneton House offers spacious accommodation in three comfortable, south-facing bedrooms, each individually designed and equipped to the highest standards, with beverage facilities and a radio. There is a separate TV lounge overlooking a pretty cottage garden and the stunning Pulham Valley.

SB

A full English breakfast is included in the nightly rate, and evening meals are available by arrangement, using fresh local produce whenever possible. Meal times are flexible and special diets can be catered for.

Brompton Regis nestles on the southern edge of Exmoor National Park, within easy reach of the north and south Devon coasts, where you will find beautiful beaches, fishing villages, and countless attractions for all the family. Set in some of the most beautiful countryside in the British Isles, Bruneton House is an ideal base for rambling, riding, twitching and fishing.

Tariff: from £27.50 - £32pppn
Children under 12 half price.

For further information contact Mrs Jennifer Stringer Tel: 01398 371224 or e-mail: brunetonhouse@hotmail.com

SB

SB

Taunton

Somerset shares in the wild, heather-covered moorland of Exmoor, along with the Quantock Hills to the east, ideal for walking, mountain biking, horse riding, fishing and wildlife holidays. The forty miles of coastline with cliffs, sheltered bays and sandy beaches includes family resorts like Weston-super-Mare, with its famous donkey rides and brand new pier with 21st century facilities and entertainment for everyone. More family fun can be found at Minehead and Burnham-on-Sea, or opt for the quiet charm of Clevedon. With theatres, festivals, museums, galleries, gardens, sporting events and of course, shopping, the city of Bath has everything for a short break or longer stay. Attracting visitors from all over the world, this designated World Heritage Site boasts wonderful examples of Georgian architecture and of course, the Roman Baths.

Weston-super-Mare, Woodford (near Williton)

Malmesbury

Wiltshire

The Old Bell Hotel
Abbey Row, Malmesbury
Wiltshire SN16 0BW
Tel: 01666 822344
www.oldbellhotel.com
info@oldbellhotel.com

SB

Wi-Fi

Built in 1220 and reputed to be the oldest purpose-built hotel in England, **The Old Bell Hotel** is still offering quintessentially English warmth, comfort and hospitality nearly 800 years later.

Standing alongside Malmesbury's medieval Abbey, in England's first capital, the hotel provides outstanding levels of service and retains the ambience of a bygone age.

There are 33 en suite bedrooms, 18 in the main house, each furnished in an individual style, some with antique furniture, and a further 15 in the Coach House

- En suite facilities
- TV with DVD player and Freeview
- Wired broadband internet access.

For the greatest concentration of prehistoric sites in Europe, visit Wiltshire. Most famous is the UNESCO World Heritage Site, Stonehenge, on Salisbury Plain, dating back at least five thousand years, while the stone circle at Avebury is the largest in the world. Salisbury, as well as the famous medieval cathedral, has plenty to choose from in arts and entertainment, while, Swindon, with its railway heritage, is the place to go for shopping and a lively nightlife. In the countryside there are interesting old market towns to explore, stately homes and gardens, including the safari park at Longleat, to visit, and ample opportunities for walking and cycling

Jackie & James Macbeth

Manor Farm

Collingbourne Kingston,
Marlborough,
Wiltshire SN8 3SD

B&B from £32.50 pppn

• Attractive Grade II Listed farmhouse on working family farm, very easy to find, 12 minutes south of Marlborough on the A338 Salisbury Road.
• Comfortable, spacious and well equipped rooms, all en suite or with private bathroom, including double, twin and family (for four).
• Sumptuous traditional, vegetarian, and other special diet breakfasts.
• Beautiful countryside with superb walking and cycling from the farm.
• Ample private parking
• Non-smoking
• Credit cards welcome

Tel: 01264 850859
e-mail: stay@manorfm.com
www.manorfm.com

Manor Farm B&B

SB

Off A36, three miles west of Warminster; 16 miles from historic city of Bath. Close to Longleat, Cheddar and Stourhead. Reasonable driving distance to Bristol, Stonehenge, Glastonbury and the cathedral cities of Wells and Salisbury.

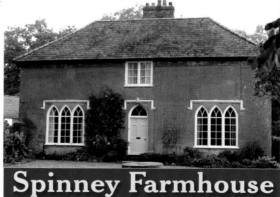

Spinney Farmhouse

• *Washbasins, tea/coffee-making facilities and shaver points in all rooms.*
• *Family room available.* • *Guests' lounge with colour TV.* • *Central heating.*
• *Children and pets welcome.* • *Ample parking.* • *Open all year.* • *No smoking.*
• *Discount on Longleat tickets.*
Enjoy farm fresh food in a warm, friendly family atmosphere.
Bed and Breakfast from £28 per night. Reduction after 2 nights. Evening Meal £12.

Thoulstone, Chapmanslade, Westbury BA13 4AQ
Tel: 01373 832412 • e-mail: isabelandbob@btinternet.com

London

London
(Central & Greater)

London has it all - theatres, shopping, concerts, museums, art galleries, pageantry and sporting events, a magnet for visitors from all over the world. In 2012, with the staging of the Olympic Games, the focus is on sport, but for visitors with other interests, there's plenty to see and do, from all the hands on activities of the Science Museum and the Natural History Museum, the National Gallery with one of the largest art collections in the world, the thought-provoking artworks at the Tate Modern, the splendour of Buckingham Palace and the magnificent gardens at Kew, to a sumptuous afternoon tea at a top hotel. With a wide range of accommodation at prices to suit every pocket, it's easy to spend a weekend here or a take a longer break. Take a bird's eye view of the city on the London Eye, the world's highest observation wheel, or meet celebrities (or at least their wax doubles) at Madame Tussauds. There are fashion and designer shops to suit all ages and tastes, markets for all kinds of goods, entertainment for all tastes, with over 400 venues where you can listen to the music of your choice, or watch musicals and plays, and eating places of all kinds offering menus from all over the world.

The Athena

110-114 SUSSEX GARDENS, HYDE PARK, LONDON W2 1UA

Tel: 0207 706 3866; Fax: 0207 262 6143

e-mail: stay@athenahotellondon.co.uk • www.athenahotel.co.uk

TREAT YOURSELVES TO A QUALITY HOTEL AT AFFORDABLE PRICES

The Athena is a newly completed family run hotel in a restored Victorian building. Professionally designed, including a lift to all floors and exquisitely decorated, we offer our clientele the ambience and warm hospitality necessary for a relaxing and enjoyable stay. Ideally located in a beautiful tree-lined avenue, extremely well-positioned for sightseeing London's famous sights and shops; Hyde Park, Madame Tussaud's, Oxford Street, Marble Arch, Knightsbridge, Buckingham Palace and many more are all within walking distance.

Travel connections to all over London are excellent, with Paddington and Lancaster Gate Stations, Heathrow Express, A2 Airbus and buses minutes away.
Our tastefully decorated bedrooms have en suite bath/shower rooms, satellite colour TV, bedside telephones, tea/coffee making facilities. Hairdryers, trouser press, laundry and ironing facilities available on request. Car parking available.

We offer quality and convenience at affordable rates.

A VERY WARM WELCOME AWAITS YOU.

Single Rooms from £50-£89
Double/Twin Rooms from £64-£99
Triple & Family Rooms from £25 per person
All prices include full English breakfast plus VAT.

All major credit cards accepted, but some charges may apply.

Windsor

Berkshire

Buckinghamshire

Aylesbury

SB

Lymington

Hampshire

SB

Efford
Cottage

Everton, Lymington, Hampshire SO41 0JD

Tel: 01590 642315

Guests receive a warm and friendly welcome to our home, which is a spacious Georgian cottage. All rooms are en suite with many extra luxury facilities. We offer a four-course, multi-choice breakfast with homemade bread and preserves. Patricia is a qualified chef and uses our home-grown produce. An excellent centre for exploring both the New Forest and the South Coast, with sports facilities, fishing, bird watching and horse riding in the near vicinity. Private parking. Dogs welcome. Sorry, no children. Bed and Breakfast from £25–£35 pppn. Mrs Patricia J. Ellis.

AA

★★★★
Accommodation

Winner of " England For Excellence 2000"
FHG Diploma 1997/1999/2000/2003 / Michelin / Welcome Host
Awards Achieved: Gold Award / RAC Sparkling Diamond & Warm Welcome
Nominated Landlady of Year & Best Breakfast Award.
Enquiries and bookings by telephone only.
e-mail: pellis48@btinternet.com • www.effordcottage.co.uk

Idyllic countryside, sandy beaches, beautiful gardens and historic houses, country parks, museums and castles, and wildlife parks, are all there to enjoy in Hampshire. There are museums full of military heritage on land, sea and air, including the HMS Victory at Portsmouth, where a trip to the top of the Spinnaker Tower provides spectacular views of the surrounding area. Outdoors walk, cycle or ride on horseback over the heathland and through the ancient woodlands of the New Forest, and in the South Downs National Park, or try out one of the many watersports available along the coast. Boating enthusiasts will make for one of the many marinas, and the annual regatta on the River Hamble, and for courses on sailing, rockclimbing, and even skiing, where better to learn more than the Calshot Activities Centre on the shores of the Solent.

SB

Tiverton B and B is a large chalet-style bungalow featuring two delightful
Bed and Breakfast Suites, each with its own sitting room and en suite facilities.
Located at the end of a quiet cul-de-sac in the village of Sway in the New Forest, Tiverton
B and B is just three minutes' walk from Sway railway station and from ArtSway art centre and
gallery. The coast near Lymington is just four miles away and Brockenhurst three miles.

**Ron and Thelma Rowe, Tiverton, 9 Cruse Close,
Sway, Hampshire SO41 6AY • Tel/Fax: 01590 683092
thelma.ronrowe@hotmail.co.uk • www.tivertonnewforest.co.uk**

SB

Wi-Fi

Woodlands Lodge • New Forest
A little piece of luxury in the heart of the New Forest

A privately owned 3 star country house hotel, the Woodlands Lodge is ideally situated on the edge of the
New Forest. The Hotel is perfectly placed to explore the forest, which can be accessed directly from the
hotel gardens, or to visit the city of Southampton, or the many local museums and gardens.
Of course if you prefer you can just sit back and relax and unwind with us in the Hotel's picturesque
setting and let us spoil you. Pets welcome. All of our rooms and suites are en suite.
For that special occasion, why not book one of our
four-poster bedrooms. You deserve to be spoilt!

Bartley Road, Woodlands, New Forest,
Southampton, Hampshire SO40 7GN
Tel: 0238 029 2257
e-mail: reception@woodlands-lodge.co.uk
www.woodlands-lodge.co.uk

New Forest

SB

Wi-Fi

Bramble Hill Hotel

unpretentious and welcoming ....

...in the heart of the New Forest

Peacefully located in tranquil surroundings, this country house hotel, noted for its wonderful collection of rhododendrons and other flowering shrubs and trees, is set in ancient woodlands, with 15 acres of glades, lawns and shrubbery to enjoy.
Bramble Hill, a former Royal Hunting Lodge, looks out across a valley designated as a nature reserve, where deer, badgers and other wild life of the New Forest abound.

A short drive from Lyndhurst, the hotel is only three miles from Junction 1 of the M27, and is ideal for country walks and horse riding.
All bedrooms have en suite bathrooms and some have antique four-poster beds.
A warm, friendly welcome and a hearty home-cooked breakfast assured.

**Bramshaw, New Forest,
Hampshire SO43 7JG
Telephone: 023 80 813165
bramblehill@hotmail.co.uk
www.bramblehill.co.uk**

symbols 🐕🐎SB♿🍷Wi-Fi

🐕	Pets Welcome	🐎	Children Welcome
SB	Short Breaks	♿	Suitable for Disabled Guests
🍷	Licensed	Wi-Fi	Wi-Fi available

Isle of Wight

Lower Bonchurch

Shore Road, Lower Bonchurch, Isle of Wight PO38 1RF
Tel: 01983 852613 • e-mail: info@lakehotel.co.uk • www.lakehotel.co.uk
*"Truly unbeatable value for money". This lovely country house is set in a beautiful
2-acre garden on the seaward side of the 'olde worlde' village of Bonchurch, just
400 yards from the sea. Run by the same family for over 45 years, we offer first class
bed & breakfast, service and comfort, all in a very relaxed and friendly atmosphere.
All rooms are decorated in a mix of traditional and contemporary styles. All are
en suite and have large flat screen TVs and tea/coffee making. Please look at our
comprehensive website with lots of photos, or request a brochure from us.*

*We can offer special car ferry breaks starting from
just £185 for 4 nights including breakfast.
We really do believe that you will not find better
value on our beautiful island.*

Kent

Ashford

Bolden's Wood Fiddling Lane, Stowting, Near Ashford, Kent TN25 6AP

Between Ashford/Folkestone. Friendly atmosphere – modern accommodation (one double, one single) on our Smallholding, set in unspoilt countryside. No smoking throughout. Full English breakfast. Country pubs (meals) nearby. Children love the old-fashioned farmyard, free range chickens, friendly sheep and... Llamas, Alpacas and Rheas. Treat yourself to a Llama-led Picnic Trek to our private secluded woodland and downland and enjoy watching the bird life, rabbits, foxes, badgers and occasionally deer. Easy access to Channel Tunnel and Ferry Ports.

Bed and Breakfast £28.00 per person.
Contact: Jim and Alison Taylor
e-mail: StayoverNight@aol.com

Tel: 01303 812011

Canterbury, Dover

Upper Ansdore

Beautiful secluded Listed Tudor farmhouse with various livestock, situated in an elevated position with far-reaching views of the wooded countryside of the North Downs.
The property overlooks a Kent Trust Nature Reserve, is five miles south of the cathedral city of Canterbury and only 30 minutes' drive to the ports of Dover and Folkestone. The accommodation comprises one family, three double and one twin-bedded rooms. All have shower and WC en suite and tea making facilities. Dining/sitting room, heavily beamed with large inglenook. Pets welcome. Car essential.

Tel: 01227 700672

Bed and Breakfast from £35 per person. Credit cards accepted.
Mr and Mrs R. Linch, Upper Ansdore, Duckpit Lane, Petham, Canterbury CT4 5QB
e-mail: rogerd@talktalk.net • www.bedandbreakfastupperansdore.co.uk

---

SB

Wi-Fi

South Wootton House
Capel Road, Petham, Canterbury CT4 5RG

A lovely farmhouse with conservatory set in extensive garden, surrounded by fields and woodland.
Fully co-ordinated bedroom with private bathroom.
Tea/coffee facilities, colour TV.
Children welcome. Canterbury four miles.
Non-smoking. Open all year.
Bed and Breakfast from £35.

Frances Mount
Tel: 01227 700643 • Mobile: 07885 800843
e-mail: mountfrances@btconnect.com

SB

Blériots
GUEST HOUSE, DOVER

AA RATING ★ ★ ★ HIGHLY COMMENDED

01304 211 394
BELPER HOUSE, 47 PARK AVENUE, DOVER, KENT CT16 1HE

Welcome to Bleriot's, a family-run guesthouse in Dover

Our AA Highly Commended three gold star non-smoking Victorian residence is set in a tree-lined avenue, in the lee of Dover Castle, within easy reach of trains, bus station, town centre, ferries and cruise terminal. Channel Tunnel approximately 10 minutes' drive. Off-road parking. Single, double, twin and family rooms with full en suite. All rooms have flat screen Freeview TV, tea and coffee making facilities, and are fully centrally heated. Full English breakfast served from 7am to 9am. Open all year. MasterCard, Visa and debit cards accepted. AA Centenary Awards B&B Friendliest Landlady Finalist.

Room only £28-£30* • Breakfast £5 per adult and £3 per child.
Bleriot's, 47 Park Avenue, Dover CT16 1HE • Tel: 01304 211394
e-mail: info@bleriots.net • www.bleriots.net
*Rates: per person, per night based on two people sharing. Single and family rates: POA

Maidstone, Tenterden

Kent, the 'Garden of England', yet with such easy access to London, is a county of gentle, rolling downlands, edged by the famous White Cliffs and miles of sands and shingle beaches along the Channel coast. Walk along the North Downs Way through an Area of Outstanding Natural Beauty stretching from Kent through Sussex to Surrey, or enjoy the stunning scenery from the Saxon Shore Way with views to the coast of France, and the wildlife of the Medway Estuary and Romney Marsh. The resorts of the Isle of Thanet and the south-east coast, like Ramsgate, Margate, Herne Bay and Deal have plenty to offer for a traditional family seaside holiday, and there are steam trains, animal parks and castles full of history to explore too. At Leeds and Hever Castles visitors can even play a round of golf, just two of the wide choice of links, urban and countryside courses throughout the county.

LITTLE / SILVER

C O U N T R Y　 H O T E L

SB

Wi-Fi

Versatility combined with efficiency, friendliness and a personal regard for detail are the hallmarks offered by the management and staff. Each of the bedrooms is stamped with its own identity, including standard rooms, four-posters and suites with spa baths. Bespoke bedrooms are offered to those guests with mobility needs, and the hotel is totally accessible for wheelchair users.

The excellent Oaks Restaurant offers locally sourced foods with plenty of surprises to keep our menus exciting.

The wine list is varied and offers a selection of new world wines as well as wines from local vineyards.

Pre-dinner drinks are served in the oak-beamed lounge, where log fires burn on those cold winter nights.

Morning coffee, light lunches and afternoon tea are served in the Orangery overlooking the landscaped gardens.

Licensed for wedding ceremonies and partnerships, the magnificent Kent Hall holds up to 120 guests.
Al fresco weddings are held in the beautiful garden gazebo on those warm summer days.

The hotel is ideally suited for anyone wishing to explore the beautiful countryside, castles and gardens which abound in the area. The medieval town of Rye and the wonderful city of Canterbury are within easy reach, whilst Tenterden, one of the loveliest towns in the Weald and steeped in history, is just up the road.

Little Silver Country Hotel, the Jewel in the Weald

Ashford Road, St Michaels, Tenterden, Kent TN30 6SP
Tel: 01233 850321 • Fax: 01233 850647
e-mail: enquiries@little-silver.co.uk • www.little-silver.co.uk

Tunbridge Wells

SB

Wi-Fi

Manor Court Farm • Bed and Breakfast

Manor Court Farm Bed & Breakfast is offered in a spacious, Listed Georgian farmhouse on a 350-acre family farm.

We aim to create a warm and friendly atmosphere so guests can relax and enjoy the farm and the surrounding lovely countryside of Kent and Sussex.

One double and two twin rooms are available throughout the year and are tastefully and comfortably furnished to a high standard. Each room has hot and cold water, tea-making facilities, TV and wonderful views of the gardens and surrounding countryside. Our spacious bedrooms are complemented by two large bathroom/shower rooms, exclusively for guests' use.

A lounge/sitting room with an open fire, TV and DVD is available.

Rates: from £28 per person per night.
Reduced rate for children. Babies free.

Mrs Julia Soyke, Manor Court Farm
Ashurst, Tunbridge Wells, Kent TN3 9TB
Telephone: 01892 740279
e-mail: jsoyke@jsoyke.freeserve.co.uk
www.manorcourtfarm.co.uk

Oxfordshire

Oxford

Oxfordshire, with the lively, historic university city of Oxford, the 'city of dreaming spires', at its centre, is ideal for a relaxing break. Quiet countryside is dotted with picturesque villages and busy market towns, while the open downland to the south is covered by a network of footpaths connecting up with the ancient Ridgeway Trail and the riverside walks of the Thames Path. Hire a rowing boat or a punt for a leisurely afternoon on the River Thames or explore the Cotswold villages to the west. Stretching from Oxford to the Cotswolds, the mysterious Vale of the White Horse is named after the oldest chalk figure in Britain, dating back over 3000 years. The historic market towns like Abingdon and Wantage make good shopping destinations, and all the family will enjoy the history, activities and beautiful gardens at Blenheim Palace.

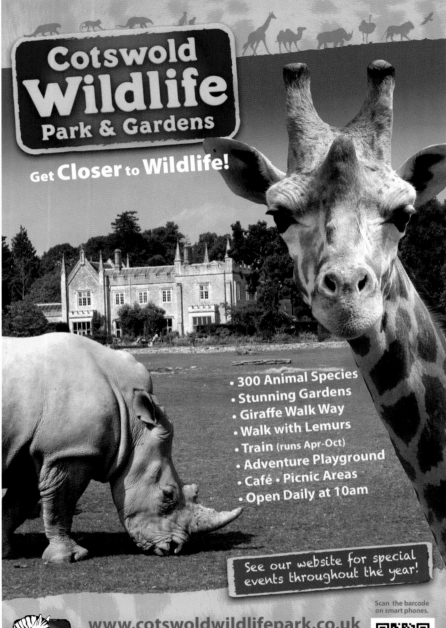

symbols SB Wi-Fi

🐕	Pets Welcome	🐎	Children Welcome	
SB	Short Breaks	♿	Suitable for Disabled Guests	
♉	Licensed	Wi-Fi	Wi-Fi available	

Surrey

Crowborough, Eastbourne

East Sussex

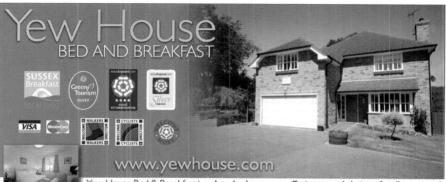

Battle

SB

Wi-Fi

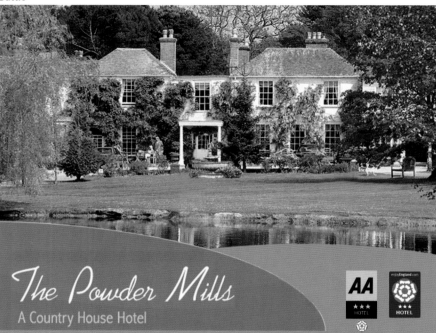

The Powder Mills
A Country House Hotel

The Powder Mills is a privately owned 18thC Listed country house hotel in 150 acres of beautiful parklands, woods and lakes, adjoining the famous battlefield of 1066. Once a famous gunpowder mill, it has been skilfully converted into a fascinating country hotel. The Orangery Restaurant, with its marble floor, Greek statues and huge windows looking out onto the terrace and pool, has been awarded an AA Rosette for fine dining. There is a range of 40 individually decorated en suite bedrooms and Junior Suites, many with 4-poster beds. The Pavilion is a delightful conference centre, accommodating up to 200 persons, situated away from the main hotel with its own parking facilities, and suitable also for concerts, events and weddings. The Powder Mills is open to non-residents every day for luncheon, light lunches and dinner.

Powder Mills Hotel & The Orangery Restaurant
Powdermill Lane, Battle TN33 0SP • Tel: 01424 775511
www.powdermillshotel.com • e-mail: powdc@aol.com

Paskins
town house

Distinctive, different, comfortable

SB

Wi-Fi

PASKINS is a small, green hotel that has found its own way. It's an eclectic, environmentally friendly hotel with nice and sometimes amusing rooms, with the bonus of brilliant breakfasts. You arrive at the Art Nouveau reception to be shown to one of the 19 slightly out of the ordinary rooms, each individual in design, perhaps a little quirky, but not at the expense of being comfortable. For example, one room has a genuine Victorian brass bed with several mattresses, just as Queen Victoria's did, which enabled her to sleep higher than all her subjects. Having been welcomed royally, you will sleep like a monarch, and come down to a regal spread at breakfast, prepared with mainly organic, fair trade or locally sourced produce. The Art Deco breakfast room continues the charming theme of the hotel, and has a menu of celebrated choice, including a variety of imaginative vegetarian and vegan dishes, some intriguing signature dishes, and a blackboard full of specials.

PASKINS TOWN HOUSE • 18/19 Charlotte Street, Brighton BN2 1AG
Tel: 01273 601203 • Fax: 01273 621973
www.paskins.co.uk • welcome@paskins.co.uk

RYE LODGE HOTEL

The Stylish Place to Stay in Rye

"A little gem of an Hotel"

From the moment you arrive at Rye Lodge you will enjoy the attentive service and attention to detail that only a small, family-run hotel can offer. The friendly reception staff will be pleased to greet you and help you to settle in. They have a wealth of information to offer you about Rye and the surrounding area and will be pleased to help you with any queries or special requirements you may have throughout your stay.

From spacious superior de luxe rooms with private balconies and family rooms to a cosy bedroom with shower en suite, all of the bedrooms at Rye Lodge offer luxury accommodation. Whatever standard of room you choose, you are assured of comfortable and stylish accommodation. Every room has remote-control TV with satellite channels, hospitality tray, radio and direct-dial telephone. De luxe rooms all have well stocked mini-bars and, in the bathroom you will find quality toiletries, bathrobes for your use and complimentary slippers. Standard rooms have en suite shower rooms or bathrooms.

Enjoy the luxury of breakfast in bed (or on your balcony if your room has one), without extra charge for room service.

A new **Champagne Bar** has opened recently and guests can enjoy a chilled glass of champagne at any time - there is also a menu of light dishes served throughout the day.

With a heated swimming pool, spa bath, and sauna you can relax or exercise in Rye Lodge's Venetian Leisure Centre. Rye Lodge is the only hotel with a swimming pool in Rye, and guests have exclusive and unlimited complimentary use of the centre throughout their stay.

"One of the finest small luxury hotels in the country"

Recommended by Signpost and designated a "Best Loved Hotel of the World"

RYE LODGE HOTEL

Hilder's Cliff, Rye, East Sussex TN31 7LD

Tel: 01797 223838 • Fax: 01797 223585

www.ryelodge.co.uk

Henfield, Selsey

West Sussex

SPRINGWELLS HOTEL

9 High Street, Steyning, West Sussex BN44 3GG

Once a Georgian merchant's town house, now an elegant ten-bedroom Bed and Breakfast hotel. All rooms have Freesat televisions and free Wi-Fi; two have four-poster beds. The bar and adjoining conservatory lead to a patio and walled garden with outdoor heated swimming pool. At the front of the hotel there is a sunny dining room and elegant lounge.

Tel: 01903 812446 • Fax: 01903 879823
contact@springwells.co.uk • www.springwells.co.uk

From the dramatic cliffs and sandy beaches of the Sussex coast to the quiet countryside of the Weald and the South Downs, there's an endless choice of the things to do and places to explore. Sailing, walking, cycling, horse riding, golf are all available for an active break, while the fascinating history of 1066 country, castles like Bodiam and the seaside ports will attract all the family. If you're looking for beaches, the 100 miles of coast offer something for everyone, whether your preference is for action-packed fun at a family resort or a quiet, remote spot. Best known for a combination of lively nightlife and all the attractions of the seaside, Brighton has everything from its pebble beach, classic pier, Royal Pavilion and Regency architecture, to shopping malls, art galleries, antique shops, and the specialist boutiques and coffee shops of The Lanes. There's so much to choose from!

Cambridgeshire

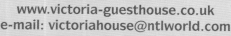

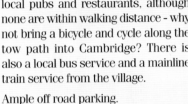

Essex

Seven Arches Farm

Georgian farmhouse set in large garden close to the ancient town of Colchester. The farm extends to 100 acres and supports both arable crops and cattle. Private fishing rights on the River Colne, which runs past the farmhouse. This is a good location for visits to North Essex, Dedham and the Stour Valley which have been immortalised in the works of John Constable, the landscape painter.

- Children and pets welcome.
- Open all year.
- Static caravan on caravan site also available.

◆ Bed and Breakfast from £30
◆ Twin room £60
◆ Family room en suite

Mrs Jill Tod, Seven Arches Farm,
Chitts Hill, Lexden, Colchester CO3 9SX
01206 574896 • www.sevenarchesfarmbandb-colchester.co.uk

From the historic port of Harwich in the north to the Thames estuary in the south, the 300 miles of coastline and dry climate of maritime Essex have attracted holiday makers since early Victorian times. Nowadays there's plenty for everyone, from the fun family resorts with plenty of action like Clacton, on the Essex sunshine coast, and Southend-on-Sea, with over six miles of clean safe sand and the world's longest pleasure pier to quiet walks through country nature reserves. Along the coast there are quiet clifftop paths, sheltered coves, long beaches, mudflats, saltmarshes and creeks. Previously the haunt of smugglers, these are now a great attraction for birdwatchers, particularly for viewing winter wildfowl. At Maldon take a trip on a Thames barge to see the seal colonies or cross the Saxon causeway to Mersea Island to taste the oysters, washed down by wine produced on the vineyard there, but watch the tides!

Colchester

Rye Farm

Rye Lane, Layer de la Haye,
Colchester CO2 0JL
Tel: 01206 734350/07976 524276
e-mail: peterbunting@btconnect.com
www.ryefarm.org.uk

Wi-Fi

This 17thC moated farmhouse enjoys a quiet location adjacent to Abberton Reservoir, one of Europe's most important wildfowl havens. Ideal for a relaxing break and a good base for exploring Colchester with its castle and museums, Colchester Zoo, Mersea Island, Layer Marney Towers, Beth Chatto Gardens, Maldon and Constable Country. 30 mins from the coast; 50 mins from Stansted Airport/Harwich Port. London 50 minutes by train.

Three comfortable en suite rooms, with central heating, colour TV/DVD, tea and coffee making facilities, fridge and hairdryer. Substantial farmhouse breakfast. No smoking. No pets. Children over 12 years only

Norfolk

Cromer

Wi-Fi

THE OLD PUMP HOUSE

LUXURY BED & BREAKFAST ACCOMMODATION

This comfortable 1750s house, owned by Marc James and Charles Kirkman, faces the old thatched pump and is a minute from Aylsham's church and historic marketplace.

It offers five en suite bedrooms (including one four-poster and two family rooms) in a relaxed and elegant setting, with colour TV, tea/coffee making facilities, bath robes, hairdryers and CD radio alarm clocks in all rooms. Wireless internet access in all rooms.

English breakfast with free-range eggs and local produce (or vegetarian breakfast) is served in the pine-shuttered sitting room overlooking the peaceful garden.

Aylsham is central for Norwich, the coast, the Broads, National Trust houses, steam railways and unspoilt countryside.

• Well behaved children welcome. • Non-smoking.

• Off-road parking for six cars.

• *B&B: single £80-£98, double/twin £98-£120, family room £123-£145*

Holman Road, Aylsham, Norwich
NR11 6BY
Tel: 01263 733789
theoldpumphouse@btconnect.com
www.theoldpumphouse.com

Along the Norfolk coast from King's Lynn to Great Yarmouth the broad, sandy beaches, grassy dunes, nature reserves, windmills, and pretty little fishing villages are inviting at all times of year. Following the routes of the Norfolk Coastal Path and Norfolk Coast Cycle Way, walk or cycle between the picturesque villages, stopping to visit the interesting shops and galleries, or to enjoy the seafood at a traditional pub or a restaurant. Take lessons in surfing at Wells-next-the-Sea, then enjoy the challenge of the waves at East Runton or Cromer, or go sea fishing here, or at Sheringham or Mundesley. An important trade and fishing port from medieval times, the historic centre of King's Lynn is well worth a visit, and take a break at Great Yarmouth for family entertainment, 15 miles of sandy beaches, traditional piers, a sea life centre and nightlife with clubs and a casino.

SB

A Charming 16th Century Manor House

Located Between Hunstanton and Heacham on the beautiful West Norfolk Coast.

■ Luxury Accommodation
■ 18 hole Golf Course ■ Exquisite Cuisine ■ Beautiful Gardens
■ Additional Cottages ■ Wedding Receptions ■ Coastline Sunsets

Open to non-residents, fine dining restaurant.
We look forward to welcoming you soon.

Heacham Manor Estate, Hunstanton Road, Heacham, West Norfolk. PE31 7JX
Tel: 01485 536 030   www.heacham-manor.co.uk

Well-next-the-Sea, Wymondham

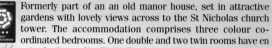

The many RSPB and other nature reserves always attract birdwatchers to the region, whether for the migrating birds on the coastal sandspits and marshes, or inland on the low-lying Fens, the Norfolk Broads or the ancient pine forests and heathland of The Breck. Follow the walking, cycling and horse riding trails, or explore interesting market towns and villages from the calm waterways of the Broads to see the Norman churches, take part in the fun of a village fete, watch traditional morris dancing, or visit the one of the few remaining windmills, at Denver, Letheringsett or Great Bircham. In contrast, in the medieval city of Norwich with its historic streets and half-timbered houses, cathedral, Norman castle and museums you'll find not only history, but opera, ballet, theatre, music and restaurants as well as all kinds of shopping.

Suffolk

Bungay

HIGH HOUSE FARM

Farmhouse Bed & Breakfast

High House Farm is a family-run farm in the heart of rural Suffolk, offering quality Bed & Breakfast in our 15th Century listed farmhouse.

Featuring: exposed oak beams • inglenook fireplaces • generous Full English Breakfast with locally sourced ingredients • tea and coffee making facilities • flat screen TVs • one double room, en suite and one large family room with double and twin beds and private adjacent bathroom

children's cots • high chairs • books • toys • outside play equipment • attractive semi-moated gardens • farm and woodland walks.

Explore the heart of rural Suffolk, local vineyard, Easton Farm Park, Framlingham and Orford Castles, Parham Air Museum, Saxtead Windmill, Minsmere, Snape Maltings, Woodland Trust.

High House Farm
Cransford, Framlingham, Woodbridge IP13 9PD
Tel: 01728 663461
e-mail: b&b@highhousefarm.co.uk www.highhousefarm.co.uk

Hintlesham Hall

Hintlesham, Ipswich, Suffolk IP8 3NS

AA ★★★★ HOTEL

Hintlesham Hall Hotel is a 21st century haven of comfort and friendly service within a Grade I listed Elizabethan Manor House. The heart of Hintlesham Hall is the opportunity simply to relax and perhaps wander around the grounds or countryside before enjoying chef's latest menus and depleting the award-winning wine cellar.

Hintlesham Health Club is in uniquely charming and peaceful surroundings with plenty of fresh air, light, room to relax and a warm welcome.

Tel: 01473 652334

www.hintleshamhall.co.uk • reservations@hintleshamhall.com

Suffolk's 40 miles of unspoilt World Heritage coastline is perfect for a seaside holiday. Whether you're looking for a quiet weekend break or an active family fortnight in a well established resort, a music festival - rock and pop or classical, farm parks and fun parks or just to indulge in the wonderful local food, it's all to be found here. Wander through the coastal forests or along the shingle and sandy beaches admiring the scenery, or hire bicycles for a family bike ride. Rent a gaily painted beach hut at Felixstowe, where the level esplanade and beaches are ideal both for small children and older family members, try crabs fresh from the sea at Walberswick, or enjoy the annual music and literature festivals at Aldeburgh. Eat oysters at Orford, and explore the Norman castle, or follow the Suffolk Coastal Churches Trail. At Woodbridge visit the Tide Mill and Buttrum's Mill, the tallest remaining windmill in Suffolk, and the nearby Anglo-Saxon burial site at Sutton Hoo. River yachting is another option, and of course right along the coast there are opportunities for all forms of boating, sailing, and diving holidays. Fishing is particularly popular on the Waveney and on many other rivers as well, and there are plenty of opportunities for still water angling or sea fishing too. Golfers are not neglected, with a choice between short local courses to some of championship standard, with luxury hotel accommodation on site. Horse racing enthusiasts can't miss Newmarket, whether for a fun day out, to visit the National Horseracing Museum or to take a guided tour round the National Stud.

Ashbourne

Derbyshire

THROWLEY HALL FARM
ILAM, ASHBOURNE DE6 2BB
01538 308202/308243

Bed and Breakfast in farmhouse.
Near Alton Towers and stately homes.
4 double/twin rooms (3 en suite).
Dining/sitting room with TV.
Tea/coffee making • full central heating • open fire.
Terms from £32pppn • Reduced rates for children.
Cot and high chair available.

www.throwleyhallfarm.co.uk
e-mail: throwleyhall@btinternet.com

Self-catering accommodation in farmhouse for up to
12 and cottages for five and seven people
ETC ★★★★

SB

The Clarendon Guest House

Located near the town centre and within easy reach of the Peak District, this Victorian town house offers a warm and cheerful welcome, whether on business or pleasure.

Comfortable, cosy rooms, each with TV and tea/coffee facilities; free Wi-Fi. Two single rooms, one single en suite; one twin en suite, one double en suite.

The rear walled garden offers a peaceful summer retreat.

Full English breakfast; special diets catered for. Non-smoking throughout.

Bed and Breakfast from £25 single, from £50 double/twin room en suite.

Mr & Mrs A. Boardman • 01246 235004
The Clarendon Guest House,
32 Clarence Road, Chesterfield S40 1LN
www.clarendonguesthouse.com

Moseley House Farm
Maynestone Road, Chinley, High Peak SK23 6AH
Tel: 01663 750240

A stunning location in the Peak District is where you will find this quality farmhouse. Lovely bedrooms, en suite or with private bathrooms, charming ground floor suite with own entrance. Relax in the garden. Village half mile – good pubs and restaurants. Ideal spot for a holiday on a working farm.
Double or twin from £29 per person, single £30.
Also self-catering cottage. Farmhouse, sleeps six.

e-mail: goddardbromley@aol.com
www.visitderbyshire.co.uk

Mayfield, Peak District National Park

SB

i

MONA VILLAS
Church Lane
Middle Mayfield
Mayfield
Near Ashbourne
DE6 2JS
Tel: 01335 343773

A warm, friendly welcome to our home with purpose-built en suite accommodation. Beautiful views over open countryside. A local pub serves excellent food within a five minute walk. Situated near Alton Towers, Dove Dale, etc. Three en suite rooms available, single supplement applies. Family rooms available. Parking.

Bed and Breakfast from £28.00 to £35.00 per night.

e-mail: info@mona-villas.fsnet.co.uk
www.mona-villas.fsnet.co.uk

BIGGIN HALL

Tranquilly set 1000ft up in the White Peak District National Park, 17th century Grade II* Listed Biggin Hall – a country house hotel of immense character and charm where guests experience the full benefits of the legendary Biggin Air – has been sympathetically restored, keeping its character while giving house room to contemporary comforts. Rooms are centrally heated with bathrooms en suite, colour television, tea-making facilities, silent fridge and telephone. Those in the main house have stone arched mullioned windows, others are in converted 18th century outbuildings. Centrally situated for stately homes and for exploring the natural beauty of the area. Return at the end of the day to enjoy your freshly cooked dinner alongside log fires and personally selected wines.

Well behaved pets are welcome by prior arrangement

Biggin-by-Hartington, Buxton, Derbyshire SK17 0DH
Tel: 01298 84451
www.bigginhall.co.uk

Mrs Jane Ball

Brae Cottage

East Bank, Winster DE4 2DT

Tel: 01629 650375

In one of the most picturesque villages in the Peak District National Park this 300-year-old cottage offers independent accommodation across the paved courtyard. Breakfast is served in the cottage. Rooms are furnished and equipped to a high standard; both having en suite shower rooms, tea/coffee making facilities, TV and heating.

The village has two traditional pubs which provide food.

Local attractions include village (National Trust) Market House, Chatsworth, Haddon Hall and many walks from the village in the hills and dales.

Ample private parking • Non-smoking throughout
Bed and Breakfast from £60 per double room

For walking, climbing, cycling, horse riding, mountain biking and caving, visit Derbyshire. Take part in one of the walking festivals, with themed walks at every level, cycle the recently restored Monsal Trail through spectacular scenery along the old railway line from Bakewell to Buxton, or hire an electric bike to enjoy the countryside, whatever your level of fitness. Visit Poole's Cavern to see the best stalagmites and stalactites in Derbyshire (and discover the difference!), and the Blue John Cave at Castleton where this rare mineral is mined, and perhaps buy a sample of jewellery in one of the local shops. Buxton was a spa from Roman times, but the main attractions now are concerts, theatre and the opera, music and literature festival held every year. Go to Wirksworth in spring for the annual well dressings or try out a wizard's wand at Hardwick Hall near Chesterfield, the market town with the church with the crooked spire. No stay in Derbyshire is complete without visiting Chatsworth, the best known of the stately homes, with impressive interiors and magnificent gardens and grounds, and for a contrasting step back in time go to Crich Tramway Village for a tram ride down a period street and on into the countryside.

The FHG Directory of Website Addresses
on pages 531-541 is a useful quick reference guide for
holiday accommodation with e-mail and/or website details

Belton-in-Rutland, Melton Mowbray

Leicestershire & Rutland

Michelin Star

RELAIS & CHATEAUX.

HAMBLETON HALL

The county of Rutland is verdant, undulating, and largely unspoilt, making it an ideal place to spend a tranquil vacation. No better venue for such an excursion exists than this fine hotel, perched in the very centre of man-made Rutland Water.

The superb cuisine exhibits flair and refreshing originality, with the emphasis very much on seasonal, freshly sourced ingredients. Beautifully furnished in subtle shades, elegant and profoundly comfortable, with 17 individually and lavishly decorated bedrooms. Hambleton is within easy reach of numerous places of historic interest, wonderful gardens and antique shops. On-site tennis, outdoor heated swimming pool and croquet lawn, and within a short drive, horse riding, golf, sailing, fishing and boating.

Hambleton, Oakham, Rutland LE15 8TH

Tel: 01572 756991 • Fax: 01572 724721

hotel@hambletonhall.com • www.hambletonhall.com

Barton-Upon-Humber, Gainsborough

Lincolnshire

West Wold Farmhouse

Deepdale, Barton-upon-Humber DN18 6ED

Tel: 01652 633293

Friendly farmhouse set in the hamlet of Deepdale.
Rooms have en suite or private bathroom.
We offer the 'Great British' breakfast, with fresh, locally
sourced produce where possible; vegetarian and other
diets as requested.
Dogs and horses welcome by arrangement.
We have plenty of off-road parking. Special breaks and long term discounts available

e-mail: pam@westwoldfarmhouse.co.uk • **www.westwoldfarmhouse.co.uk**

The *Black Swan* *Guest House*

As resident proprietors, Judy and John Patrick offer a
warm welcome at our delightfully converted former
18th century coaching inn. The property has been
fully refurbished, using much of the original materials
and retaining many original features.
The house and stable block now offer comfortable
rooms which are en suite, with digital TV and
tea/coffee making facilities. There is a guest lounge
where you can enjoy a drink in the evenings, or just
relax. Our breakfasts are all freshly cooked to order using locally sourced best quality produce.
The local area is steeped in history, from Roman times through to the old airfields of the Second World
War, and the city of Lincoln is only 12 miles away, with its stunning cathedral and old city centre in the
Bailgate area.For those of you who need to keep in touch, wireless broadband is available.
We are a non-smoking establishment. **Single from £45, double/twin from £68.**

21 High Street, Marton, Gainsborough, Lincs DN21 5AH
Tel: 01427 718878 • **email: info@blackswanguesthouse.co.uk**
www.blackswanguesthouse.co.uk

Baumber Park
Farmhouse B&B and Self Catering Cottage

Spacious elegant farmhouse of character in quiet parkland setting, on a mixed farm. Large colourful and inspiring plantsman's garden with extensive vistas and wildlife pond. Fine bedrooms with lovely views, period furniture, log fires and books. Central in the county and close to the Lincolnshire Wolds, this rolling countryside is little known, quite unspoilt, and ideal for walking, cycling or riding. Championship golf courses at Woodhall Spa. Well located for historic Lincoln, interesting market towns and many antique shops. Enjoy a relaxing break, excellent breakfasts, and a comfortable, homely atmosphere. *Two doubles, one twin, all en suite or private bathroom. Bed and Breakfast from £30. Discounts on stays of 3 nights or more.*

Gathman's Cottage
Across the field, self-catering accommodation available in picturesque, 18th Century thatched cottage lovingly restored and with enough 'mod-cons', but retaining its great character. Surrounded by parkland and grazing cattle in summer; warm and cosy in winter, Lovely distant views, as far as Lincoln Cathedral. Three bedrooms –double and twin upstairs, small double downstairs suitable for those with limited mobility. Private gardens and parking. *Short Break weekends: 3 nights, Friday - Monday OR Mid Week Breaks: 4 nights, Monday - Friday for the same price. From £200.*

Mrs Clare Harrison, Baumber Park, Baumber, Near Horncastle LN9 5NE
Tel: 01507 578235 • Fax: 01507 578417 • mobile: 07977 722776
e-mail: mail@baumberpark.com • www.baumberpark.com

SB

Wi-Fi

Redhurst B&B & Self-Catering

Exchange the buzz of city traffic for the birdsong of the countryside whilst staying at Redhurst B&B, set in gardens and orchard in a small village nestling on the edge of the Lincolnshire Wolds. Ideal setting for visiting the many and varied attractions of Lincolnshire.
Two twin en suite (one ground floor).
From £28 and £31pppn.
One single with private facilities. From £28pn.
Open all year • Sorry no pets • Non-smoking
• Self-catering also available in house
and in "The Shed", sleeps 4.

Mrs Vivienne Klockner, Redhurst,
Holton-cum-Beckering,
Market Rasen LN8 5NG
Tel: 01673 857927
www.RedhurstBAndB.co.uk
e-mail: Vivienne@RedhurstBAndB.co.uk

Coast or country, the choice is yours for a holiday in Lincolnshire. With award-winning beaches, miles of clean sand, theme parks, kite surfing, jet skiing and seaside nature reserves, there's action, excitement and interests for everyone right along the coast. At Skegness, as well as all the fun on the beach, children will love watching the seals being fed at the seal sanctuary, and the Parrot Zoo nearby. There's a seal sanctuary at Mablethorpe too, and all the fun of the fairground, as well as beach huts to hire if the sun goes behind a cloud. Further north, at Cleethorpes with its wonderful beaches and Pleasure Island, take a ride on the Cleethorpes Coast Light Railway, or a guided tour of the sand dunes and saltmarshes at the Discovery Centre to find out about local wildlife habitats. Inland spend a peaceful break exploring the quiet countryside of the Wolds. Keen fishermen can always find a peaceful spot along the extensive network of rivers and canals and for golfers there's a wide variety and standard of courses, with the home of amateur golf in England at the National Golf Centre at Woodhall Spa. In Lincoln walk round the battlements at the Castle, explore the cobbled streets lined with medieval buildings and visit the imposing Gothic cathedral, one of the finest in Europe. Cruise on the Roman canal that flows through the city, shop at the boutiques, eat at the restaurants and cafes, and in the evening enjoy a concert or a visit to the theatre.

Daventry, Kettering

Northamptonshire

SB

Wi-Fi

Murcott Mill Farmhouse
Murcott, Long Buckby, Northampton NN6 7QR
• Tel: 01327 842236 •

Imposing Georgian mill house set within a working farm.
Large garden and lovely outlook over open countryside. All rooms
are en suite with colour TV. Central heating throughout and
visitors have their own lounge and dining room with woodburner.
An ideal stopover, close to M1, and good location for touring.
Children and pets welcome.
Bed and Breakfast from £40 single; double £70. Open all year.

Credit cards accepted

e-mail: carrie.murcottmill@virgin.net • www.murcottmill.com

SB

ENJOY A HOLIDAY in our comfortable 17th century farmhouse with
oak beams and inglenook fireplaces. Four-poster bed now available.
Peaceful surroundings, large garden containing ancient circular
dovecote. Dairy Farm is a working farm situated in a beautiful
Northamptonshire village just off the A14, within easy reach of many
places of interest or ideal for a restful holiday. Good farmhouse food and
friendly atmosphere. Open all year, except Christmas.
B&B from £27 to £38 (children under 10 half price); Evening Meal £18.

Mrs A. Clarke
Dairy Farm
Cranford St Andrew
Kettering NN14 4AQ
Tel: 01536 330273

Burton Joyce

Nottinghamshire

Willow House Bed and Breakfast

A period house (1857) in quiet village two minutes' walk from beautiful river bank, yet only five miles from City. Attractive, interesting accommodation with authentic Victorian ambience. En suite available. Bright, clean rooms with tea/coffee facilities, TV.
Off-road parking. Porch for smokers.
Ideally situated for Holme Pierrepont International Watersports Centre; golf; National Ice Centre; Trent Bridge (cricket); Sherwood Forest; Nottingham Racecourse; Shelford Pony Trials and the unspoiled historic town of Southwell with its Minster and Racecourse.
Good local eating. Please phone first for directions.
Rates: From £26 per person per night.

**Mrs V. Baker, Willow House,
Burton Joyce NG14 5FD
Tel:0115 931 2070; Mob: 07816 347706
www.willowhousebedandbreakfast.co.uk**

SB

In Nottinghamshire the myths, legends and facts all play a part in the stories of Robin Hood, but visit Sherwood Forest, the hiding place of outlaws in medieval times, and make up your own mind from the evidence you find there. Watch cricket at Trent Bridge, horse racing at Nottingham and the all-weather course at Southwell, and ice hockey at Nottingham's National Ice Centre, or try ice skating yourself. There are golf courses from municipal and pay & play to championship standard, fishing in canals, lakes and fisheries, walking by rivers and canals and cycling in the woodland and country parks, and everyone is welcome to play at the Nottingham Tennis Centre. The city of Nottingham is a wonderful place to shop, with designer outlets, independent shops and department stores, and don't miss the traditional Lace Market.

The Grange • Elton

The Grange offers traditional Farmhouse breakfast with mainly local produce used, served in a sunny conservatory looking out onto a beautiful garden.

Owned by ex Scottish International Footballer, Don Masson and his wife Brenda, The Grange is set in the scenic Vale of Belvoir, only 200 metres off the A52 between Nottingham and Grantham. There is an excellent pub and restaurant within a three minute walk away and a five minute drive to Bingham or Bottesford where there are many good eating places. The Grange is ideal for events at Belvoir Castle and also only a 20 minute drive to Trent Bridge cricket ground. Why not try The Grange where Don and Brenda will give you a very warm welcome.

Free wi-fi at The Grange

Please note that we do not accept credit/debit cards - cash and cheques only.

AA
★★★★★
Bed &
Breakfast
Highly Commended

Terms from £45-£55 single, £70-£75 double/twin.

The Grange Bed & Breakfast, Sutton Lane, Elton NG13 9LA
Mobile: 07887 952181

A house of uncommon charm in the beautiful Vale of Belvoir

Standing in quiet seclusion overlooking lovely gardens and parkland, this charming hotel combines the standards of good hotelkeeping with the hospitality of an informal country house.
Most bedrooms enjoy lovely views, and all are comfortable and very well equipped.
Relax in the study or the sitting room; then dine in the elegant pillared hall, which is open daily for lunch and dinner, with the emphasis on fresh seasonal food – game in winter and fish in summer. The hotel is conveniently situated for visiting Nottingham and the many places of historic interest in the East Midlands.

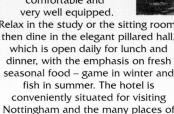
Langar Hall

LANGAR HALL, LANGAR,
NOTTINGHAMSHIRE NG13 9HG
TEL: 01949 860559
FAX: 01949 861045
e-mail: info@langarhall.co.uk
www.langarhall.co.uk

Hereford, Ledbury

Herefordshire

Ross-on-Wye

Outdoor activities, creative arts and crafts, wonderful food - Herefordshire, on the border with Wales, will appeal whatever your interest. With its rolling countryside and green meadows dotted with woodland and meandering streams, there are endless opportunities for all kinds of outdoor activities, from white water canoeing on the Yat Rapids through the steep-sided gorge at Symonds Yat, to longer, more gentle trips on the quieter sections of the River Wye. Footpaths, bridleways and traffic-free cycle trails through countryside rich in wildlife are perfect for families as well as the more experienced. The Black and White Village Trail takes visitors through beautiful countryside to pretty little villages, each with its own individual characteristics and shops, or follow the Cider Route in this county of apple orchards.

Shropshire

Malt House Farm

Olde worlde beamed farmhouse situated amidst spectacular scenery at the lower slopes of the Long Mynd Hills.

We are a working farm producing beef cattle and sheep. One double bedroom and one twin, both with en suite bathroom, hairdryer and tea tray. Good farmhouse cooking is served in the dining room.

Private guests' sitting room.

- *Non-smoking* • *Regret no children or pets*
- *Bed and Breakfast from £29.50pppn*

**Malt House Farm, Lower Wood,
Church Stretton SY6 6LF
Tel: 01694 751379 • Proprietor: Mrs Lyn Bloor**

SB

Wi-Fi

Acton Scott Farm

Lovely 16th century farmhouse in peaceful village amidst the beautiful South Shropshire Hills, an Area of Outstanding Natural Beauty where Victorian Farm was filmed. The farmhouse is full of character and all rooms have heating and are comfortable and spacious. The bedrooms are either en suite or private bathroom with hairdryers, tea/coffee making facilities, patchwork quilts and colour TV.

There is a lounge with colour TV and inglenook fireplace. Children welcome. We are a working farm, centrally situated for visiting Ironbridge, Shrewsbury and Ludlow, each being easily reached within half an hour. Touring and walking information is available for visitors. Bed and full English Breakfast from £29pppn. Non-smoking. Open all year excluding November, December, January and February.

**Mrs Mary Jones, Acton Scott Farm, Acton Scott,
Church Stretton SY6 6QN • Tel: 01694 781260
e-mail: fhg@actonscottfarm.co.uk • www.actonscottfarm.co.uk**

Mynd House

Bed and Breakfast in an Edwardian Guest House near Church Stretton in Shropshire

An Edwardian house built at the turn of the century, it provides 7 spacious en suite bedrooms with stunning views of the surrounding Shropshire hills - an ideal location for pleasure or business. All the spacious en suite bedrooms, including a four-poster suite and a de luxe family room, have TV, mini-bar fridge and tea/coffee making. Wi-Fi available. Licensed residents' bar.
Many National Trust and other historic properties are within easy reach.

Mynd House, Ludlow Road, Little Stretton, Church Stretton, Shropshire SY6 6RB
Tel: 01694 722212 • www.myndhouse.co.uk
e-mail: info@myndhouse.co.uk

Family-run B&B with 7 en suite bedrooms
Comfortable guest lounge
Residential licensed bar

HAYNALL VILLA

Haynall Villa is set in a quiet position in the picturesque Teme Valley on the borders of Shropshire, Herefordshire and Worcestershire, near historic Ludlow, famed for its architecture, and food too. Ironbridge and mid-Wales are within easy reach. Nearby there are lots of attractive towns and villages, gardens and National Trust properties. There is a choice of good walks, stroll by the pretty brook running through the farm, or cycle around the quiet country lanes.

The farmhouse, built approx in the 1820s as a gentleman's residence, is set in large gardens. An oak staircase leads to the comfortable bedrooms, a double and twin en suite, and a family room with private bathroom, all with good views, TV and hot beverage facilities. Relax in the lounge, with a fire on cooler evenings. Enjoy a traditional English farmhouse breakfast using local produce.

In 2008 we were awarded Highly Commended by the AA Member Shropshire Nature Trust.

Mrs Rachel Edwards, Haynall Villa, Little Hereford, Near Ludlow SY8 4BA
Tel & Fax: 01584 711589
e-mail: rachelmedwards@hotmail.com
www.haynallvilla.co.uk

Eccleshall

Staffordshire

Situated right in the middle of England, for an active holiday Staffordshire is difficult to beat. There are forest walks and cycle trails for all the family in the National Forest and over the historic heathlands and woodlands of Cannock Chase, and everything from canoeing to climbing in the Staffordshire Peak District. The exciting theme parks, stately homes and castles, miles of canals and the largest street-style skate park in Europe at Stoke-on-Trent, ensure thrills, interest and fun for every age group. Take a look at life in the past at the complete working historic estate at Shugborough near Stafford, with working kitchens, dairy water mill and brewhouse, shop at the retail village or walk with the monkeys in Trentham's historic estate or just take a leisurely boat trip down one of the many canals, there's so much of interest to see and do!

Kingsley, Tamworth

symbols 🐾🎠 SB ♿ ♉ Wi-Fi

🐾 *Pets Welcome* 🎠 *Children Welcome*

SB *Short Breaks* ♿ *Suitable for Disabled Guests*

♉ *Licensed* **Wi-Fi** *Wi-Fi available*

Stratford-Upon-Avon

Warwickshire

SB

Holly Tree Cottage
Birmingham Road, Pathlow, Stratford-upon-Avon CV37 0ES
Tel & Fax: 01789 204461

Period cottage dating from 17th Century, with antiques, paintings, collection of porcelain, fresh flowers, tasteful furnishings and friendly atmosphere. Picturesque gardens, orchard, paddock and pasture with wildlife and extensive views over open countryside. Situated 3 miles north of Stratford-upon-Avon towards Henley-in-Arden on A3400.

Rooms have television, radio/alarm, hospitality trays and hairdryers. Breakfasts are a speciality. Pubs and restaurants nearby.

Ideally located for Theatre, Shakespeare Country, Heart of England, Cotswolds, Warwick Castle, Blenheim Palace and National Trust Properties. Well situated for National Exhibition Centre, Birmingham and National Agricultural Centre, Stoneleigh.

Children welcome, pets by arrangement. Non-smoking.

Bed and Breakfast from £30 per person.

e-mail: john@hollytree-cottage.co.uk • www.hollytree-cottage.co.uk

Warwickshire and Shakespeare's birthplace, Stratford-on-Avon, go hand in hand. A great way to view this interesting town of black and white, half-timbered buildings is from the tower of the newly rebuilt Royal Shakespeare Theatre next to the river. For a closer look take a guided walking tour, or for a more gentle approach to sightseeing cruise down the River Avon. Round off the day with a performance by the RSC of a favourite Shakespearian play. As well as Sir Basil Spence's Coventry Cathedral and two other churches designed by him, Coventry is home to Warwick Arts Centre, the largest in the Midlands, and of course, in the birthplace of the British motor transport industry, Coventry Transport Museum. For football fans, Coventry is hosting several of the London 2012 Olympic matches, and the city's Live Site with an interactive screen means no-one need miss any of the Olympic action.

Stratford-Upon-Avon

West Midlands

Awentsbury Hotel

Victorian Country House Hotel set in its own grounds in peaceful surroundings, only 2½ miles from the city centre. Close to University Hospitals, Cadbury World, Indoor Arena, Convention Centre. Easy access to NEC and University of Central England.

Wi-Fi

- Dating from 1882
- Cooked breakfasts
- Vintage cars to view
- Easy access to NEC
- A warm welcome awaits you

21 Serpentine Road, Selly Park,
Birmingham B29 7HU
Tel: 0121 472 1258
e-mail: ian@awentsbury.com
www.awentsbury.com

SB
Wi-Fi

Featherstone Farm Hotel

New Road, Featherstone, Wolverhampton WV10 7NW

A small, high-class country house hotel set in five acres of unspoiled countryside, only one mile from Junction 11 on the M6 or Junction 1 on the M54. The main house has nine en suite bedrooms with all the facilities one would expect in a hotel of distinction. Kings Repose Indian Restaurant, serving freshly prepared dishes, and licensed bar. Secure car park.

- Self-contained fully furnished cottages with maid service are also available.

Tel: 01902 725371 • Fax: 01902 731741

Mobile: 07836 315258

e-mail: featherstonefarmhotel@yahoo.co.uk

www.featherstonefarmhotel.co.uk

Droitwich Spa

Worcestershire

Worcestershire, stretching south-east from the fringes of Birmingham, is a county of Georgian towns, Cotswold stone villages and a Victorian spa, all centred on the cathedral city of Worcester. To the north canals were cut to satisfy the need for transport that grew with industrialisation, and now provide a wonderful opportunity for a leisurely break on a narrowboat, or take a restful look at the countryside from the Severn Valley Railway between Bromsgrove and Kidderminster. Long distance trails like the 100-mile Millenium Way cross the countryside in all directions, or follow one of the many shorter local circular walks. In the Malvern Hills choose between gentle and more strenuous exercise to appreciate the wonderful views of the surrounding countryside, or for a different kind of challenge, try mountain boarding in the hills near Malvern.

Great Malvern

SB

Wi-Fi

Copper Beech
HOUSE

Great Malvern is renowned for its annual music festivals, prestigious theatres, garden shows, mineral water, and Morgan Cars. The area is a haven of elegant landscapes, open spaces, and fantastic walks. **Copper Beech House** is conveniently located a few minutes' walk from Great Malvern Station, a short distance from the theatres and town centre, and a few minutes by car to the Three Counties Showground.

Family-owned and run late Victorian property with 7 en suite guest rooms. All rooms have flat-screen TVs, tea/coffee making facilities, hairdryer, radio alarm, and free Wi-Fi access. A large guest lounge with writing desk, widescreen Freesat television, and a wide range of books, overlooks the south-facing garden. The breakfast room comfortably seats a full house, and an extensive menu with vegetarian and other options is always available. There is ample on and off-road parking and a good choice of restaurants and pubs within walking distance. Non-smoking throughout and open all year. Our website shows availability and allows on-line bookings to be made 24 hours a day.

Copper Beech House
32 Avenue Road, Malvern WR14 3BJ • 01684 565013
www.copperbeechhouse.co.uk • enquiries@copperbeechhouse.co.uk

---

SB

The health-giving properties of Malvern are well documented, the town retaining the popularity which made it a favourite Victorian spa and cultural centre.

Very much part of this scenario, this beautiful house reposes peacefully in mature gardens and is but a short stroll from the town centre. The hotel has an aura of tranquillity allied to style and impeccable taste in its appointments. It has recently been refurbished to AA Three Star (79%) standard, and has a Rosette for its 'L'Amuse-Bouche' Restaurant. It is the ideal retreat for a weekend away or a business break in a family-owned and run hotel.

THE COTFORD HOTEL
51 Graham Road, Great Malvern, Worcestershire WR14 2HU
Tel: 01684 572427 • Fax: 01684 572952 • www.cotfordhotel.co.uk • e-mail: reservations@cotfordhotel.co.uk

Tenbury Wells, Worcester

Please note...

Beverley, Bridlington

East Yorkshire

Coverdale, Harrogate

North Yorkshire

Middle Farm

🐴
🐕
SB

Peacefully situated 'traditonal' Dales farmhouse, away from the madding crowd.

Two double rooms and one twin room, all en suite, guests' own lounge, dining room in a converted adjoining stable block.

Bed & Breakfast with optional Evening Meal. Home cooking. Pets and children welcome. Off-road parking. Ideally positioned for walking and touring in the beautiful Yorkshire Dales. Open all year.

Mrs Julie Clarke, Middle Farm, Woodale, Coverdale, Leyburn, North Yorkshire DL8 4TY Tel: 01969 640271

e-mail: j-a-clarke@hotmail.co.uk

www.yorkshirenet.co.uk/stayat/middlefarm/index.htm

Homely, comfortable, Christian accommodation. Spacious stone built bungalow in beautiful Nidderdale which is very central for touring the Yorkshire Dales; Pateley Bridge two miles, Harrogate 14 miles, Ripon nine miles. Museums, rocks, caves, fishing, bird watching, beautiful quiet walks, etc all nearby. En suite rooms (one twin, two double), TV. Private lounge. Tea making facilities available. Choice of breakfast. Evening meals available one mile away. Ample parking space on this working farm. Open Easter to end of October.

Mrs C.E. Nelson, Nidderdale Lodge Farm, Fellbeck, Pateley Bridge, Harrogate HG3 5DR • Tel: 01423 711677

Hawes, Helmsley

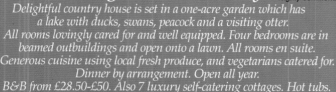

Dominated by the magnificent York Minster, the largest medieval Gothic cathedral in northern Europe, the city of York in North Yorkshire is full of attractions for the visitor. Have fun finding your way through the Snickelways, the maze of hidden alleyways, and enjoy a morning – or longer – in the array of independent shops and boutiques as well as all the top high street stores. Explore York's past at Jorvik, the recreation of the original Viking city from 1000 years ago or become an archaeologist for the day at Dig! and excavate for yourself items from Viking, Roman, medieval and Victorian times. Outside the city the vast open stretches of the North York Moors and Yorkshire Dales National Parks and the golden sandy beaches of the coast are perfect for an active holiday.

THE OLD STAR
West Witton, Leyburn
DL8 4LU
Tel: 01969 622949
enquiries@theoldstar.com
www.theoldstar.com

Formerly a 17th century coaching inn, now a family-run guest house, you are always welcome at the Old Star.

The building still retains many original features. Comfortable lounge with oak beams and log fire. Bedrooms mostly en suite with central heating, TV and tea/coffee making facilities.

Two good food pubs in village. In the heart of the Yorkshire Dales National Park we are ideally situated for walking and touring the Dales. Large car park. Open all year except Christmas.

En suite Bed and Breakfast from £29pppn.

Lovesome Hill Farm
Mary & John Pearson
Tel: 01609 772311
Lovesome Hill,
Northallerton DL6 2PB

SB

Wi-Fi

Central location for exploring the Dales and Moors, Durham and York. Enjoy the comfort and welcome we have to offer you at our traditional working farm with en suite bedrooms of various combinations and styles, some on ground floor. Gate Cottage, our luxurious suite, with its antique half-tester bed and its own patio, has views towards the Hambleton Hills. Enjoy home-made produce including our own free-range eggs cooked on the Aga. Brochure available.

Seasonal breaks incl. Lambing & Apple Juicing.
Open all year except Christmas and New Year
B&B from £36-£42 twin/double,
£40-£50 single.
Evening Meal available £15-£20.

www.lovesomehillfarm.co.uk
e-mail: lovesomehillfarm@btinternet.com

Nawton, Pickering

Pickering

Farfields Farm

*Steve and Liz offer a warm welcome to this working
farm, with a chance to relax and enjoy the peace and
tranquillity within the magnificent National Park.
A walkers' paradise, with spectacular views of the North
York Moors Railway. Central for exploring the moors,
Whitby and the Heritage Coast, and historic York.
Very comfortable accommodation in five en suite
rooms, two in the farmhouse and three in
a lovely barn conversion adjacent.
All rooms have colour TV and tea/coffee making
facilities; one with small kitchenette.
Lovely Yorkshire breakfasts using local produce
wherever possible. Five minute stroll to local inn.
Tariff £35-£45pppn.*

Wi-Fi

**Mrs E. Stead, Farfields Farm, Lockton,
Pickering YO18 7NQ • Tel: 01751 460239
e-mail: stay@farfieldsfarm.co.uk
www.farfieldsfarm.co.uk**

Banavie

is a large semi-detached house set in a quiet part
of the picturesque village of Thornton-le-Dale, one
of the prettiest villages in Yorkshire with its famous
thatched cottage and bubbling stream flowing
through the centre. We offer our guests a quiet
night's sleep and rest away from the main road, yet
only four minutes' walk from the village centre. One large
double or twin bedroom and two double bedrooms, all
tastefully decorated with en suite facilities, colour TV, hairdryer,
shaver point etc. and tea/coffee making facilities. There is a large
guest lounge, tea tray on arrival. A real Yorkshire breakfast is served
in the dining room. Places to visit include Castle Howard, Eden Camp,
North Yorkshire Moors Railway, Goathland ("Heartbeat"), York etc.
There are three pubs, a bistro and a fish and chip shop for meals.
Children and dogs welcome. Own keys. Car parking at back of house.

B&B from £29 pppn
• SAE please for brochure • Welcome To Excellence
• Hygiene Certificate held • No Smoking
Mrs Ella Bowes

**BANAVIE, ROXBY ROAD, THORNTON-LE-DALE, PICKERING YO18 7SX
Tel: 01751 474616 • e-mail: info@banavie.uk.com • www.banavie.uk.com**

Scarborough

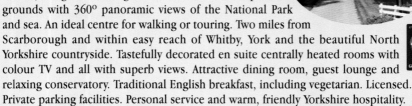

Scarborough, Skipton

Skipton

BECK HALL
Malham • North Yorkshire

*18th century B&B on the Pennine Way,
log fires and huge breakfasts.
Midweek and 4-night specials.
Ideal for exploring the Yorkshire Dales.*

Built in 1710, Beck Hall has been providing accommodation since the 1930s. There are now 10 double/twin en suite rooms and 8 with four-poster. Spacious guest lounge with log fire. Full English breakfast, fish, vegetarian or lighter continental selection. Malham is one of the most visited villages in the Yorkshire Dales, with plenty of things to do for the walker, cyclist or family. The market towns of Settle and Skipton are nearby and the Settle-Carlisle Railway is a good bet for a day out. If the weather palls there are caves nearby and other indoor attractions. The Lake District, Kendal and Windermere are an hour's drive.

**Beck Hall, Cove Rd, Malham, North Yorkshire BD23 4DJ
Tel: 01729 830332
e-mail: alice@beckhallmalham.com
www.beckhallmalham.com**

LOW SKIBEDEN FARMHOUSE

Detached 16th century farmhouse in private grounds. Quiet, with safe parking. One mile east of Skipton, Gateway to the Dales, and close to many places of beauty and interest. Luxury B&B with fireside treats in the lounge.

All rooms are quiet and spacious, with panoramic views, washbasin and toilet (some full en suite), tea/coffee facilities and electric overblankets.

Sorry, no smoking, no pets, no children.

*Terms: £32-£38pppn;
single occupancy £40-£56*

Open all year. Credit cards accepted. Farm cottage sometimes available.

**HARROGATE ROAD, SKIPTON, NORTH YORKSHIRE BD23 6AB
Tel: 01756 793849 • www.lowskibeden.co.uk**

BROOKLYN B & B

Wi-Fi

Situated on a quiet terrace in the old part of the picturesque, historic village of Staithes, with its artistic and Captain Cook associations, Brooklyn is a solid, red brick house, built in 1921 by a retired sea captain.

It has three letting rooms (2 doubles, 1 twin) which are individually decorated with views across the rooftops to Cowbar cliffs. All have a television and tea /coffee making facilities, and although not en suite, do have washbasins.

The dining room doubles as a sitting room for guests, and breakfasts are generous, vegetarians catered for, and special diets by arrangement. Pets and children are most welcome.

MS M.J. HEALD, BROOKLYN B&B, BROWN'S TERRACE, STAITHES, NORTH YORKSHIRE TS13 5BG
Tel: 01947 841396 • margaret@heald.org.uk
www.brooklynuk.co.uk

Golden Fleece Hotel

Market Place - Thirsk - York YO7 1LL
Tel: 01845 523108   Fax: 01845 523996

HOTEL

The Golden Fleece Hotel is a 400-year-old Coaching Inn overlooking the cobbled market place in Thirsk, situated between two outstanding areas of natural beauty, the Yorkshire Moors and Dales National Parks. The hotel has a range of 25 individually designed en suite rooms equipped with all the amenities that make today's traveller feel completely at home.

Food is home cooked using local produce and the service is relaxed and friendly.

For information about our Shortbreaks please contact the reception team at the hotel.

www.goldenfleecehotel.com • reservations@goldenfleecehotel.com

SB

One twin and one double en suite rooms, one single; all with tea/coffee making facilities and TV; alarm clock/radio and hairdryer also provided; diningroom; central heating.

ETC ★★★★

Very clean and comfortable accommodation with good food. Situated in a quiet part of this picturesque village, which is in a good position for Moors, countryside, coast, North York Moors Railway, Flamingo Park Zoo and Dalby forest drives, mountain biking and walking. Good facilities for meals provided in the village. Open Easter to October for Bed and Breakfast from £32-£36pp. Private car park. Secure motorbike and cycle storage.

Tangalwood

Roxby Road, Thornton-le-Dale, Pickering YO18 7TQ

TELEPHONE: **01751 474688** • **www.accommodation.uk.net/tangalwood**

York

York

SB

Wi-Fi

Sheffield

South Yorkshire

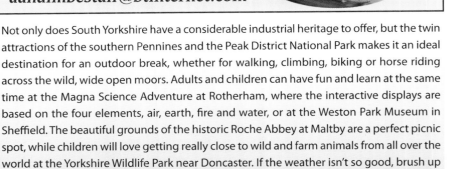
Not only does South Yorkshire have a considerable industrial heritage to offer, but the twin attractions of the southern Pennines and the Peak District National Park makes it an ideal destination for an outdoor break, whether for walking, climbing, biking or horse riding across the wild, wide open moors. Adults and children can have fun and learn at the same time at the Magna Science Adventure at Rotherham, where the interactive displays are based on the four elements, air, earth, fire and water, or at the Weston Park Museum in Sheffield. The beautiful grounds of the historic Roche Abbey at Maltby are a perfect picnic spot, while children will love getting really close to wild and farm animals from all over the world at the Yorkshire Wildlife Park near Doncaster. If the weather isn't so good, brush up your mountaineering skills at a choice of indoor climbing walls, and there's swimming and ice skating and for relaxation, a tropical spa, at Doncaster Dome.

Bingley

West Yorkshire

Large Victorian house tucked away in tranquil area, but close main roads, tourist sites, cities. Good views, individual decor, informal style. Comfy sofas, interesting artworks. Antidote to chain hotels. Historic canal locks and excellent walking (dogs and humans) close by.

THE FIVE RISE LOCKS HOTEL & RESTAURANT,
BECK LANE, BINGLEY, YORKSHIRE BD16 4DD
Tel: 01274 565296 • e-mail: info@five-rise-locks.co.uk
www.five-rise-locks.co.uk

West Yorkshire is a mix of wild moorland and towns and cities with an historic industrial heritage. Spend some time in one of the many fascinating museums of past working life, then stride out over the moors, taking in the dramatic scenery, before a shopping spree or a wonderful afternoon tea. Visit the Rhubarb Triangle near Wakefield early in the year to see the crop being harvested by candlelight. At the model Victorian village for mill workers at Saltaire UNESCO World Heritage Site, Salts Mill has been transformed into the Hockney Gallery, with a restaurant and everything from musical instruments to carpets for shoppers to browse and buy. From there, wander along the banks of the Leeds-Liverpool Canal, so vital for trade in a past age, and watch the Five Rise Locks in action. Leeds is the destination for a lively city break. Theatres, ballet, opera, festivals, restaurants, clubs, and of course, one of the best shopping experiences in the country.

If you are looking for a warm and comfortable environment in which to relax and enjoy your stay whilst visiting Yorkshire then The Manor will be perfect for you. This luxurious 5 Star Gold Award retreat offers a relaxing and refreshing base from which to explore some of the most beautiful countryside in Yorkshire. Lovingly restored, this 18th Century Manor House is enhanced by many original features. Ideally situated for exploring the rugged Pennine moorland or Bronte Country, the Yorkshire Dales and beyond.

- Ample off-road car parking
- Centrally heated en suite rooms
- Welcome tray with homemade biscuits
- Top quality beds and linen
- Satellite TV with DVD player
- Wi-Fi Internet access
- Extensive DVD library
- Hairdryer, CD player & radio alarm clock
- Easy access to all major attractions
- Debit & credit cards accepted
- Private guest lounge
- Thick fluffy towels
- Extensive complimentary toiletries
- Iron & ironing board available
- Packed lunches available on request
- Hearty Yorkshire breakfast menu

The Manor Guest House
Sutton Drive, Cullingworth, Bradford BD13 5BQ
Tel: 01535 274374
e-mail: info@cullingworthmanor.co.uk
www.cullingworthmanor.co.uk

The Bank House Hotel & Restaurant
11/13 Bank Street, Westgate, Wakefield WF1 1EH
Tel: 01924 368248 • Fax: 01924 363724
www.thebankhousehotelandrestaurant.com

We are a small family-run business with a warm and friendly welcome to all our guests. Our staff are always happy to help ensure your stay is a pleasant one. Our rooms are all en suite, with tea/coffee making facilities and Sky TV. All parties are welcome and are catered for.

We are two miles from the M1 and M62 and five miles from the A1. The main Westgate rail station and bus station are five minutes away. Our location is in the city centre, based near the Ridings shopping complex, the Theatre Royal Opera House, and all the popular Westgate nightlife. We have many local attractions nearby, which our staff will be happy to direct you to.

Durham

Northumberland

Waren House Hotel

   AA

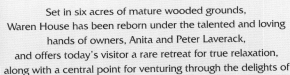

Set in six acres of mature wooded grounds, Waren House has been reborn under the talented and loving hands of owners, Anita and Peter Laverack, and offers today's visitor a rare retreat for true relaxation, along with a central point for venturing through the delights of North Northumberland and the Scottish Borders.

Breakfast and dinner are served in the beautiful and romantic dining room where food is presented with the utmost care. Our cellar is stocked with a huge choice of reasonably priced fine wines. All public rooms and bedrooms are non-smoking.

Relax in the gardens or in the comfortable lounge and adjacent library. For those seeking the simple pleasures of walking - the sandy shore offers mile upon mile of beautiful scenery.

From this tranquil setting it is easy to find the treasures of the Heritage Coast, including the magnificent castle at Bamburgh, just two miles away.

Waren Mill, Belford, Near Bamburgh, Northumberland NE70 7EE
Tel: 01668 214581 • Fax: 01668 214484
e-mail: enquiries@warenhousehotel.co.uk
www.warenhousehotel.co.uk

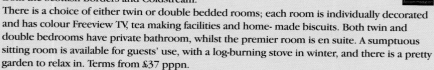

Greenhead, Hadrian's Wall

Holmhead

Standing directly on The Hadrian's Wall Path and Pennine Way, Holmhead is built with stones from Hadrian's Wall and stands on the foundations of this World Heritage Site.
Ideal for exploring Hadrian's Wall, the Lake District, Scottish Borders and North Pennines.

All bedrooms en suite. Beautiful country views.

Self-catering cottage sleeps four. Camping Barn also available.

Holmhead Guest House
Hadrian's Wall
Greenhead
Northunberland CA8 7HY
Tel: 016977 47402
e-mail:
holmhead@forestbarn.com
www.bandbhadrianswall.com

❖ Struthers Farm ❖
Bed & Breakfast

Catton, Allendale, Hexham NE47 9LP

Struthers Farm offers a warm welcome, with many splendid local walks from the farm itself.
Situated in an area of outstanding beauty, with panoramic views.
Double/twin rooms,
en suite bathrooms, central heating.
Good farmhouse cooking.
Ample safe parking.

Come and share our home and enjoy beautiful countryside. Near Hadrian's Wall (½ hour's drive). Children welcome, pets by prior arrangement. Open all year.

Bed and Breakfast from £30

Optional Evening Meal from £12.50.

Contact Mrs Ruby Keenleyside - 01434 683580
email: r.keenleyside121@btinternet.com
www.struthersfarmbandb.com

SB

Wi-Fi

Hospitality, comfort and simply breathtaking views set the atmosphere for your visit to Dunns Houses. Welcome to our farmhouse, built in the 1400s in Border Reiver country, on a 960 acre stock farm in an Area of Outstanding Natural Beauty. Panoramic views of the Rede Valley and the Cheviot Hills. Private fishing for brown trout and salmon. Lockup garage for cycles and boiler house for walkers' clothing and boots.

Many activities available close by including golf, cycling and walking on the Pennine Way, as well as Kielder Water and Forest for all sorts of outdoor activities and water sports.
Spacious en suite bedrooms and guests' lounge in self-contained part of our home with fantastic views of the Rede Valley, Otterburn and the foothills of the Cheviots.
TV, snooker/pool table, games and rocking horses for the younger children.
Tasty, farm-reared or organic breakfast using good quality local bacon, sausage and eggs.
Open all year. Children and pets welcome. Terms from £30 twin/double, £45 single.

**Mrs Jane Walton, Dunns Houses, Otterburn,
Newcastle Upon Tyne NE19 1LB
01830 520677 • 07808 592701
e-mail: dunnshouses@hotmail.com
www.northumberlandfarmholidays.co.uk**

Katerina's Guest House

High Street, Rothbury NE65 7TQ • 01669 620691

Wi-Fi

Charming old guest house, ideally situated for the amenities of pretty Rothbury village, and to explore Northumberland's hills, coast, Alnwick Castle and gardens. Beautiful bedrooms, each decorated and colour co-ordinated to enhance its individual character; some with original stone fireplaces/beamed ceilings, all en suite, with four-poster beds, TV, and superbly stocked tea tray. Free Wi-Fi. Wide, interesting choice of breakfasts; licensed evening meals also available — sample Cath's bread, 'whisky porridge', vegetarian nutballs, or Steak Katerina.

Bed and Breakfast from £68-£78 per room per night, depending on number of nights booked.

e-mail: ian.mills6@btopenworld.com
www.katerinasguesthouse.co.uk

Warkworth

FAIRFIELD HOUSE
16 Station Road,
Warkworth NE65 0XP
Tel: 01665 714455

Fairfield House is an elegant Victorian property quietly situated on the edge of the picturesque village of Warkworth - an ideal location for exploring the Alnwick district and Northumberland's stunning coastline. We offer bed and breakfast accommodation in the main house where we have four tastefully decorated, spacious en suite bedrooms. Self catering accommodation is available in our studio style Garden Apartment. All guests are welcome to enjoy our lovely terraced garden.

mandy@fairfield-guesthouse.com • www.fairfield-guesthouse.com

Rambling over the heather-clad Cheviot moorlands, exploring the castles and pele towers built to ward off invading Scots, watching the feast of wildlife on the coast and in the countryside, breathing in the wonderful sea air on a golden sandy beach, you'll find it all in Northumberland. On the coast, a designated Area of Outstanding Natural Beauty, keen walkers can take the Coast Path from the walled Georgian market town of Berwick-on-Tweed to Cresswell, stopping at little fishing villages on the way. Follow the section along Embleton beach from Craster, best known for its traditionally smoked kippers, to get the best views of the ruins of Dunstanburgh Castle. At the lively market town of Alnwick visit the castle, Hogwarts in the Harry Potter films, with its redeveloped gardens, magnificent water features and even a poison garden! Howick Hall gardens are beautiful from the spring snowdrops onwards. Rare and endangered wildlife is found all along the coast and the ultimate destination for enthusiasts is the Farne Islands, with boat trips from the family resort of Seahouses to watch the grey seals and seabirds, including puffins, in the breeding seasons. Wildlife is abundant in the uplands to the west too. In the heather moorlands of the Cheviot Hills there are plenty of opportunities for birdwatching, as well as horse riding, fishing, canoeing and rock climbing, while at Kielder Water and Forest Park watch the red squirrels and ospreys, follow forest trails and mountain bike tracks or watch the stars in the dark night skies. Learn too about the Romans by watching a re-enactment of Roman life at one of the settlements along Hadrian's Wall, or walk along its length from coast to coast. Hexham and Haltwhistle are good bases for a visit, and these and other market towns and villages dotted all over the county make a stay here a very pleasant one.

Cheshire

Mitchell's of Chester Guest House
28 Hough Green, Chester CH4 8JQ
Tel: 01244 679004 • Fax: 01244 659567
e-mail: mitoches@dialstart.net
www.mitchellsofchester.com

Visit Chester & Cheshire Annual Awards 2006
Best B&B - Commended

SB
♀
Wi-Fi

This elegantly restored Victorian family home is set on the south side of Chester, on a bus route to the city centre.

Guest bedrooms have been furnished in period style, with fully equipped shower room and toilet, central heating, TV, refreshment tray and other thoughtful extras.

An extensive breakfast menu is served in the elegant dining room, and the guest lounge overlooks the well-maintained garden. Wi-Fi available.

The historic city of Chester is ideally placed for touring Wales and the many attractions of the North West of England.

symbols 🐕🎠SB♿♀Wi-Fi

🐕	*Pets Welcome*		🎠	*Children Welcome*
SB	*Short Breaks*		♿	*Suitable for Disabled Guests*
♀	*Licensed*		**Wi-Fi**	*Wi-Fi available*

Chester

In Cheshire, just south of Manchester, combine a city break in historic Chester with a day or two at one of relaxing spas either in the city itself or in one of the luxury resorts in the rolling countryside. A round at an on-site golf course offers an alternative way of enjoying the break, and while out in the country, why not visit one of the many gardens open to the public? Time your visit to the historic Georgian mansion at Tatton Park to coincide with one of the wide choice of events held there throughout the year, including the annual RHS Flower Show. All the family will be fascinated by a visit to the giant Lovell Telescope at Jodrell Bank Visitor Centre near the old silk weaving town of Macclesfield or a ride on the Anderton Boat Lift at Northwich. The walkways in nearby Delamere Forest provide pleasant and not too challenging walks, or hire a mountain bike to ride round the forest trails. Enjoy the views of the wilder countryside from the more challenging Gritstone Trail in the Peak District National Park to the east. A less energetic alternative is to hire a boat and sail round the 'Cheshire Ring' of canals through the tranquil countryside right into Manchester city centre, following these formerly vital trade routes. Chester, with its wonderful array of Roman, medieval and Georgian buildings is a fascinating place to visit. Walk round the most complete example of city walls in the whole country, past the beautiful cathedral, before browsing through the wonderful range of shops, art galleries and museums, making sure you visit The Gallery, a 700 year-old mall with two tiers of boutiques, jewellers and eateries. Explore the history of the area at the Dewa Roman Experience, with reconstructed Roman streets, and take the opportunity to see the Roman, Saxon and medieval remains on view.

Ambleside

Cumbria

The Dower House

Wray Castle, Ambleside, Cumbria
LA22 0JA • Tel: 015394 33211

SB

Lovely old house, quiet and peaceful, stands on an elevation overlooking Lake Windermere, with one of the most beautiful views in all Lakeland. Its setting within the 100-acre Wray Castle estate (National Trust), with direct access to the Lake, makes it an ideal base for walking and touring. Hawkshead and Ambleside are about ten minutes' drive and have numerous old inns and restaurants. Ample car parking; prefer dogs to sleep in the car. Children over five years welcome. Open all year.

Bed and Breakfast from £39.00pp
Dinner, Bed & Breakfast from £58.00pp
e-mail: margaret@rigg5.orangehome.co.uk
www.dowerhouselakes.co.uk

The stunning scenery of the region now known as Cumbria, in England's north west, from the Solway Firth in the north to the coasts of Morecambe Bay in the south, the ports and seaside villages in the west to the Pennines in the east, and including the Lake District National Park, has been attracting tourists since the end of the 17th century, and the number of visitors has been increasing ever since. All kinds of outdoor activities are available, from gorge walking and ghyll scrambling to a trek through the countryside on horseback or a quiet afternoon rowing on a tranquil lake. The area is a walkers' paradise, and whether on foot, in a wheelchair or a pushchair there's a path and trail for everyone. Whether you're following one of the 'Miles without Stiles' on relatively level, well laid tracks around the towns and villages, climbing in the Langdales or tackling Scafell Pike, the highest mountain in England, you won't miss out on all the Lake District has to offer.

Ambleside

Ees Wyke

• COUNTRY HOUSE •

Near Sawrey, Ambleside, Cumbria LA22 0JZ

Ees Wyke is an elegant and comfortable Georgian Country House overlooking Esthwaite Water in the centre of the Lake District. Once a holiday home of Beatrix Potter, Ees Wyke offers superb bed and breakfast, and dinner. Just a short walk away is Hill Top, where she made her home and wrote many of her Peter Rabbit books.

Many bedrooms, the lounge and the restaurant have stunning lake views and fells, from Coniston Old Man to the Langdale Pikes and Grizedale Forest. There are excellent walks nearby, from the easy and relaxing to the more challenging. Lavish Lakeland breakfasts and a daily five-course dinner menu offer dishes featuring local produce.

Tel: 015394 36393 • www.eeswyke.co.uk

e-mail: mail@eeswyke.co.uk

Good Food Guide • Good Hotel Guide Recommended

Ambleside

Ambleside

SB
Wi-Fi

A relaxing hotel break in the Lake District

The Rothay Manor Hotel & Restaurant offers a relaxed, warm and friendly atmosphere in a luxury country house setting, with large, individually designed en suite bedrooms, spacious comfortable lounges, delicious fresh food and outstanding service.

We offer well appointed bedrooms, homemade jams and marmalades with breakfast, our famous buffet-style afternoon tea, and a candlelit restaurant, whilst providing modern amenities - flatscreen TVs, DVDs, iPod docks and free Wi-Fi. Free use of nearby **Leisure Club** with sauna and jacuzzi.

Situated in attractive landscaped gardens just 15 minutes' walk from the head of Windermere and 10 minutes from the centre of Ambleside.

Special offers, packages and a wide range of special interest breaks available.

ROTHAY MANOR
HOTEL & RESTAURANT

**Rothay Bridge, Ambleside,
Cumbria LA22 0EH
Tel: 015394 33605
e-mail: hotel@rothaymanor.co.uk
www.rothaymanor.co.uk**

Ambleside, Appleby-in-Westmorland

AMBLESIDE HOUSE

Church Street, Ambleside LA22 0BU

Tel: 015394 32209

Ambleside House is a non-smoking guest house situated on a quiet street just a minute's walk from the main bus stop and centre of Ambleside, a popular Lakeland village offering a wide range of shops, restaurants and inns catering for all tastes. The en suite rooms have colour TV, tea/coffee making facilities; some have views of Loughrigg and Fairfield Horseshoe.

A generous home-cooked breakfast is served and special diets catered for by arrangement. Enjoy home baked scones and cakes, light lunches and afternoon teas in our adjacent Tea Rooms. Freshly made packed lunches by arrangement

Guests have use of private car park.

B&B from £30 - £45 pppn.
Spring and Autumn Offers
Groups Welcome

email: diana.cameron@btconnect.com

Wi-Fi

www.orangesatthelimes.co.uk

Bed & Breakfast in the Eden Valley

Situated in the heart of the Eden Valley, 20 minutes from Penrith and two miles from Appleby. We have the Pennines to the east, the Lake District to the west, Howgill Fells and the Yorkshire Dales to the south and Hadrian's Wall to the north.

Three lovely centrally heated bedrooms, one en suite with king-size bed, one downstairs king-size/twin bed en suite room, and one double/single room with private bathroom. All have TV with Freeview and coffee/tea making facilities.

Full English Breakfast with sausages made by our local butcher and local free-range eggs, or Continental Breakfast, both with home-made bread and fresh coffee. Sandwiches and packed lunches available on request. B&B from £33 pppn.

Penny Orange
The Limes, Colby
Appleby-in-Westmorland CA16 6BD
01768 351605
e-mail: info@orangesatthelimes.co.uk

Bowness-on-Windermere, Broughton-in-Furness

There's so much to find out about the creatures who live in the water both nearby and in distant parts of the world at the Lakes Aquarium at Newby Bridge. From here too see more of the scenery from the Lakeside and Haverthwaite Railway, or from the Ravenglass and Eskdale Railway which runs inland from the coast. Visit nearby haunted Muncaster Castle for a ghostly experience, enjoy the wonderful collection of rhododendrons in spring, watch the wild herons feeding and 'meet the birds' at the World Owl Centre, with more than 200 species of owl to see. Just along the coast the Edwardian resort of Grange-over–Sands, in a sheltered spot with a mild climate, is a good base from which to explore the South Lakes, with the Lakeland Miniature Village and the award-winning gardens at Holker Hall close by. Children of all ages will want to visit The Beatrix Potter Attraction at Bowness-on-Windermere and Hilltop, the author's home on the other side of the lake. Find out all about the area at Brockhole, the National Park Visitor Centre overlooking Windermere, with an adventure playground and lovely gardens. For the central Lakes stay at Ambleside or one of the many traditional Lakeland villages, like Grasmere, the home of Wordsworth. The busy market town of Keswick is the ideal centre for exploring the north Lakes, including the historic port of Whitehaven, the former centre for the rum trade. Stay in Penrith, Appleby-in-Westmorland or Kirkby Lonsdale to explore the western Pennines or Silloth-on-Solway to discover the Solway Firth coast. Finally don't miss out Carlisle and its cathedral and castle, the stronghold involved in so many battles with the Scots, the Jacobite rebellions and the Civil War.

Bridge Hotel

Set between Buttermere and Crummock Water and surrounded by the famous Buttermere Fells, in an Area of Outstanding Natural Beauty. Buttermere is the ideal location for exploring the quieter and more scenic northern area of the English Lake District - "the real Lake District"! It is also close enough to the busier southern areas for easy access and therefore makes an ideal holiday base.

Comfortable accommodation is available in 21 individually designed en suite bedrooms - Standard. Superior and Four-poster.

A selection of traditional bar meals can be enjoyed along with a choice of real ales, or more formal dining is available in the restaurant. Relax in the residents' lounge with morning coffee, afternoon tea or pre-dinner drinks.

Free Wi-Fi is available here or in the reception area.

Comfortable, well equipped self-catering apartments are also available, sleep 2/4.

**Buttermere, Lake District,
Cumbria CA13 9UZ**
Tel: 017687 70252 • Fax: 017687 70215
enquiries@bridge-hotel.com
www.bridge-hotel.com

Dalegarth Guest House

SB

Hassness Estate, Buttermere CA13 9XA

e-mail: dalegarthhouse@hotmail.co.uk • www.dalegarthguesthouse.co.uk

Dalegarth is a beautiful 9 bedroom guesthouse set in stunning grounds with private parking on the edge of Buttermere Lake. Here at Dalegarth we always offer a warm welcome and a choice of comfortable rooms including doubles, family, twin, en suite and standard, all with tea and coffee making facilities. A hearty full English breakfast, continental choice, cereals, juices and fruit are also on offer as are packed lunches and a variety of sweet treats.

Our large 35-pitch campsite with showers, toilets and drying room is set in the beautiful grounds of Dalegarth House, nestled below the Peak of Robinson in a tranquil woodland setting, only two minutes' walk from the lake edge.

Tel: 01768 770233

Swaledale Watch,

Whelpo, Caldbeck CA7 8HQ
Tel & Fax: 016974 78409

AA
★★★★

Wi-Fi

A working farm situated in beautiful countryside within the Lake District National Park. Central for Scottish Borders, Roman Wall, Eden Valley and the Lakes. Primarily a sheep farm (everyone loves lambing time). Visitors are welcome to see farm animals and activities. Many interesting walks nearby or roam the peaceful Northern fells. Enjoyed by many Cumbrian Way walkers. Very comfortable accommodation with excellent breakfasts. All rooms have private facilities. Central heating. Tea making facilities. We are a friendly Cumbrian family and make you very welcome. Bed and Breakfast from £27 to £35. Contact: **Mr and Mrs A. Savage**

e-mail: nan.savage@talk21.com • www.swaledale-watch.co.uk

GRAHAM ARMS HOTEL
Longtown, Near Carlisle, Cumbria CA6 5SE

A warm welcome awaits at this 250-year-old former Coaching Inn. Situated six miles from the M6 (J44) and Gretna Green, The Graham Arms makes an ideal overnight stop or perfect touring base for the Scottish Borders, English Lakes, Hadrian's Wall and much more. 16 comfortable en suite bedrooms, including four-poster and family rooms with TV, radio etc. Meals and snacks served throughout the day. Friendly 'local's bar' and new 'Sports bar' serving real ale, extra cold lagers and a fine selection of malt whiskies. Secure courtyard parking for cars, cycles and motorcycles. Beautiful woodland and riverside walks. Pets welcome with well behaved owners!

• **Tel: 01228 791213** • **Fax: 01228 794110** •
• **e-mail: office@grahamarms.com** • **www.grahamarms.com** •
Bed and full traditional breakfast £35– £40.
Special rates for weekend and midweek breaks.

ABBERLEY HOUSE

33 Victoria Place, Carlisle CA1 1HP
Tel: 01228 521645

A charming Victorian Guest House located in the centre of Carlisle offering single, double/twin and family en suite rooms with flat screen TV, tea and coffee facilities, free Wi-Fi and private parking. We are only a short walk from the city centre with its fine variety of shops, restaurants, pubs and of course the cathedral, castle and award-winning Tullie House museum. Also close by are Stoney Holme and Swift golf courses, the Sands sports and leisure centre and the splendid River Eden. *A short drive takes you to historic Hadrian's Wall and the magnificent Lake District; a convenient place to stay over en route to Scotland.*

Our rates start from only £25 per person which includes English breakfast and taxes.

e-mail: info@abberleyhouse.co.uk • www.abberleyhouse.co.uk

The Rook Guesthouse
9 Castlegate Cockermouth
Cumbria CA13 9EU

SB

Interesting 17th century town house, adjacent to historic castle. We offer comfortable accommodation with full English, vegetarian or Continental breakfast.

All rooms are en suite with colour TV, beverage tray and central heating.

Cockermouth is an unspoilt market town located at the North Western edge of the Lake District within easy reach of the Lakes, Cumbrian Coast and Border country.

We are ideally situated as a base for walkers, cyclists and holidaymakers.
Open all year, except Christmas.

B&B from £50 Double,
£30 Single.

Mrs V. A. Waters • Tel: 01900 828496
e-mail: sarahwaters1848@btinternet.com
www.therookguesthouse.gbr.cc/

The Old Homestead is a sympathetically renovated, award-winning, 16thC Cumbrian longhouse. Situated in the Vale of Lorton in peaceful countryside, with a backdrop of the Lakeland fells and easy access to the unspoilt Western Lakes. The accommodation can be booked for B&B or as a whole for SELF CATERING with a large dining room, kitchen and lounge facilities. All 10 bedrooms are en suite, with underfloor heating throughout. Enjoy local bottled ales, wines and spirits by the log fire. This is the perfect location for walkers and cyclists, and has amenities nearby for riding, fishing, golf and outdoor pursuits. Also suitable for groups and large family bookings.

The Old Homestead
Byresteads, Cockermouth CA13 9TW
Tel: 01900 822223 • mobile: 07795 823385 • *Zen & Jayne*

Simply elegant.

Tel: 07795 823385
info@byresteads.co.uk
www.byresteads.co.uk

THE YEWDALE HOTEL • CONISTON

Yewdale Road, Coniston LA21 8DU • Tel: 015394 41280

The Yewdale Hotel is a situated in the centre of Coniston, central for the scenic delights of the Lake District. Accommodation is available in eight centrally heated en suite bedrooms, with TV and tea-making facilities, and an excellent Cumbrian breakfast starts the day. In the bar and dining room fresh seasonal produce features on a varied menu which includes plenty of choice for vegetarians, as well as children's dishes.

Fishing, boating, canoeing, walking and pony trekking are all available on or around Coniston Water, and those with energy to spare can tackle the climb up the 2,600ft Old Man of Coniston. The Ruskin Museum in the village celebrates the life and work of the Victorian artist John Ruskin, and a short ferry trip across the Lake takes visitors to Brantwood, Ruskin's home.

The hotel is open daily for breakfast, morning coffee, snacks, lunches, afternoon tea and evening meals. Non-residents welcome.

info@yewdalehotel.com • www.yewdalehotel.com

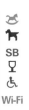

Keswick

Keswick

SB

Wi-Fi

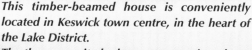

SB

In the heart of the Lake District, in acres of mature gardens and woodland, award-winning Dale Head Hall sits alone on the shores of Thirlemere. With Helvellyn rising majestically behind, this family-run hotel and award-winning restaurant is an ideal base for exploring this most beautiful corner of England.

Superb views. Wildlife in abundance.
Luxury self-catering suites are also available.

Dale Head Hall Lakeside Hotel
and luxury self-catering suites

Lake Thirlmere, Keswick CA12 4TN • Tel: 017687 72478 • Fax: 017687 71070
e-mail: onthelakeside@daleheadhall.co.uk www.daleheadhall.co.uk

AA ★★★ HOTEL   ★★★ HOTEL   *Gold* AWARD

In a quiet village location, in SW Cumbria, Black Combe House offers hearty breakfasts and comfortable rooms with rural views. There are 5 double rooms, 1 twin room, 1 single room and 1 family room, all en suite with TV, DVD, hospitality tray, shaver plug and hair dryer. The very comfortable guests' lounge has TV, books, magazines and games and internet access is available. Directly opposite Black Combe House, there is the village green and in front of the house, ample parking space. The popular tourist towns and villages of The Lake District are not far away for visits.

Black Combe House
Kirksanton, Cumbria LA18 4NW

Ed & Dot Williams.
Please ring us on **01229 776683 or 07879 531290**
e-mail: **dotwilliams1@ukonline.co.uk**
www.blackcombehousebandb.co.uk

Visit the FHG website
www.holidayguides.com
for all kinds of holiday
acccommodation in Britain

Penrith

Windermere

The **Wild Boar**

Inn, Grill & Smokehouse

Nestling in a peaceful setting in the Gilpin Valley, The Wild Boar benefits from beautiful surrounding countryside, including its own private 72 acres of woodland, and many other Lake District attractions close by.

A special venue for many an occasion, whether that be a romantic or adventurous break, family get-together, intimate business meeting or as one of our very valued frequent diners.

After undergoing a refurbishment The Wild Boar now offers individually designed bedrooms, Grill and Smokehouse with an open kitchen and chef's table.

THE WILD BOAR
INN, GRILL & SMOKEHOUSE
NEAR WINDERMERE
CUMBRIA LA23 3NF
RESERVATIONS: 08458 504 604
www.wildboarinn.co.uk

English Lakes Hotels Resorts & Venues

Wi-Fi

Luxury in the Lakes –

The Queen's Head Hotel

The Queen's Head Hotel
Townhead, Troutbeck
Near Windermere, Cumbria, LA23 1PW
Tel 015394 32174
www.queensheadtroutbeck.co.uk

The UK has some of the most stunning landscape in the world, boasting superb scenery, rolling hills, and views to remember. No more so is this true than in the Lake District, so we've found the ideal base from which you can experience all this and more - The Queen's Head Hotel.

Tucked away in the Troutbeck Valley near Windermere (only three miles away), this warm and welcoming accommodation awaits your arrival, where you'll experience first hand the luxurious rooms on offer, as well as an array of tantalising dishes. Plus, you'll have no trouble discovering all the area has to offer, with a maze of footpaths linking ancient hamlets, as well as luring you into some beautiful gardens.

Take a break from the stresses and strains of everyday life and savour the moment within comfortable and attractive surroundings. You can expect a choice of double and fabulous four-poster beds, as well as being enticed by the textures and themes that complement each room. From the original coaching inn to the beautifully transformed ancient barn, your room will just be the tip of the iceberg when it comes to comfort.

During your stay you'll also no doubt want to sample the extensive menu on offer, with locally sourced produce, including poached local duck eggs, prime cut fillet steak, slowly braised ham hock parcel, locally reared braised lamb shank, as well as the old favourite of real ale battered fish and chips! With so much choice, it seems that the most stressful part of your break will be what to choose from the menu and there's even a selection of local ales to wash everything down!

So, take advantage of The Queen's Head Hotel NOW and book your next Lakeland adventure.

Windermere

symbols ★ 🐎 SB ♿ ♟ Wi-Fi

🐕	Pets Welcome		🐎	Children Welcome
SB	Short Breaks		♿	Suitable for Disabled Guests
♟	Licensed		Wi-Fi	Wi-Fi available

Bolton

Lancashire

Generations of excited holiday-makers have visited Lancashire's coastal resorts, and amongst them Blackpool stands out as the star attraction. For seaside fun, amusements and entertainment it's difficult to beat, but the quieter resorts along the coast with traditional seaside attractions have their own appeal. For an outdoor break there are all kinds of activities from hot air ballooning to fishing on offer inland, from the lowland plain, along the winding valleys of the Ribble and the Lune, up into the Forest of Bowland and on to the moors of the western Pennines. Further north at Morecambe take part in the Catch the Wind Kite Festival held on the sands in July, just one of a number of events in the town each year. With the winds blowing in every direction conditions on this Irish Sea coast are perfect for kite-surfing, and instruction is available at Fleetwood, a family-orientated Victorian resort where the Fylde Folk Festival is held every September.

Cornwall

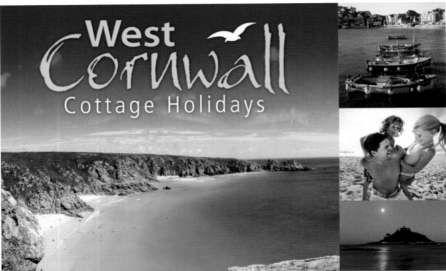
Bude

SB

Granary Cottage • Bude

A lovely ground floor cottage in the quiet hamlet of Rosecare, on the North Cornwall Coast. Ideal for four people, this well equipped barn conversion opens onto a small courtyard by a tranquil village green. Lots of doorstep walking (some farm land). Dog and child-friendly pubs nearby serving great food. Two lovely sandy beaches at Widemouth Bay and Bude - dog-friendly all year.

Terms from £255 to £545 per week.

Short Breaks available out of season. Complimentary cream tea on arrival.

Contact: L. Hunt • Tel: 01384 878287 or 07941 148340
e-mail: lynneh@ethicaltraining.co.uk • www.cottagenearbude.com

Penrose Burden Holiday Cottages

St Breward, Bodmin, Cornwall PL30 4LZ
Tel: 01208 850277 / 850617; Fax: 01208 850915
www.penroseburden.co.uk

Situated within easy reach of both coasts and Bodmin Moor on a large farm overlooking a wooded valley with own salmon and trout fishing. These stone cottages with exposed beams and quarry tiled floors have been featured on TV and are award-winners. All are suitable for wheelchair users and dogs are welcomed. Our cottages sleep from two to seven and are open all year.

Please write or telephone for a colour brochure.   *Nancy Hall*

Close to The Eden Project

Forget-Me-Not Farm Holidays

Situated on Trefranck, our 340-acre family-run beef and sheep farm, in North Cornwall, on the edge of enchanting Bodmin Moor and six miles from the spectacular North Cornwall Heritage Coast. We offer all year round luxury, 4-star, self-catering acccommodation.

Forget-Me-Not Cottage can comfortably sleep 6 and is tastefully decorated and superbly equipped, with a real log fire and central heating. **The Old Wagon House** is a stylish barn conversion and sleeps 2, with a 4-poster bed – ideal for romantic breaks. Mobility rating. **The Stable** is an en suite twin annexe to the Old Wagon House. **Honeysuckle Cottage** sleeps 5. Lovely views of the moor; beautiful garden. Well equipped.

Meadowsweet Cottage (Okehampton, Devon) - barn conversion, sleeps 4, surrounded by own woodlands. Abundance of wildlife. Excellent for cycling and walking holidays.

Trefranck is within easy reach of the Eden Project, the Lost Gardens of Heligan, Padstow and the Camel Trail.

Visit Bude, Crackington Haven, Padstow, Tintagel & The Eden Project.

Trefranck Farm, St Clether, Launceston PL15 8QN
Mobile: 07790 453229
Tel: 01566 86284
e-mail: holidays@trefranck.co.uk
www.meadowsweetcottage.co.uk OR
www.forget-me-not-farm-holidays.co.uk

farm STAY UK

Green Tourism SILVER

SELF CATERING

SB

Coombe Cottages

Crackington Haven is a small unspoilt cove overlooked by 400 foot cliffs, with rock pools and a sandy beach at low tide – ideal for swimming or surfing.

Coombe Cottages are situated within this Area of Outstanding Natural Beauty, only 300 yards from the beach, coastal path or pub.

Little Coombe sleeps two, *Rivercoombe* sleeps four and both cottages have their own fenced gardens with picnic table and BBQ. Inside, they are well equipped and have open fires for those more chilly evenings.

Along the private drive there is a laundry room, and easy off-road parking is available outside each cottage.

Paul & Helen Seez, Coombe Cottages, Crackington Haven, Bude EX23 0JG Tel: 01840 230664

SB

Wi-Fi

CREEKSIDE HOLIDAY HOUSES

- Spacious houses, sleep 2/4/6/8.
- Peaceful, picturesque water's edge hamlet.
- Boating facilities
- Use of boat. • Own quay, beach.
- Secluded gardens • Near Pandora Inn.
- Friday bookings • Dogs welcome.

**PETER WATSON,
CREEKSIDE HOLIDAY HOUSES,
RESTRONGUET, FALMOUTH TR11 5ST**
TEL: **01326 372722**

www.creeksideholidayhouses.co.uk

Falmouth

Creekside Cottages • Cornwall

SB

Wi-Fi

A fine selection of individual water's edge, village and rural cottages, sleeping from 2-8, situated around the creeks of the Carrick Roads, near Falmouth, South Cornwall.
Set in enchanting and picturesque positions, with many of the cottages offering panoramic creek views.

38 Exclusive Holiday Cottages in South Cornwall

Just come and relax

Perfect locations for family holidays, all close to superb beaches, extensive sailing and boating facilities, Cornish gardens and excellent walks.
The majority of the cottages are available throughout the year, and all offer peaceful, comfortable and fully equipped accommodation; most have open fires.
Dogs welcome.

• **Flushing • Restronguet • Mylor • Feock •**
• **Falmouth •**

For a colour brochure please phone
01326 375972
www.creeksidecottages.co.uk

Fowey

Renowned for its wonderful coastline, the longest in the UK, Cornwall has everything to offer for lovers of watersports, whether sailing, surfing, windsurfing, water-skiing, scuba diving or simply enjoying a family holiday on the beach. In busy fishing towns like Looe and Padstow, and traditional villages such as Polperro, there are plenty of inns and restaurants where you can sample the fresh catch. The best-known centre for the arts is St Ives, with the Tate St Ives, and artists and galleries are also to be found in Fowey, St Agnes and Penzance. In summer, when the seaside towns are at their busiest, visit the Rame Peninsula in the south east of the county for a quieter break, or take a trip to the Isles of Scilly for a traditional and relaxing stay. The magnificent coast is ideal for birdwatchers, artists and photographers, golfers of every standard will find a wide choice of courses.

Liskeard

SB

Butterdon Mill Holiday Homes

Idyllic rural site set in 2.5 acres
of mature gardens.
Two-bedroom detached bungalows sleeping
up to six. Games barn and children's play areas.
Ideal for touring coasts and moors of Cornwall and Devon.
Located 3 miles from Liskeard, 8 miles from Looe.
Discounts for Senior Citizens/couples Sept to June.
Children and pets welcome. Brochure available.

**Butterdon Mill Holiday Homes,
Merrymeet, Liskeard, Cornwall PL14 3LS
Tel: 01579 342636 • e-mail:butterdonmill@btconnect.com
www.bmhh.co.uk**

SB

Away from it all, yet close to everything

Get away from it all at Rosecraddoc Lodge, Liskeard, a well maintained, purpose-built
holiday retreat on the edge of Bodmin Moor. Pub/restaurant on site, but NOT 'holiday
camp' style. Ideally located for visiting attractions, including the Eden Project.

Liskeard 2 miles • Looe 9 miles • Plymouth 20 miles

Several well equipped and comfortable bungalows available, sleeping 4, 5 or 6.
Everything you need including bed linen, etc.
Available March-December. Weekly rates £130-£480. Discounts available.

Visit our website at **www.gotocornwall.info** or **Freephone 0800 458 3886**
or **E-mail: rosecraddoc@uwclub.net**

Looe

Looe

- All accommodation dog friendly - 2 dogs maximum
- Individual fenced gardens
- Dog walk and off-lead paddock on site
- Many dog friendly beaches
- Dog friendly local pubs
- Day kennelling nearby
- Open all year
- Short breaks available

Valleybrook

Villas & Cottages

Nestling in a tranquil country valley in the heart of Cornish farmlands, bordered by a sparkling stream, the 6 superb villas and 2 delightful cottages are located between Fowey, Polperro and Looe and just 2½ miles from the SW Coastal path. At Valleybrook you can enjoy the space and freedom of luxury self-catering accommodation, with all of life's little luxuries and everyday convenience at your fingertips. Internet ordered food from Waitrose, Tesco, Sainsbury's or Asda can be delivered to your accommodation.

Valleybrook Peakswater Lansallos
Looe Cornwall PL13 2QE

Tel: 01503 220493
www.valleybrookholidays.com

Talehay Holiday Cottages

Pelynt, Near Looe PL13 2LT

A Quiet Haven in the Countryside near the Sea

Beautiful, traditional cottages with many original features retained provide superb holiday accommodation on 17C non-working farmstead.

Set in 4 acres of unspoilt countryside offering peace and tranquillity with breathtaking coastal and country walks on your doorstep. This is an ideal location for dogs and their owners alike. Close to the Eden Project.

Tel: Mr & Mrs Dennett • 01503 220252
e-mail: infobookings@talehay.co.uk • www.talehay.co.uk

Raven Rock and Spindrift

Contact: Mrs S. Gill,
Bodrigy, Plaidy,
Looe PL13 1LF
Tel: 01503 263122

- *Two bungalows adjacent to Plaidy Beach. Spindrift has en suite bedroom, sleeps two; Raven Rock has two bedrooms and sleeps four. Own parking spaces, central heating. Semi-detached bungalows are fully furnished, well equipped and have sea views. Set in peaceful surroundings at Plaidy. Open plan lounge-diner-kitchen. Colour TV. Patio garden. Electricity and gas included in rent. Pet by arrangement. Personally supervised.*

- *Looe is a fishing port with a variety of shops and restaurants and is only a few minutes by car or a 15 to 20 minute walk.*

- *Weekly terms: Spindrift from £290 to £380; Raven Rock from £325 to £490. Short breaks (three days minimum) before Easter and after end of October.*

Badham Farm

Holiday Cottages

★★★★ SELF CATERING

Green Tourism BRONZE

SB

Once part of a Duchy of Cornwall working farm, now farmhouse and farm buildings converted to a high standard to form a nine cottage complex around former farmyard. Sleeping from two to ten. All cottages are well furnished and equipped and prices include electricity, bed linen and towels. Most cottages have a garden. Ten acre grounds, set in delightful wooded valley, with tennis, putting, children's play area, fishing lake, animal paddock, games room with pool and table tennis. Gym & Spa pool. Separate bar. Laundry. Barbecue. Railcar from Liskeard to Looe stops at end of picnic area. Have a 'car free' day out. Children and well behaved dogs welcome (no dogs in high season, please). Prices from £120 per week.

Badham Farm, St Keyne, Liskeard PL14 4RW
Tel: 01579 343572
e-mail: badhamfarm@yahoo.co.uk
www.badhamfarm.co.uk

Newquay, Perranporth

Retorrick Mill • *Self-catering accommodation*

offers two cottages, six chalets, traditional camping and licensed bar.
Set in 30 acres and nestled within the tranquil Lanherne Valley,
perfectly located for Cornwall's finest beaches, attractions and activities.
Pets, including horses, are very welcome.
For a brochure or further assistance contact Chris Williams.

The Granary, Retorrick Mill, St Mawgan, Cornwall TR8 4BH
Tel: 01637 860460
www.retorrickmill.co.uk • e-mail: wilf@retorrickmill.co.uk

On the outskirts of picturesque St Mawgan village between Newquay and Padstow

Cornwall's best kept secret

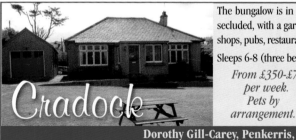

The bungalow is in the centre of Perranporth and yet is secluded, with a garden and parking. It is near the park, shops, pubs, restaurants and the magnificent sandy beach.

Sleeps 6-8 (three bedrooms. only one bathroom).

*From £350-£795
per week.
Pets by
arrangement.*

**Dorothy Gill-Carey, Penkerris,
Penwinnick Road, St Agnes TR5 0PA**
Tel & Fax: 01872 552262 • e-mail: penkerris@gmail.com • www.penkerris.co.uk

symbols 🐕🎠SB♿🍷Wi-Fi

🐕	*Pets Welcome*	🎠	*Children Welcome*
SB	*Short Breaks*	♿	*Suitable for Disabled Guests*
🍷	*Licensed*	**Wi-Fi**	*Wi-Fi available*

Polperro, Port Isaac

PEAK HOUSE
POLPERRO • CORNWALL PL13 2RY

SB

Directly overlooking the picturesque fishing harbour of Polperro with sea views, between Looe and Fowey, on the South Cornish Coast. 25 miles Plymouth, 12 miles A38.

Let for 30 years for family holidays as well as for friends and couples to enjoy.
Pets and children are very welcome. Sleeps 2-8

A lovely, comfortable 250-year-old village property, Terraced gardens, parking, superb views stretching to the Eddystone Lighthouse.

Only 3 minute walk from shops, restaurants, tea rooms, olde-worlde pubs, small sandy beach, quay, pier and rock fishing

NO CHARGE FOR PETS • PRIVATE PARKING FREE

VIEW FROM PEAK HOUSE

For details, please telephone GRAHAM WRIGHTS on
01579 344080

CARN-AWN & POP'S PLACE
PORT GAVERNE • PORT ISAAC

SB

CARN AWN and POP'S PLACE stand privately tucked away in the quiet cove of Port Gaverne, with fantastic sea views. Port Isaac is only a short walk away. The accommodation is situated next to the South West Coastal Path, an ideal base for exploring the area. Both properties have their own patios and gated area; ample parking.

CARN AWN is a 4 Star rated property. It has two double en suite rooms, twin room with separate toilet/shower. Lounge dining area and fully fitted kitchen.

POP'S PLACE has a double en suite, twin/single en suite; large lounge, fully fitted kitchen.

Open all year. Short breaks available. Pets welcome.
For terms contact: Mrs S. A. May, Orcades House,
Port Gaverne, Port Isaac, Cornwall PL29 3SQ • Tel or Fax: 01208 880716
e-mail: orcades@mays364.wanadoo.co.uk • www.carn-awn.co.uk

The Garden House   near Port Isaac, Cornwall

SB

Wi-Fi

Lovely far-reaching view across open countryside. Very warm and cosy for all year round. Full central heating, electricity, bed linen and towels included. One bedroom with twin or double. Lounge/kitchen/dining and shower room all fully equipped to very high standards.
Central location in small quiet hamlet near Michaelstow and within 8 miles of Port Isaac, Boscastle, Tintagel, Polzeath, Rock, Wadebridge, Bodmin Moor and Camel Trail. From £188 pw.
Pets welcome.
Contact David & Jenny Oldham • 01208 850529
Trevella, Treveighan, St Teath, Cornwall PL30 3JN
email. david.trevella@btconnect.com   www.trevellacornwall.co.uk

Prices held for previous 5 years

Rock, St Austell

Courier Cottage • Rock • Cornwall

"Self-catering beach side house that sleeps up to 8 people and has superb views over the estuary"

Recently renovated to a very high standard, the cottage has one of the prime views over the estuary from all three levels. Accommodation includes two double, one twin, and one bedroom with bunk beds and a single bed. Bathrooms are very modern, and the shower room has a superb high-power shower. Fully equipped kitchen with dishwasher and laundry facilities. Parking space for two cars. There are many coastal walks along miles of sandy beach and coastal paths. Surfing, water-skiing, boating and fishing available. Sailing club directly opposite the cottage.

Courier Cottage, 2 Slipway Cottages Rock, Cornwall PL27 6LD
Tel: - 01491 638309 • Office: 01491 410716
Mob: 07974 714520/1

BOSINVER FARM COTTAGES

Best Self-catering Establishment 2005, 2006 & 2007
Cornwall Tourism Awards

Bosinver's individual detached farm cottages are so nice our guests often don't want to leave. Here you can relax in real comfort on our small farm in a hidden valley, with 30 acres of wildflower meadows to walk your dog and a short stroll to the village shop and pub. Located near St Austell and the sea, Bosinver is a great base for glorious coast and inland walks. Heligan Gardens and the Eden Project are on our doorstep but nowhere in Cornwall is more than one hour away. Bosinver is an ideal all-year-round holiday venue, particularly spring, autumn and winter when the crowds are gone, the colours are changing and the cottages are as warm as the welcome.

Brochure from: Mrs Pat Smith, Bosinver Farm,
Trelowth, St Austell, Cornwall PL26 7DT
Tel: 01726 72128

e-mail: reception@bosinver.co.uk
www.bosinver.co.uk

If it's views, golf or walking you want, this is the place for you!

- Magnificent location alongside and overlooking West Cornwall Golf Course, Hayle Estuary and St Ives Bay.
- Both flats have lovely views. Wonderful spot for walking.
- Five minutes from the beach and dogs are allowed there all year round.
- Two well-equipped flats which are open all year.

The Links
Lelant, St Ives
Cornwall TR26 3HY

Your hosts are Bob and Jacky Pontefract
Phone 01736 753326
e-mail: bobandjackyp@btinternet.com

Cheriton Self-Catering, St Ives

In the centre of beautiful St Ives,
four apartments, sleep 2 to 5.
Also three Fishermen's Cottages
nearby (max 5 persons each).
All well equipped, clean and
comfortable. Inspected annually.
Only 30 yards from harbour.
Parking available. Very competitive
rates. Graded 3 or 4 stars.

*Short Breaks available October to May at
special price of £120 for two persons for
two nights - additional nights £35 per night.*

Under the personal supervision of proprietors:

**Mr & Mrs A. Luke, Cheriton Self-Catering,
Cheriton House, Market Place,
St Ives, Cornwall TR26 1RZ
Tel: 01736 795083**

CHAPEL COTTAGES • ST TUDY

Four traditional cottages, sleeping 2 to 5, in a quiet farming area. Ideal for the
spectacular north coast, Bodmin Moor, and the Eden Project. Comfortable and
well-equipped. Garden and private parking. Rental £205 to £485 per week.
Also two cottages for couples at Hockadays, near
Blisland - converted from a 17th century barn in
a quiet farming hamlet. Rental £205 to £380 per
week. Shop and pub/restaurant within walking
distance. Regretfully, no pets. Brochure available.

**Mrs M. Pestell, 'Hockadays',
Tregenna, Blisland PL30 4QJ
Tel: 01208 850146
www.hockadays.co.uk**

Please quote FHG when enquiring

Wadebridge

Great Bodieve Farm Barns
Luxury Cottages in beautiful North Cornwall

SB

Wi-Fi

Four spacious, luxury barns close to the Camel Estuary.

Furnished and equipped to a very high standard. Wi-Fi.

Most bedrooms en suite (king-size beds). Sleep 2-8.

Excellent area for sandy beaches, spectacular cliff walks, golf, Camel Trail and surfing. One mile from Wadebridge towards Rock, Daymer and Polzeath.

Contact: Thelma Riddle or Nancy Phillips,
Great Bodieve Farm Barns, Molesworth House,
Wadebridge, Cornwall PL27 7JE
enquiries@great-bodieve.co.uk
www.great-bodieve.co.uk
Tel: 01208 814916 • Fax: 01208 812713

Devon

Wooder Manor

SB

Tel & Fax: 01364 621391
e-mail: angela@woodermanor.com
www.woodermanor.com

Widecombe-in-the-Moor, Near Ashburton TQ13 7TR

Cottages, converted coach house and stables nestled in the picturesque valley of Widecombe, surrounded by unspoilt woodland, moors and granite tors. Half-a-mile from village with post office, general stores, inn with dining room, church and National Trust Information Centre. Excellent centre for touring Devon with a variety of places to visit and exploring Dartmoor by foot or on horseback.

Accommodation is clean and well equipped with colour TV/DVD, central heating, laundry room. Children welcome. Large gardens and courtyard for easy parking. Open all year, so take advantage of off-season reduced rates. Short Breaks also available.
Two properties suitable for disabled visitors.
Brochure available.

Think of Devon, and wild moorland springs to mind, but this is a county of contrasts, with the wild moors of the Exmoor National Park to the north fringed by dramatic cliffs and combes, golden beaches and picturesque harbours, and busy market towns and sleepy villages near the coast. An experience not to be missed is the cliff railway between the pretty little port of Lynmouth and its twin village of Lynton high on the cliff, with a backdrop of dramatic gorges or combes.In the centre of the county lies Dartmoor, with its vast open spaces, granite tors and spectacular moorland, rich in wildlife and ideal for walking, pony trekking and cycling. The Channel coast to the south, with its gentle climate and scenery, is an attractive destination at any time of year.

This delightfully converted thatched cider barn, with exposed beams, adjoins main farmhouse overlooking the outstanding beauty of the orchards, pools and pastureland, and is ideally situated for touring Devon, Dorset and Somerset.

Bathing, golf and tennis at Lyme Regis and many places of interest locally, including Wildlife Park, donkey sanctuary and Forde Abbey. Membury Village, with its post office and stores and church is one mile away.

The accommodation is of the highest standard with the emphasis on comfort. Two double rooms; shower room and toilet; sitting/diningroom with colour TV; kitchen with electric cooker, microwave, washing machine, fridge. Linen supplied. Pets by arrangement. Car essential. Open all year. No smoking.

Terms from £200 to £400. Short Breaks available out of season £25pp.

SAE, please, to **Mrs Pat Steele,**
Hasland Farm, Membury, Axminster EX13 7JF
Tel: 01404 881 558
davidsteele887@btinternet.com
www.ciderroomcottage.com

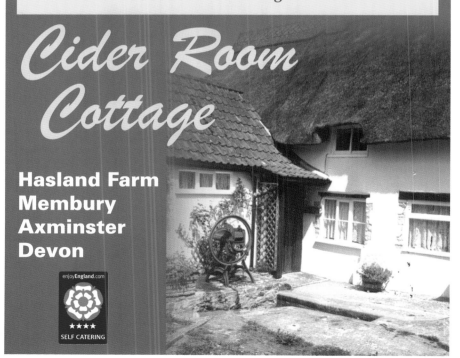

Cider Room Cottage

Hasland Farm
Membury
Axminster
Devon

enjoyEngland.com
★★★★
SELF CATERING

SB

Barnstaple

Bigbury-on-Sea, Bradworthy

A delightful family working farm, situated on the coast, overlooking the sea and sandy beaches of Bigbury Bay. Farm adjoins golf course and River Avon. Lovely coastal walks. Ideal centre for South Hams and Dartmoor. The spacious wing (sleeps 2/6) comprises half of the farmhouse, and is completely self-contained. All rooms attractively furnished. Large, comfortable lounge overlooking the sea. There are three bedrooms: one family, one double and a bunk bed; two have washbasins. The kitchen/diner has a fridge/ freezer, electric cooker, microwave, washing machine and dishwasher. There is a nice garden, ideal for children. Reduction for two people staying in off peak weeks. Please write or telephone for a brochure to Mrs Jane Tucker.

e-mail: info@bigburyholidays.co.uk
www.bigburyholidays.co.uk
Tel: 01548 810267

SB

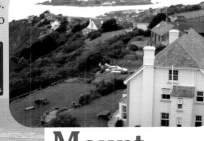

Mount Folly Farm
Bigbury-on-Sea,
Kingsbridge TQ7 4AR

Lake House *Cottages and B&B*
Lake Villa, Bradworthy, Devon EX22 7SQ
Brochure: Peter & Lesley Lewin on 01409 241962
e-mail: lesley@lakevilla.co.uk • www.lakevilla.co.uk

SB

Wi-Fi

Enjoy the peace and tranquillity in this rural spot with countryside, cliff and beach walks close by. Four cosy, well equipped, period cottages sleeping 2 to 5/6. One acre garden with tennis, 6-acre meadow with lakes (coarse fishing available). Half-a-mile from village shops and pub.

Off-road parking. Well behaved pets welcome. Short breaks available.

TWO EN SUITE B&B ROOMS WITH BALCONY ALSO AVAILABLE IN OUR FARMHOUSE

Brayford, Broadwoodwidger

Little Bray House · North Devon

SB

Situated 9 miles east of Barnstaple, Little Bray House is ideally placed for day trips to North and East Devon, the lovely sandy surfing beaches at Saunton Sands and Woolacombe, and many places of interest both coastal and inland. Exmoor also has great charm. Come and share the pace of life and fresh air straight from the open Atlantic.

THE BARN COTTAGE • This cottage is built in the south end of one of the old barns, and enjoys beautiful views across to Exmoor. Kitchen, with microwave, cooker and fridge. Large living room with dining area and colour TV. Main double bedroom, a bunk room and a single bedroom.

THE ORCHARD COTTAGE • A pretty cottage. Kitchen, with microwave, cooker and fridge. Large sitting room with dining area and stairs. Three bedrooms (sleeps up to 5) and a bathroom.

FLATLET FOR TWO • Self catering accommodation located within the oldest part of the main house, with access through the main front door. Twin beds. The kitchen/dining room is well equipped and the traditional-style bathroom is private to the flatlet.

Brayford, near Barnstaple EX32 7QG
Tel: 01598 710295
e-mail: holidays@littlebray.co.uk
www.littlebray.co.uk

SB

West Banbury Farm Cottages...

Have it all! Dartmoor tors, coastal paths, water sports, family attractions, fishing, cycling, bird watching, beaches, market towns, castles, cream teas, relaxing, pampering... West Banbury is ideally located for Dartmoor, North Devon and Cornwall, within easy reach of all of the above and more!

10 charming self-catering cottages, spacious and well-equipped, sleeping 2-8. Heated indoor swimming pool, sauna and games room on site. • Children's play area • Grass tennis court • Dogs welcome • Short Breaks available • 9 hole miniature golf course.

Nigel and Karen Dua
West Banbury Farm Cottages
Broadwoodwidger, Lifton, Devon PL16 0JJ

Tel. 01566 780423 • Mob. 07791 395039
e-mail info@westbanbury.co.uk • www.westbanbury.co.uk

where relaxation is a way of life

Brixham

DEVONCOURT HOLIDAY FLATS

SB

BERRYHEAD ROAD, BRIXHAM, DEVON TQ5 9AB

Devoncourt is a development of 24 self-contained flats, occupying one of the finest positions in Torbay, with unsurpassed views.

At night the lights of Torbay are like a fairyland to be enjoyed from your very own balcony.

EACH FLAT HAS:
Heating
Sea Views over Torbay
Private balcony
Own front door
Separate bathroom and toilet
Separate bedroom
Bed-settee in lounge
Lounge sea views over Marina
Kitchenette - all electric
Private car park
Opposite beach
Colour television
Overlooks lifeboat
Short walk to town centre
Double glazing
Open all year
Mini Breaks October to April

Harbour view from Devoncourt

Tel: 01803 853748
(or 07802 403289 after office hours)
www.devoncourt.info

Colyton

SB

Situated beside the village church, the cottages (sleep 4/5) have been tastefully renovated to maintain the old style of the barn. With panoramic views over the Coly valley, they provide a quiet holiday and offer many interesting walks. Riding stables and ancient monuments are within walking distance. Honiton Golf Course, swimming pool and bowling green are four miles away. Lyme Regis, Sidmouth and Exmouth plus many other quaint scenic coastal resorts and the Jurassic Coast are all within half an hour's drive; situated on the route of the East Devon (Foxglove) Way.

Each cottage has a modern kitchen complete with washing machine, dishwasher and microwave as well as a conventional cooker, comfortable lounge with colour TV and DVD/Digibox, two bedrooms, and bathroom with bath and shower. Central heating • Electricity by £1 meter • Bed linen supplied • Games room • Brochure on request.

Church Approach Cottages
Church Green, Farway, Colyton
Devon EX24 6EQ

For further details please contact: Sheila & Liz Lee
Tel: 01404 871383/871202
e-mail: lizlee@eclipse.co.uk • www.churchapproach.co.uk

SB

BONEHAYNE FARM
COLYTON, DEVON EX24 6SG   **COTTAGE: CARAVAN: BOARD**

- Family 250 acre working farm • Competitive prices • Spectacular views
- Our two self-catering caravans are located on an exclusive site. Each on its own special area with stunning views over the enclosed garden and the Devon countryside.
- The 4-star farm cottage is full of character and adjoins Bonehayne farmhouse. South-facing with glorious views over the garden and the Devon countryside.
- Rooms are available for Bed and Breakfast in part of the farmhouse.
- Relax outside the cottage in the deckchairs provided.
- Four miles to the beach • Five minutes from Colyton
- Spacious lawns/gardens • Laundry room, BBQ, picnic tables
- Good trout fishing, woods to roam, walks
- Spacious enclosed lawn where children can play croquet and table tennis.

Mrs Gould • Tel: 01404 871396/871416
www.bonehayne.co.uk • e-mail: gould@bonehayne.co.uk

Crediton, Cullompton

Hope Cove, Kingsbridge

symbols ⚐ 🎠 SB ♿ ♟ Wi-Fi

🐕	Pets Welcome	🎠	Children Welcome
SB	Short Breaks	♿	Suitable for Disabled Guests
♟	Licensed	Wi-Fi	Wi-Fi available

Partridge Arms Farm

Yeo Mill, West Anstey, South Molton, North Devon EX36 3NU

Times gone by...For those who want to enjoy a break in more unusual circumstances, Partridge Arms Farm has a converted, self-catering railway carriage. The carriage is situated on the old Taunton to Barnstaple railway line and, as well as being fully equipped, it sleeps up to 6 people. Children are welcome to stay in the carriage, as are dogs. The railway line offers a delightful and fascinating walk. Visitors can also explore at their leisure the 200 acres of surrounding farmland, which is situated in the Southern foothills of Exmoor. Prices start from £490 per week (no hidden extras). Daily rates available.

Now a working farm of over 200 acres, four miles west of Dulverton, "Partridge Arms Farm" was once a coaching inn and has been in the same family since 1906. Genuine hospitality and traditional farmhouse fare await you. Comfortable accommodation in double, twin and single rooms, some of which have en suite facilities. There is also an original four-poster bedroom. Children welcome. Animals by arrangement. Residential licence. Open all year. Fishing and riding available nearby. FARM HOLIDAY GUIDE DIPLOMA WINNER *Bed and Breakfast from £30 • Evening Meal from £16.*

For further information contact Hazel Milton
Tel: 01398 341217 • Fax: 01398 341569
bangermilton@gmail.com

NEWHOUSE FARM COTTAGES

Superior Quality Self-catering Accommodation

Nine beautifully converted, well equipped, Grade II Listed stone barns,
with a choice of accommodation ranging from a one-bedroom cottage with
four-poster bed through to our spacious five-bedroom barn sleeping 10.
Take a stroll through 23 acres of flower-filled meadows and woodland,
or simply relax in our heated indoor swimming pool and games room.

For long or short breaks and more information, please call us on
01884 860266 or visit our website at www.newhousecottages.com
Newhouse Farm, Witheridge, Tiverton, Devon EX16 8QB

West Millbrook

ADJOINING EXMOOR. Two fully-equipped bungalows and one farmhouse annexe (properties sleep 2/8) in lovely surroundings bordering Exmoor National Park. Ideal for touring North Devon and West Somerset including moor and coast with beautiful walks, lovely scenery and many other attractions. North Molton village is only one mile away. All units have electric cooker, fridge/freezer, microwave and digital TV; two bungalows also have washing machines/dryers. Children's play area; cots and high chairs available free. Linen hire available. Games room. Car parking. Central heating if required. Electricity metered. Out of season short breaks. Weekly prices from £100 to £520. Colour brochure available.

SB

Mike and Rose Courtney, West Millbrook, Twitchen, South Molton EX36 3LP
Tel: 01598 740382 • e-mail: wmbselfcatering@aol.com
www.visitsouthmolton.co.uk • www.westmillbrook.co.uk

SOUTH DEVON • NEAR TORBAY

A quiet secluded farm park welcoming tents, motor caravans and touring caravans. It is less than one mile from the riverside village of Stoke Gabriel and within four miles of Torbay beaches. Central for touring South Devon. Facilities include modern toilet/shower block with dishwashing and family rooms. Electric hook-ups and hard standings. Launderette, shop and payphone. Also static caravans to let from £180 per week or £26 per night.

SB

J. & E. BALL, HIGHER WELL FARM HOLIDAY PARK
Stoke Gabriel, Totnes, South Devon TQ9 6RN
Tel: 01803 782289 • www.higherwellfarmholidaypark.co.uk

CROSSWAYS AND SEA VIEW
COTTAGES & APARTMENTS
Teignmouth Road, Maidencombe, Torquay TQ1 4TH

SB

In a countryside location, but only ten minutes from the centre of Torquay, and within walking distance of a peaceful bathing cove.

Sailing, fishing, water-skiing, windsurfing, diving, swimming, tennis, bowls, ten-pin bowling, golf and walking all within easy reach.

Dartmoor only a half-hour car journey away.

Properties sleep 2-6 and are well equipped with colour TV, fridge, cooker, kettle, toaster & microwave. Cots and Highchairs available. Non Smoking. Large private car park. Large garden. Children's play area & picnic areas

Tel: 01803 328369 • www.crosswaysandseaview.co.uk

SB

WEST PUSEHILL FARM COTTAGES

Resident proprietors, The Violet Family have been welcoming visitors to West Pusehill Farm for over twenty years, and many return time and time again.

Ideal for family summer holidays, restful spring/winter breaks, or a perfect base to explore Devon's outstanding coast and countryside and many outdoor activities.

West Pusehill Farm Cottages not only give you the freedom and independence of a self-catering holiday, but the local area offers a wide range of excellent restaurants and cafes, so your holiday can be enjoyed by every member of the family.

- ❖ Located in an Area of Outstanding Natural Beauty
- ❖ Eleven sympathetically converted cottages
- ❖ BBQ area
- ❖ Children's playground
- ❖ On-site heated outdoor pool
- ❖ Laundry room
- ❖ Golf, fishing, walking, exploring, shopping
- ❖ Family attractions

West Pusehill Farm
Westward Ho!
North Devon EX39 5AH
Tel: 01237 475638/474622
e-mail: info@wpfcottages.co.uk
www.wpfcottages.co.uk

Resthaven
Holiday Flats

On the sea front overlooking the beautiful Combesgate beach. Fantastic views of Morte Point and the coastline.
**Contact Brian Watts for details and brochure.
Tel: 01271 870248**

★ Two self contained flats, sleeping 5 & 9 ★ Family, double and bunk bedrooms all with washbasins ★ All-electric kitchens. Electricity on £1 meter ★ Bathrooms with bath & shower ★ Colour TVs with DVD players ★ Free parking, lighting, hot water, laundry and Wi-Fi ★ Terms £180 to £1100 per week

**The Esplanade, Woolacombe, Devon EX34 7DJ
e-mail: rhflats@orange.net • www.resthavenflats.co.uk**

Woolacombe

CHICHESTER HOUSE HOLIDAY APARTMENTS

SB

Quiet, relaxing, fully furnished apartments. Opposite Barricane Shell Beach – central seafront position with outstanding sea and coastal views.
Open all year

FLATLETS • Lundy Lights and Bay Views • both situated on the first floor, with balconies with magnificent views over the Bay. **SLEEP 2.**

SELF CONTAINED APARTMENTS • all with sea views.

The Retreat • on the first floor with bathroom, bedroom with double bed, sitting room and combined kitchen, split level apartment. **SLEEPS TWO**

Shell Bay • on the second floor with double bedroom, bathroom, living room/kitchen overlooking the sea. **SLEEPS TWO PLUS**

Hartland View • very large apartment on second floor with lounge overlooking the sea, two bedrooms, each with a double and single bed. Kitchen diner. Bathroom. **SLEEPS UP TO SIX**

Morte View • on the first floor, with bathroom, sitting room/kitchen opening onto a balcony, double bedroom. **SLEEPS TWO**

Sea Spray • on the ground floor, with bathroom, dining/bed-sitting room with foldaway double bed, large bedroom with double and single beds. Kitchen. **SLEEPS FOUR.**

Well behaved dogs are welcome by prior arrangement • Resident Proprietor: Joyce Bagnall

The Esplanade, Woolacombe EX34 7DJ • Tel: 01271 870761
www.chichesterhouse.co.uk

Pubs & Inns

See the Supplement on pages 483-530

The FHG Directory of Website Addresses
on pages 531-541 is a useful quick reference guide for holiday accommodation with e-mail and/or website details

Please note...

Dorset

Orchard End & The Old Coach House
Hooke, Beaminster, Dorset

Orchard End is a stone-built bungalow, with electric central heating and double glazing. Four bedrooms, two bathrooms; sleeps 8. Well-equipped and comfortable. Enclosed garden and off-road parking.

For details contact: Mrs Pauline M. Wallbridge, Watermeadow House, Hooke, Beaminster, Dorset DT8 3PD • Tel: 01308 862619

Hooke is a quiet village nine miles from the coast. Good walking country and near Hooke Working Woodland with lovely woodland walks. Coarse fishing nearby.
Terms from £350 to £770 inclusive of VAT, electricity, bed linen and towels.
enquiries@watermeadowhouse.co.uk • www.watermeadowhouse.co.uk

Both properties ETC ★★★★ • Wi-Fi available

The Old Coach House, a cottage sleeping 9, is also finished to a high standard. Four bedrooms, two bathrooms; central heating. Large garden; off-road parking. Both properties (on a working dairy farm) are equipped with washing machine, dryer, dishwasher, fridge/freezers, microwaves and payphones.

In Dorset on the south coast, there are resorts to suit everyone, from traditional, busy Bournemouth with 10 kilometres of sandy beach and a wide choice of entertainment, shopping and dining, to the quieter seaside towns of Seatown, Mudeford and Barton-on-Sea, and Charmouth with its shingle beach. Lulworth Cove is one of several picturesque little harbours. In 2012 attention will be focussed on Weymouth, the venue for the Olympic and Paralympic sailing events, and one of several very popular sailing centres along the coast. Fossil hunters of all age groups are attracted by the spectacular cliffs of the Jurassic Coast, a World Heritage Site, and walkers can enjoy the wonderful views from the South West Coast Path at the top. With almost half the county included in Areas of Outstanding Natural Beauty, walking enthusiasts have downs, heathland, woodlands and river valleys, country villages and market towns to explore.

Six stunning cottages in a private hidden valley, surrounded by extensive gardens, grounds and ponds. Situated at Dorset's very centre, close to Milton Abbas, with a fine pub and restaurant (01258 880233), we make a great touring base not too far from anywhere.

Superior self-catering Holiday Cottages

Luccombe Country Holidays

Try our indoor pool, jacuzzi, swim jet and sauna, or gymnasium and games room on wet days. Play tennis, explore our farm on foot or bike, followed by a lakeside barbecue on dry ones. Go riding (01258 880057), shoot a clay, fish or just relax in a very peaceful setting.

There is something for everyone here at Luccombe

• Terms from £305 to £1500.

Please check our availability at www.luccombeholidays.co.uk or telephone 01258 880558

• Dogs welcomed by arrangement.

enjoyEngland.com

2 ★ - 3 ★
SELF CATERING

Luccombe, Milton Abbas, Blandford Forum, Dorset DT11 0BE

e-mail: luccombeh@gmail.com
www.luccombeholidays.co.uk

Bournemouth, Burton Bradstock

White Horse Farm

★ Self-Catering Holidays in Rural Dorset ★

SB

Four self-catering barn conversion cottages, a 4-star converted farmhouse annexe "The Willows", and a luxury 4-star 3 bedroom lodge "Otter's Holt".

Our holiday cottages were formerly part of the old courtyard. Tastefully converted with exposed stone walls and beams, providing comfortable accommodation.

- **Toad Hall** sleeps 4 • **Ratty's** sleeps 2/4
- **Moley's** and **Badger's** sleep 2

The Willows, converted 4 star 3 bedroom self-catering annexe for up to six people. Each en suite bedroom has lovely views over the surroundings fields and gardens. Surrounded by willow trees with a patio and private entrance to the duck pond.

Otter's Holt, 4 star luxury Wessex-built Milbourne lodge for 6 people in 3 bedrooms, with master bedroom en suite, a family bathroom and a large lounge diner with a vaulted ceiling, exposed beams and a rustic hearth with wood burner-style electric fire.

Surrounded by 2 acres of gardens and paddock with a large duck pond.

Fully equipped recreation room with table football, videos, books, indoor/outdoor games and much more.

Delightful walks in the surrounding area and many tourist attractions locally.

Fishing, walking, horse-riding and golfing facilities within a short drive.

Within easy travelling distance is the lovely Dorset coast including Lulworth Cove, Weymouth and Lyme Regis.

White Horse Farm, Middlemarsh, Sherborne, Dorset DT9 5QN

e-mail: enquiries@whitehorsefarm.co.uk

Tel: 01963 210222

www.whitehorsefarm.co.uk

enjoyEngland.com
3★ - 4★
SELF CATERING

PETS WELCOME

Weymouth

Grade II Listed Cottage with 3 bedrooms, 2 bathrooms, approx. one minute walk to beach, close to harbour.

VB ★★★

Other properties available weekly or short breaks.

Weymouth has a lovely sandy beach and picturesque harbour with pavement cafes. There is plenty to do all year round.

**Phone: 01305 836495 • Mobile: 0797 1256160
e-mail: postmaster@buckwells.plus.com
www.holidaycottagesweymouth.co.uk**

Gloucestershire

Weymouth

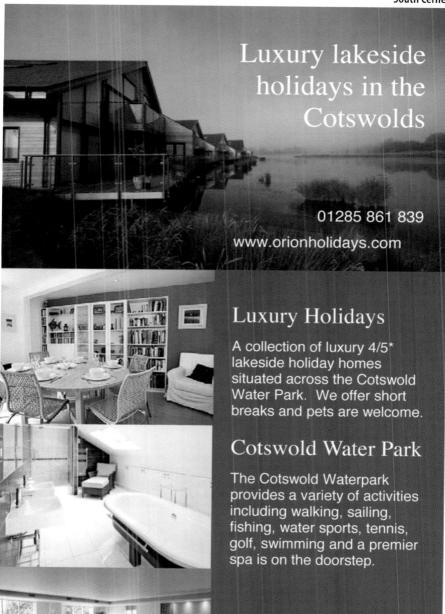

SB

Wi-F

Luxury lakeside holidays in the Cotswolds

01285 861 839

www.orionholidays.com

Luxury Holidays

A collection of luxury 4/5* lakeside holiday homes situated across the Cotswold Water Park. We offer short breaks and pets are welcome.

Cotswold Water Park

The Cotswold Waterpark provides a variety of activities including walking, sailing, fishing, water sports, tennis, golf, swimming and a premier spa is on the doorstep.

Somerset

Chard

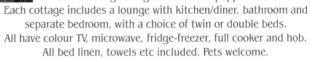

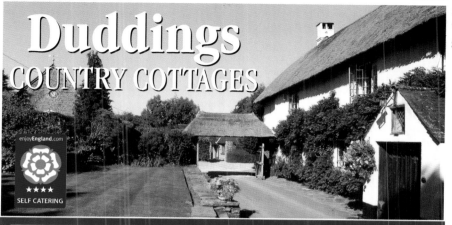

Duddings
COUNTRY COTTAGES

SB

As resident owners, we personally guarantee immaculate presentation of cottages on arrival. Each cottage has tasteful decor with matching, highest quality fabrics and is fully central heated. Amenities include comfortable lounges with colour TV/video/DVD, fully fitted modern kitchens with fridge-freezer, cooker and microwave. Our facilities include heated indoor pool, hard tennis court, putting green, pool and table tennis, trampoline, football net and play centre. Trout stream in 8.5 acres for fishing or picnics. Families and pets welcome, walking, riding, beaches nearby. Short breaks available off season, open all year. Full details and plans of the cottages together with up to date prices and availablity can be found on our website, or please call for brochure.

Thatched longhouse and 12 cottages for 2-16 persons, beautifully converted from old stone barns and stables. Original beams and exposed stonework retain the character of the buildings. Two miles from the picturesque village of Dunster in the Exmoor National Park.

Luxury Cottages

Indoor Heated Pool

Tennis Court

Duddings Country Cottages
Timberscombe Dunster, Somerset TA24 7TB

Telephone: 01643 841123
www.duddings.co.uk
e-mail: richard@duddings.co.uk

Exmoor

SB

Hope Farm Cottages

SB

Wi-Fi

Four Award-Winning Cottages in a beautiful part of England's West Country

Hope Farm Cottages are four 4-star, self-catering holiday cottages which are great for families, also particularly ideal for dog lovers and the disabled.

Set in peaceful countryside on the edge of picturesque Lympsham, Hope Farm dates back to the mid 16th Century. The four holiday cottages have been sympathetically converted from the old farmyard outbuildings and have views across the pretty, manicured, lawned courtyard to the front and to open fields behind. Each cottage has tasteful and relaxing accommodation for four people and a baby, with an open plan living room/kitchen, two bedrooms (one with a double bed and one with twin beds) and two bathrooms. A Z-bed is available for a fifth person.

All the cottages are on the ground floor and have easy wheelchair access throughout. Front door ramps and other aids for the elderly or disabled are available.

HOPE FARM COTTAGES
Brean Road, Lympsham
Near Weston-super-Mare
Somerset BS24 0HA
Tel: 01934 750506
e-mail: hopefarmcottages@gmail.com
www.hopefarmcottages.co.uk
Resident owners: Malcolm & Aline Bennett

Minehead

SB

Stay in Real Farm Style...

Idyllic award-winning organic working stock farm

Quality Farm Accommodation

18th Century Farmhouse or S/C Cottage

Both with charm and 21st century comforts

Real Farm – Real Food – Relax

Organic Producers of the Year Award Winners.
Own Produce – Rick Stein Food Heroes
National Trust Fine Food Awards
Aromatherapy Relaxing Pamper Breaks.
Hot Tub under the Exmoor sky.

" A little piece of heaven on earth" Escape to our hidden 500 acres within the Holnicote Estate on Exmoor National Park....where the countryside meets the sea. Farming with Care and Conservation. Peace for country lovers. Minehead 3 miles – Dunster Castle 5 miles – Porlock 7 miles.

Wonderful walks from our door to the heather moor and SW Coast Path, with wandering Exmoor ponies, then next door Selworthy village for 'scrummy' cream teas.

Crisp all cotton linen • Fresh flowers • Natural toiletries • Organic & Free-range produce • Aga-cooked farmhouse breakfasts also available for s/c cottage guests • Fresh baked organic bread • Own eggs Fresh picked garden fruits • Penny's home-made Muesli • Hand-made sausages and bacon.

Well behaved dogs welcome by arrangement

Penny & Roger Webber & Family, Hindon Organic Farm, Near Selworthy, Minehead, Exmoor, Somerset TA24 8SH • Tel: 01643 705244

info@hindonfarm.co.uk • www.hindonfarm.co.uk

Four-star lodges and cottages sleeping from two in a cosy cottage up to 12 in our newly built Holly Lodge, all situated in two and a half acres of gardens overlooking the slopes of Exmoor.

Located between Minehead and Porlock and within five miles of Snowdrop Valley. Superb walking with National Park on two sides and with Minehead seafront, its shops, restaurants and pubs within 1½ miles, Woodcombe Lodges offer the best of both worlds. Full convector heating throughout. Dogs permitted in some lodges.

WOODCOMBE LODGES

Bratton, Near Minehead
Somerset TA24 8SQ
Tel & Fax: 01643 702789
nicola@woodcombelodge.co.uk www.woodcombelodge.co.uk

enjoyEngland.com

★★★★
SELF CATERING

Potting Shed Holidays

Potting Shed Self-catering Holiday Cottages

offer perfect retreats near Glastonbury, Cheddar and historic Wells. Our cottages are made to relax in, and we invite you to enjoy our wonderful gardens, breathtaking Somerset landscapes, wildlife and luxury spa

Potting Shed Cottage • A perfect country hideway "a deux". Situated in the centre of Somerset.

Spider's End Cottage • A cottage surrounded by nearly two acres of garden.

Middle Earth • A charming and unique little Cottage. Very quiet and beautifully appointed and fully equipped.

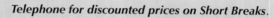

Telephone for discounted prices on Short Breaks.

**Potting Shed Holiday Cottages
Harter's Hill Cottage, Pillmoor Lane, Coxley,
Near Wells, Somerset BA5 1RF
Tel: 01749 672857
info@pottingshedholidays.co.uk
www.pottingshedholidays.co.uk**

enjoyEngland.com
★★★★
SELF CATERING

WOODLANDS FARM •• TAUNTON

SB

**Mrs Joan Greenway, Woodlands Farm,
Bathealton, Taunton TA4 2AH
Tel: 01984 623271**

You can be assured of a warm welcome at our family-run dairy farm situated in the heart of beautiful unspoilt countryside and within easy reach of both the north and south coasts and Exmoor. The wing of the farmhouse sleeps three and is furnished to a high standard. Well equipped kitchen with use of washing machine and dryer. Bathroom with bath and shower. Electricity, central heating and bed linen inclusive. Fishing, golf and horse riding nearby.

*Terms from £270 to £370 per week.
B&B also available - from £27pp*

Please write or phone for colour brochure.

www.woodlandsfarm-holidays.co.uk

Trowbridge

Wiltshire

**John and Elizabeth Moody
Gaston Farm, Holt,
Trowbridge BA14 6QA
Tel: 01225 782203**

The self-contained accommodation is part of a farmhouse, dating from the 16th century, on the edge of the village of Holt with views across open farmland. Within 10 miles of Bath, Bradford-on-Avon two miles, Lacock eight miles. Private fishing on River Avon available.

The apartment consists of a large lounge/dining room with open fire and sofa which converts into a double bed; two generously proportioned bedrooms upstairs, one twin-bedded, one with a double bed, both with washbasins; a separate toilet (downstairs); a large kitchen in the single storey wing, fitted with light oak finish units, electric cooker, microwave, refrigerator and automatic washing machine; shower room which opens off the kitchen. Electricity extra.

**Off-road parking. Choice of pubs in village.
Terms £200 to £225. Brochure and further details available.**

For the greatest concentration of prehistoric sites in Europe, visit Wiltshire. Most famous is the UNESCO World Heritage Site, Stonehenge, on Salisbury Plain, dating back at least five thousand years, while the stone circle at Avebury is the largest in the world.Salisbury, as well as the famous medieval cathedral, has plenty to choose from in arts and entertainment, while, Swindon, with its railway heritage, is the place to go for shopping and a lively nightlife. In the countryside there are interesting old market towns to explore, stately homes and gardens, including the safari park at Longleat, to visit, and ample opportunities for walking and cycling.

symbols 🐕🐎SB♿🍷Wi-Fi

🐕	*Pets Welcome*		🐎	*Children Welcome*
SB	*Short Breaks*		♿	*Suitable for Disabled Guests*
🍷	*Licensed*		**Wi-Fi**	*Wi-Fi available*

Olney

Buckinghamshire

The Old Stone Barn • Olney •

The Old Stone Barn is peacefully positioned on an arable farm 1½ miles from the beautiful market town of Olney where there is a wide variety of shops, cafes, bars and restaurants.

The accommodation is a charming combination of old character and modern facilities, and consists of seven spacious self-contained apartments (sleep 1-6), centrally heated and equipped with colour TV and payphone. Linen and towels are provided, and there is a laundry room with washing machines and a tumble dryer. Computer room and wifi available.

Guests can relax in the gardens, make use of the outdoor heated swimming pool, or take day trips to Oxford, Cambridge, London or the Cotswolds. Terms from £270 to £590 per week.

Mr & Mrs Garry Pibworth, Home Farm,
Warrington, Olney MK46 4HN
Tel: 01234 711655
e-mail: info@oldstonebarn.co.uk
www.oldstonebarn.co.uk

Only half an hour from London, the rolling hills and wooded valleys of the Buckinghamshire countryside provide a wonderful contrast to city life. Enjoy the bluebells in spring and the autumn colours of the woodland while following the innumerable footpaths, cycle paths, bridleways and two National Trails that cross the county and follow the meandering River Thames. Watch the red kites above the Chilterns, follow the Roald Dahl Trail or relax with a picnic in a country park. The excitement of the 2012 Olympics comes to Dorney Lake at Eton, for rowing, canoeing and kayaking events. Fascinating historic towns and villages include West Wycombe, owned by the National Trust, just one of many interesting properties in the area, while Milton Keynes is the destination for an all-round shopping experience.

Hampshire

SB

Hilden
Self-Catering Guest House
Tel: 01590 624444

New Forest Self-Catering between Brockenhurst and Lymington

Hilden Self-Catering Guest House is an elegant, imposing Edwardian house, situated in 2.5 acres of mature gardens and paddocks. Less than 50 yards from the open Forest, Hilden is perfectly located just 2 miles from the Georgian sailing town of Lymington and less than 2 miles from Brockenhurst, which is on the main train line from London Waterloo.

Rob and Crystal welcome you to stay in their home, offering their self-catering accommodation throughout the year. Children are welcome to play in our delightful gardens where they can meet our resident New Forest donkey!

Hilden, Southampton Road, Boldre, Lymington, Hampshire SO41 8PT
www.new-forest-self-catering.com

The Hilden Self-Catering Flat	The Hilden Self-Catering Suite
An upstairs wing of the main house, the flat benefits from its own private access. Edwardian bathroom with large, deep bath. Fitted kitchen with breakfast table. Delightful views across the lawn and paddocks. Well behaved dogs (on leads) are welcome.	*Part of the main family house, accessed via the grand hallway and full of Edwardian charm. A generous room with large bay windows, small dining and relaxing area. Separate inner-hall and full sized bathroom with Edwardian bath.*

LITTLE THATCH
15 South Street, Pennington, New Forest

Beautiful Grade II Listed thatched cob cottage in village location. Sleeps 4 in 2 bedrooms. Superbly renovated to offer traditional cottage features, tastefully combined with luxury modern comforts, including washer/dryer, dishwasher, TV, freeview, video, DVD. Secluded secure garden. Pets welcome. An ideal location for rambling country walks, cycling, horse riding, sailing and day trips. Close to shops and welcoming pubs which serve food.

Contact: Mrs Suzannah Nash (01582 842831)
e-mail: suzannah@littlethatchcottage.com • www.littlethatchcottage.com

Totland Bay

Isle of Wight

TOTLAND BAY – ISLE OF WIGHT

Modernised coastguard cottage c 1840; lovely walking; 500 yards from the sea; 6 walks start from the cottage; village shops; small town 1 mile; on regular bus route. Lounge opens onto patio and small secluded garden overlooking village bowling green and open space beyond. Family accommodation up to 5: lounge/dining kitchen area, 2 bedrooms; bathroom - separate shower and under-floor heating; heated throughout the year.   **4 days' winter rent from £60**

**Mrs C Pitts, 11 York Ave
New Milton BH25 6BT
Tel 01425 615215**
Email: Christine@gcpitts.force9.co.uk

Non-smokers only

☐ **Indicates the approximate position of the cottage**

SB

The ultimate sailing destination is of course the Isle of Wight, only a short ferry ride away from the mainland, with marinas, golden, sandy beaches, water sports centres, seakayaking, diving, sailing and windsurfing. On land there are over 500 miles of interconnected footpaths, cycleways, historic castles, dinosaur museums, theme parks and activity centres, or view it all from the skies on a paragliding adventure. To the north and east the well-known resorts of Sandown, Shanklin, Ryde and Ventnor provide all the traditional seaside activities, as well as the sailing centre, Cowes, while West Wight, an Area of Outstanding Natural Beauty will appeal to nature lovers and birdwatchers. With a thriving arts community, and of course two internationally renowned music festivals held every year, there is something for everyone!.

Kent

Kent, the 'Garden of England', yet with such easy access to London, is a county of gentle, rolling downlands, edged by the famous White Cliffs and miles of sands and shingle beaches along the Channel coast. Walk along the North Downs Way through an Area of Outstanding Natural Beauty stretching from Kent through Sussex to Surrey, including the historic Pilgrim's Way, or enjoy the stunning scenery from the Saxon Shore Way with views to the coast of France, and the wildlife of the Medway Estuary and Romney Marsh. The resorts of the Isle of Thanet and the south-east coast, like Ramsgate, Margate, Herne Bay and Deal have plenty to offer for a traditional family seaside holiday, and there are steam trains, animal parks and castles full of history to explore too.

Sunset Lodge at Great Field Farm

Stelling Minnis, Canterbury, Kent CT4 6DE
Tel: 01227 709223

SB

Ground floor Lodge in lovely private position with
panoramic views over beautiful countryside and
magnificent sunsets. Light, spacious and modern with
open-plan living, dining and kitchen area, spiral staircase
to snug/kid's room. Two en suite bedrooms, 1 double with wet
room with shower, 1 twin-bedded room with bath.
Free internet access. Open all year.
Also available in the main farmhouse on the SE corner is
a cosy flat with a double bedroom, sitting room, kitchen
and bathroom. Free internet access.
Both properties are also available for B & B, and we have
2 more en suite rooms for B & B, if required.
ETC ★★★★ and Breakfast Award
Lovely and quiet, yet easily accessible position,
approximately 15 minute drive to Canterbury, Folkestone,
Ashford and Eurotunnel.
Ample off-road parking, flexible start and finish days.
Please phone or Email for prices and availability.

Self-Catering • Bed & Breakfast
greatfieldfarm@aol.com • www.great-field-farm.co.uk

Apple Pye Self-Catering Cottage

Cottage on farm set in 45 acres, surrounded by beautiful rolling Kentish
countryside. Well away from the road and next to the farmhouse B&B, it is only
10 minutes' drive from M20, J8. Central location for visiting Kent's many
attractions, 6 miles from Leeds Castle, Canterbury half-hour drive, Dover one
hour's drive, London one and a quarter hours by train. Sleeps four.
One double room en suite, one twin with own shower room; living
room/kitchen/dining room with washer/dryer, fridge/freezer, electric cooker,
microwave, TV, DVD, wireless broadband. Full Central heating. Garden and
patio. Suitable for disabled. Rent £295-£495 per week. B&B also available.

Wi-Fi

Mr & Mrs Leat, Apple Pye Cottage, Bramley Knowle Farm, Eastwood Road, Ulcombe, Maidstone, Kent ME17 1ET
Tel: 01622 858878 • E-mail: diane@bramleyknowlefarm.co.uk • www.bramleyknowlefarm.co.uk

GOLDING HOP FARM COTTAGE
Plaxtol, Near Sevenoaks TN15 0PS

Self catering cottage on 13-acre cobnut farm in
Bourne Valley. Sleeps 5 plus cot.
Three bedrooms, living room, dining room, bathroom and
fully equipped kitchen. Children and pets welcome. Open all year. £240-£460 pw.
Set in rural Kent with easy access to channel crossings and sightseeing in London.

Tel: 07771 520229 • info@goldinghopfarm.com • www.goldinghopfarm.com

Pangbourne

Oxfordshire

Brambly Thatch

Merricroft, Goring Heath RG8 7TA
Tel: 01189 843121 • e-mail: merricroft@yahoo.co.uk

An attractive 17thC thatched cottage within easy reach of Oxford and London. The acccommodation comprises living room, dining room, fully equipped kitchen, 3 bedrooms (one downstairs), and bathroom. TV and DVD. Parking available. Sleeps 5. A variety of local attractions include National Trust properties and the Childe-Beale Wildlife Trust and further afield, Windsor Castle and Legoland Windsor and more. Open all year.

Surrey

Godalming

SB

Shepherd's Hut Shortbreaks

Bowlhead Green, Godalming, Surrey GU8 6NW

Outdoor living without roughing it - ideal for a relaxing weekend or longer break.
A beautifully kitted-out shepherd's hut with living/sleeping accommodation
and sole use of another converted shepherd's hut into a wood-lined,
warm bathroom with hot/cold water and modern drainage.
Exclusive use of hot tub/jacuzzi in its own hut, tennis court and use of 2 bicycles.
Set in the Surrey countryside, the perfect place to relax and unwind.
Excellent walking country and cycle routes nearby.

Tel: 01428 682808

heathhallfarm@btinternet.com • www.shepherds-hut-shortbreaks.co.uk

Heathfield

East Sussex

Cannon Barn

Tel: 01435 812285

Cannon Barn, a Sussex wheat barn built in 1824, has been sympathetically converted to provide modern comforts. Boring House is a small working farm with sheep. There are ponds and a stream on the farm, and plenty of footpaths in the area, including one which crosses the farm, giving plenty of choice for walkers.

Locally, there is a good selection of pubs for meals, and also a great variety of things to do and places to visit for all the family. Wireless broadband available.

Please visit our website for photographs and further information.
Short Breaks available out of season. Sleeps 8-10. Prices £200-£950.

SB

Wi-Fi

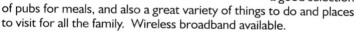

Contact: Mrs A. Reed, Boring House Farm,
Nettlesworth Lane, Vines Cross, Heathfield TN21 9AS
e-mail: info@boringhousefarm.co.uk
www.boringhousefarm.co.uk

enjoyEngland.com
★★★★
SELF CATERING

From the dramatic cliffs and sandy beaches of the Sussex coast to the quiet countryside of the Weald and the South Downs, there's an endless choice of the things to do and places to explore. Sailing, walking, cycling, horse riding, golf are all available for an active break, while the fascinating history of 1066 country, castles like Bodiam and the seaside ports will attract all the family. If you're looking for beaches, the 100 miles of coast offer something for everyone, whether your preference is for action-packed fun at a family resort or a quiet, remote spot. Best known for a combination of lively nightlife and all the attractions of the seaside, Brighton has everything from its pebble beach, classic pier, Royal Pavilion and Regency architecture, to shopping malls, art galleries, antique shops, and the specialist boutiques and coffee shops of The Lanes. There's so much to choose from!

SB

Distinctly different...

Pekes

Chiddingly
East Sussex

www.pekesmanor.com

In the grounds of a Tudor manor house, up a 350-yard drive, with unspoilt views of the Sussex countryside, Pekes offers a unique self-catering holiday. Peaceful, yet close to London, and with exceptional freedom to use the facilities: exotic indoor heated swimming pool, sauna, jacuzzi, lawn badminton, and tarmac tennis court.

Fabulous large oast house
for 7 to 11
Four period cottages
for 4 to 10

All very well equipped, with colour TV, full central heating, washing machine, tumble dryer, fridge freezer, microwave and dishwasher. Children and obedient dogs welcome. Open all year.

Contact Eva Morris
Tel: 020 7352 8088
Fax: 020 7352 8125
e-mail: pekes.afa@virgin.net

Short Breaks: 3 nights weekends or 4 nights midweek
Large Oasthouse £1004-£1232 • Mounts View Cottage £995-£1150
Cottages £258-£536. Excludes main school holidays.

Ely

Cambridgeshire

SB

Cathedral House

17 St Mary's Street, Ely
Cambridgeshire CB7 4ER

Tel: 01353 662124

The Coach House has been imaginatively converted into a delightful abode full of character and charm, situated close to Ely Cathedral.

Arranged on two floors, the accommodation downstairs comprises a sitting room and country-style kitchen. Upstairs there are two charming double rooms (one has a view of the Cathedral), and a cosy single room. All have an en suite bathroom, with a toilet, wash hand basin and a half-size bath with shower taps.

Gas central heating. Linen, towels, toilet soap, cleaning materials and some basic provisions are provided.

Prices range from £300 to £750 depending on season and length of stay. Special rates for two people.

www.cathedralhouse.co.uk
farndale@cathedralhouse.co.uk

Cambridgeshire immediately brings to mind the ancient university city of Cambridge, lazy hours punting on the river past the imposing college buildings, students on bicycles, museums and bookshops. This cosmopolitan centre has so much to offer, with theatres, concerts varying from classical to jazz, an annual music festival, cinemas, botanic gardens, exciting shops and to round it all off, restaurants, pubs and cafes serving high quality food. In the surrounding countryside historic market towns, pretty villages and stately homes wait to be explored. Visit Ely with its magnificent cathedral and museum exhibiting the national collection of stained glass, antique shops and cafes. Shopping is one of the attractions of Peterborough, along with Bronze Age excavations and reconstructed dwelling, a ghost tour of the museum and an annual CAMRA Beer Festival.

Essex

SB

Wi-Fi

Rye Farm

Three attractive holiday apartments converted from a 17thC cart lodge on a working farm adjacent to Abberton Reservoir, an internationally important wetland and wildfowl haven.

Furnished and equipped to a high standard, the apartments sleep 2-4, with central heating, colour TV/DVD. Two apartments are on the ground floor, and one is designed and equipped for disabled guests. Laundry facilities. Patio with table and chairs. Ample car parking close to the apartments. Laundry facilities. Smoking not permitted. No pets. Children over 2 years are welcome.

Rye Lane, Layer de la Haye, Colchester CO2 0JL
Tel: 01206 734350/07976 524276
e-mail: peterbunting@btconnect.com
www.ryefarm.org.uk

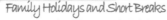

Norfolk

SB

Each Houseboat (like a floating log cabin) will sleep up to 6 people in two bedrooms, has a spacious lounge/diner, galley style kitchen and bathroom with shower. Moored in the picturesque village of Horning alongside a large sunny decking area there is lots of space to sit in the sun and watch the boats go by or do some fishing.

Horning is just 10 miles from the city of Norwich and just 15 from the busy seaside resort of Great Yarmouth. The BeWILDerwood curious treehouse adventure park is just 5 minutes away!

For a brochure call 01493 369997 or email holidays@watersideleisure.com

Norfolk Broads Houseboats

www.norfolkbroadsandcoastalholidays.com

Norfolk Broads @ Coastal Holidays

Quality accommodation both on the Norfolk Broads and on the Norfolk Coast. Whether you are looking for tranquil relaxation, beautiful scenery or exhilarating activities, Norfolk really does have something to suit everyone.

10% Discount on weekly brochure prices – quote **FHG/12** when booking

For a brochure
Call **01493 369997** or email:
holidays@watersideleisure.com

www.norfolkbroadsandcoastalholidays.com

Castaways
HOLIDAY PARK
BACTON-ON-SEA NORFOLK

For one of the best value holidays on the glorious North Norfolk Coast, welcome to Castaways Holiday Park

A small, family-run business situated in the quiet, peaceful village of Bacton, with direct access to fine sandy beach, and ideal for beach fishing and discovering Norfolk and The Broads.

Stunning sea views from most of our accommodation:
Fully equipped modern Caravans, comfortable three bedroom pine lodges and a choice of 2 ground floor and 2 first floor flats with all amenities. Licensed Club. Entertainment. Amusement Arcade. Children's Play Area.

PETS WELCOME

Enquiries and Bookings to:
Castaways Holiday Park,
Paston Road, Bacton-on-Sea,
Norfolk NR12 0JB

BH & HPA approved

on-line booking facility available

Booking Hotline: 01692 650 436
www.castawaysholidaypark.net

The Holiday Estate with a difference

Winterton Valley Holidays

A selection of modern superior fully appointed holiday chalets in a choice of locations near Great Yarmouth.

No straight lines of identical chalets on this delightfully landscaped 35 acre estate of holiday homes. It has private access to Winterton's fine sandy beaches, with no main roads for children to cross. A wonderful place for a real away from it all holiday, very quiet and yet only 8 miles from Great Yarmouth. Both the beach and valley are ideal for dog walking, and pets are very welcome.

There are no shops, amusements or clubs on the site. The village of Winterton is a short distance away, with its well stocked stores and 300 year old pub which serves excellent food and drink at the bar or in the family room and garden.

Chalets are privately owned, sleep up to 6 people and each is of individual style. All have open plan lounge and dining areas adjoining the kitchens. Electric heating and TV. Kitchens are all equipped with an electric cooker, microwave and fridge. Bathrooms have a full size bath, wash basin and WC. Most chalets have a shower over the bath.

All chalets have two bedrooms which have a double bed in one room and either twin beds or bunk beds in the second bedroom. You are asked to supply your own bed linen: duvet covers, bottom sheets, pillow cases, towels and tea towels, but these can be supplied for hire if required. Pets are very welcome in most chalets at a small additional fee.

For those wanting a livelier holiday we also have chalets at nearby **California Sands.**

For colour brochure please ring 01493 377175 or write to 15 Kingston Avenue, Caister-on-Sea, Norfolk NR30 5ET

www.wintertonvalleyholidays.co.uk

Suffolk

SB

Wi-Fi

Lodge Cottage
Laxfield, Suffolk

Set in a relaxing rural location, a 16C thatched cottage retaining some fine period features. One double en suite bedroom and one twin bedroom, shower room, sitting room with stove and kitchen. Sleeps 4. An ideal location for exploring the Suffolk countryside and coast. Plenty of rambling walks and cycling routes, bird watching, horse riding and golf are just some of the surrounding activities. Pets welcome. Fenced garden. One mile from village. 30 minutes to Southwold and coast.

For brochure phone Jane:
**01986 798830 or 07788 853884 or
e-mail: janebrewer@live.co.uk
www.lodgeholidaycottages.co.uk**

SB

Wi-Fi

Badwell Ash Holiday Lodges

A stunning resort of just four holiday lodges positioned around three fishing lakes. Set in five acres in the heart of Mid Suffolk.

As listed in The Sunday Telegraph article "The World's Best Over-Water Resorts

Badwell Ash offers the ultimate year round retreat:
a perfect place for a honeymoon, anniversary or simply
somewhere to spend time with friends and family.
Each of the 2 bedroom lodges is graded ★★★★.
VisitBritain Gold Award for 2011/12.

- Exclusively for adults.
- Personal outdoor hot tub for each lodge.
- Each lodge with a veranda over the lake.
- All furnished to a high standard with 4-poster beds,
  fully fitted kitchen and steam showers.
- Complimentary welcome hamper with Champagne,
  chocolates and many extras.
- All bedding, towels etc included.

An ideal base for exploring the historic market towns and cities,
quaint fishing villages, the beautiful coast and many other local
attractions that Suffolk has to offer.

BADWELL ASH HOLIDAY LODGES
Badwell Ash, Suffolk IP31 3DJ
Tel: 01359 258444
info@badwellashlodges.co.uk
www.badwellashlodges.co.uk

BadwellAsh
Holiday Lodges

Ashbourne

Derbyshire

Paddock House Farm Holiday Cottages

★★★★ Luxury Holiday Cottage Accommodation

Surrounded by 5 acres of delightful grounds and reached along its own long drive, Paddock House nestles peacefully in a secluded spot between the famous villages of Alstonefield and Hartington, renowned for its cheese shop. Arranged around a courtyard, these charming cottages enjoy uninterrupted views.

The area is a walker's paradise, and there are excellent cycle trails along Dovedale, Tissington and the Manifold Valley.

An ideal base for families, the surrounding area boasts a wealth of attractions to suit all tastes. Nearby the attractive market town of Ashbourne offers shops, restaurants and other town amenities. Slightly further afield, the magnificent Chatsworth House is an impressive sight to behold. The spa towns of Matlock and Buxton are as popular as their 'magical' waters have ever been. Alton Towers 20 minutes.

Peak District National Park, Alstonefield, Ashbourne, Derbyshire DE6 2FT
Tel: 01335 310282 • Mobile: 07977 569618
e-mail: info@paddockhousefarm.co.uk • www.paddockhousefarm.co.uk

For walking, climbing, cycling, horse riding, mountain biking and caving, visit Derbyshire. Visit Poole's Cavern to see the best stalagmites and stalactites in Derbyshire (and discover the difference!), and the Blue John Cave at Castleton where this rare mineral is mined, and perhaps buy a sample of jewellery in one of the local shops. Buxton was a spa from Roman times, but the main attractions now are concerts, theatre and the opera, music and literature festival held every year. Go to Wirksworth in spring for the annual well dressings or try out a wizard's wand at Hardwick Hall near Chesterfield, the market town with the church with the crooked spire. No stay in Derbyshire is complete without visiting Chatsworth, the best known of the stately homes, with impressive interiors and magnificent gardens and grounds, and for a contrasting step back in time go to Crich Tramway Village for a tram ride down a period street and on into the countryside.

Bamford, Hartington

SB

Wi-Fi

Peak District • Derbyshire
Shatton Hall Farm Cottages

On this quiet and beautiful upland farm, woodland and streamside walks, a hard tennis court and trout lake are there to enjoy, as are the gardens surrounding our three comfortable stone cottages.

Furnished in old pine, with well equipped kitchens, tiled bathrooms with showers, double and twin bedrooms in each. Open all year.

We can have a Derbyshire breakfast in your refrigerator if ordered in advance, to give you a superb start to a day's walking.

Availability and booking on-line
Low season short breaks available.

PEAK DISTRICT
ENVIRONMENTAL
QUALITY MARK
Certification Mark for Businesses

£300-£550 per week.
Sleep 4-5.

Green Tourism SILVER

Bamford, Hope Valley S33 0BG
Tel/Fax: 01433 620635
e-mail: ahk@peakfarmholidays.co.uk
www.peakfarmholidays.co.uk

Wolfscote Grange
Farm Cottages
Hartington, Near Buxton,
Derbyshire SK17 0AX
Tel & Fax: 01298 84342

enjoyEngland.com
★★★★
SELF CATERING

Charming cottages nestling beside the beautiful Dove Valley in stunning scenery.

Cruck Cottage is peaceful 'with no neighbours, only sheep' and a cosy 'country living' feel.

Swallows Cottage offers comfort for the traveller and time to relax in beautiful surroundings. It sparkles with olde worlde features, yet has all modern amenities including en suite facilities and spa bathroom.

The farm trail provides walks from your doorstep to the Dales. Open all year. Dogs by arrangement only.

Weekly terms from £180 to £490 (sleeps 4)
& £180 to £600 (sleeps 6).

e-mail: wolfscote@btinternet.com
www.wolfscotegrangecottages.co.uk

Leicester

Leicestershire & Rutland

Set in the centre of the Midlands, the rolling countryside, canals, forests, beautiful villages, interesting market towns and history make Leicestershire and Rutland well worth a visit. In the north west the 200 square miles of the new National Forest, joining the ancient woodlands of Needham and Charnwood, are transforming the landscape and giving access to this wide stretch of countryside to walkers, cyclists and horse riders. Children, and adults too, will have great fun in the discovery zones and play areas at Conkers, the award-winning attraction at the heart of the forest near Moira. Spend a peaceful hour or two cruising along the Ashby Canal past Bosworth Battlefield where the Wars of the Roses ended in 1485. With over 1000 different species there's plenty to see at Twycross Zoo at Hinckley, or take a walk through Burbage Wood to see the native fauna.

Barnoldby-Le-Beck

Lincolnshire

SB

Wi-Fi

Three well appointed cottages and riding school situated in the heart of the Lincolnshire Wolds.
The tasteful conversion of a spacious, beamed Victorian barn provides stylish and roomy cottages, one sleeping 6, and two sleeping 4 in one double and one twin bedroom, comfy sittingroom and diningroom. Fully equipped kitchen. Bathroom with bath and shower.

You don't need to ride with us, but if you do....

The Equestrian Centre offers professional tuition, an all-weather riding surface, stabling for guests' own horses, and an extensive network of bridle paths.

GRANGE FARM COTTAGES & RIDING SCHOOL
Waltham Road, Barnoldby-le-Beck, N.E. Lincs DN37 0AP
For Cottage Reservations Tel: 01472 822216 • mobile: 07947 627663
www.grangefarmcottages.com

Louth

Brackenborough Hall
Coach House Holidays

Three luxury self-catering apartments in a Listed 18th century Coach House in the beautiful county of Lincolnshire. Stables and Saddle Room sleep up to 4, Granary Apartment sleeps up to 8. Together can accommodate up to 24. Short Breaks all year round.

Winner 'Best Self-Catering Holiday in England 2009/10' Silver Award 'Best Holiday for Families in East Midlands' 2009/10

Paul & Flora Bennett,
Brackenborough Hall, Louth, Lincolnshire LN11 0NS
Tel: 01507 603193 • 07974 687779
e-mail: PaulandFlora@BrackenboroughHall.com
www.BrackenboroughHall.com

SB
Wi-Fi

Coast or country, the choice is yours for a holiday in Lincolnshire. With award-winning beaches, miles of clean sand, theme parks, kite surfing, jet skiing and seaside nature reserves, there's action, excitement and interests for everyone right along the coast. At Skegness, as well as all the fun on the beach, children will love watching the seals being fed at the seal sanctuary, and the Parrot Zoo nearby. There's a seal sanctuary at Mablethorpe too, and all the fun of the fairground, as well as beach huts to hire if the sun goes behind a cloud. Further north, at Cleethorpes with its wonderful beaches and Pleasure Island, take a ride on the Cleethorpes Coast Light Railway, or a guided tour of the sand dunes and saltmarshes at the Discovery Centre to find out about local wildlife habitats. Inland spend a peaceful break exploring the quiet countryside of the Wolds. Keen fishermen can always find a peaceful spot along the extensive network of rivers and canals and for golfers there's a wide variety and standard of courses, with the home of amateur golf in England at the National Golf Centre at Woodhall Spa. In Lincoln walk round the battlements at the Castle, explore the cobbled streets lined with medieval buildings and visit the imposing Gothic cathedral, one of the finest in Europe. Cruise on the Roman canal that flows through the city, shop at the boutiques, eat at the restaurants and cafes, and in the evening enjoy a concert or a visit to the theatre.

Ludlow

Shropshire

Sutton Court Farm

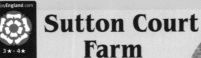

**Little Sutton,
Stanton Lacy, Ludlow
SY8 2AJ
Tel: 01584 861305**

Jane & Alan Cronin

Sympathetically converted from stone barns,
these six cottages offer the ideal centre for exploring South Shropshire and the
Marches (Ludlow 5 miles).
They are all furnished with care and attention to detail; well equipped kitchens,
central heating (two have wood burning stoves), and stable doors allowing
in sunshine and fresh air in fine weather.
Children's play room • Pets in some cottages by arrangement.
Breakfast packs, cream teas and home-cooked meals can be delivered to your
cottage by arrangement.

www.suttoncourtfarm.co.uk   enquiries@suttoncourtfarm.co.uk

'A special place to return to'

If you're looking for a break from the pace of life today, but with plenty to do and see,
Shropshire is the place to visit. For the active visitor the quiet countryside bordering on the
Welsh Marches offers opportunities for walking, cycling, horse riding, kayaking, canoeing,
and quad and mountain biking, while if the history of the region's turbulent past appeals,
there are over 30 castles to visit, as well as stately homes and beautiful gardens. Visit the
grass-roofed Shropshire Hills Discovery Centre at Craven Arms, where you can take a
simulated balloon ride and meet the Shropshire mammoth, and Stokesay Castle, the finest
13th century fortified manor house in England. To find out about the more recent past visit
the ten museums at the Ironbridge Gorge.

Ludlow

Newport

SB

Wi-Fi

Sambrook Manor
Holiday Cottages
Sambrook, Newport TF10 8AL

Set on the Shropshire/Staffordshire border,
Sambrook Manor is the ideal place to stay to
explore both counties. We have two beautifully
converted barns: the **Old Shippon** is our biggest
(sleeping 8/10), and **Churn Cottage** which
sleeps 4 is also suitable for disabled guests.
Both cottages have original exposed beams,
well equipped kitchens, the luxury of underfloor
heating, and their own gardens with fantastic
views over the farm's grassy fields.
* Short breaks. • Wi-Fi access.
* Children welcome. • Suitable for disabled.
* Non-smoking.
* Linen, towels, heat & electricity included.
e-mail: enquiries@sambrookmanor.co.uk

www.sambrookmanor.co.uk • Tel: 07811 632445

Staffordshire

Leek

THE BOTHY - RUDYARD LAKE

Find out more by calling
07957 856629 or **01565 633636**
(office hours)
or visit our website:
www.thebothy-rudyard.co.uk

The Bothy is a secluded retreat nestling on the banks of Rudyard Lake, just two miles from Leek and a million miles
from anything you know. Here the horizon is tree-top green and the air still but for the sound of birdsong.
Take time to rediscover simple pleasures - the beauty of a woodland walk, the adventure of a boat ride, the
company of friends. In this privately owned cottage you can relax knowing nothing has been overlooked
- from bathrobe to mountain bike, picnic basket to hot tub - *The Bothy has it all!*
2 double bedrooms (sleeps 5+cot) • Hot tub • Sky TV • Fully equipped kitchen • Log burning stove
Fenced garden • Private pontoon, fishing rods, rowing boat • Mountain bikes

Situated in Staffordshire Moorlands, cosy 3-bedroom cottage with four-poster (sleeps 6), overlooking picturesque countryside.
Fully equipped, comfortably furnished and carpeted throughout. An ideal base for visits to Alton Towers, the Potteries and Peak District. Patio, play area.
Cot and high chair available.
Laundry room with auto washer and dryer.
Electricity and fresh linen incl.
Terms from £230 to £375.

SB

EDITH & ALWYN MYCOCK

'ROSEWOOD COTTAGE'

LOWER BERKHAMSYTCH FARM, BOTTOM HOUSE, NEAR LEEK ST13 7QP

Tel & Fax: 01538 308213 • www.rosewoodcottage.co.uk

SB

See our latest video on our website

Silver Trees Holiday Park
Stafford Brook Road, Rugeley WS15 2TX
Tel: 01889 582185

Enjoy the peace and tranquillity at Silver Trees, set in the midst of Cannock Chase with its own Nature Reserve designated a SSSI. Open March-mid January.

Modern static caravans with all conveniences. No tourers or tents. On-site facilities include tennis court, laundry, nature reserve and indoor heated swimming pool

Birches Valley Visitor Centre 350 metres away and start of cycling/walking paths 200 metres away. Local attractions include Alton Towers. Waterworld, Twycross Zoo and many more.

info@silvertreesholidaypark.co.uk • www.silvertreesholidaypark.co.uk

Stratford-Upon-Avon

Warwickshire

SB

Weston Farm
Weston upon Avon, CV37 8JY

Five luxury holiday cottages converted from former barns and farm buildings on a working farm, four miles from Stratford upon Avon. All fully equipped including colour TV with basic Sky. Ample off-street parking. Electricity and linen included. Private fishing, golf and local cycle paths. We regret no pets. No smoking.
An ideal base from which to tour Warwickshire and Cotswold countryside or just to unwind.

Tel: 01789 750688

info@westonfarm.co.uk • www.westonfarm.co.uk

Worcestershire

Worcestershire, stretching south-east from the fringes of Birmingham, is a county of Georgian towns, Cotswold stone villages and a Victorian spa, all centred on the cathedral city of Worcester. To the north canals were cut to satisfy the need for transport that grew with industrialisation, and now provide a wonderful opportunity for a leisurely break on a narrowboat, or take a restful look at the countryside from the Severn Valley Railway between Bromsgrove and Kidderminster. Long distance trails like the 100-mile Millenium Way cross the countryside in all directions, or follow one of the many shorter local circular walks. In the Malvern Hills choose between gentle and more strenuous exercise to appreciate the wonderful views of the surrounding countryside, or for a different kind of challenge, try mountain boarding in the hills near Malvern.

Bishops Frome, Clifton-Upon-Teme

East Yorkshire

Raven Hill Holiday Farmhouse

SB

With delightful views overlooking the Yorkshire Wolds, ideally situated for touring the East Coast, Bridlington, Scarborough, Moors and York, this secluded and private four-bedroom **FARMHOUSE** is set in its own acre of woodland lawns and orchard, with garden furniture, summerhouse and children's play area. Sleeps 2-8 + 2 + cot.

Clean and comfortable and very well equipped including dishwasher, microwave, automatic washing machine and dryer; TV, DVD and games room. Fully centrally heated. Beds are made up for your arrival; cot and high chair available.

Three miles to the nearest village of Kilham with Post Office, general stores, garage and public houses. Available all year.

Terms per week from £300 to £690. Brochure on request.

Mrs P. M. Savile, Raven Hill Farm, Kilham, Driffield YO25 4EG • Tel: 01377 267217

SELF CATERING

With family-friendly beaches, dramatic coastal cliffs and the gentle uplands of the Wolds inland, East Yorkshire will appeal to all age groups and interests. Following one of the many walking trails through the quiet and beautiful countryside, ramblers will discover hidden valleys and traditional villages and market towns like Beverley, with its medieval centre, 13th century Minster, and literature, jazz and folk festivals. Driffield, known as the capital of the Wolds, is an ideal centre from which to explore both countryside and coast, or for a seaside holiday with golden sands, award-winning promenades and entertainment of all kinds at the Spa, Bridlington is ideal for a family break. Take the land train up to the top of the spectacular cliffs, summer home to huge seabird colonies, try kite-flying in the North Sea breezes, or play a round of golf on the clifftop links.

Driffield

SB

Wi-Fi

Old Cobbler's Cottage
North Dalton, East Yorkshire

A delightful mid-19th century terraced beamed cottage situated in the quiet, picturesque village of North Dalton nestling in the heart of the Yorkshire Wolds.

The cottage possesses a unique view overlooking the village pond and the 11th century village church.

Ideal for walkers as The Minster Way passes through the village, with the Wolds Way close by.

The village is a short drive from Driffield and Pocklington and the historic market town of Beverley. It is only twenty miles from York and the East Coast resort of Bridlington. Also accessible for Scarborough and Whitby.

The accommodation includes a fully equipped kitchen and living room with open fire, TV with DVD/Video/CD player and iPod player.

One double and one single bedroom, Z bed to sleep a 4th person, both with attractive views. The small conservatory leads onto a patio. Off-street parking for one car. Electric central heating is fitted throughout. Wi-Fi access available. Adjacent is an excellent, welcoming country pub serving good quality, pub grub, using locally grown produce.

Details from: Chris Wade,
2 Star Row, North Dalton,
Driffield, E Yorkshire YO25 9UX
Tel: 01377 219901/ (day) • 01377 217523
(eve) 07801 124264 (anytime)
e-mail:chris.wade@adastra-music.co.uk
www.waterfrontcottages.co.uk

enjoyEngland.com
★★★
SELF CATERING

Grosmont, Harrogate

North Yorkshire

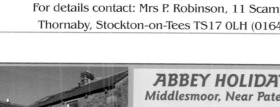

Hardraw, Harrogate

Hardraw • Hawes North Yorkshire

A delightful 18th century cottage of outstanding character. Situated in the village of Hardraw with its spectacular waterfall and Pennine Way. Market town of Hawes one mile.

This unique, traditional stone-built cottage with its beamed ceilings and open fire retains many original and unusual features. Sleeping four in comfort, in two bedrooms, it has been furnished and equipped to a high standard, using antique pine and Laura Ashley prints.

Sleeps 4

Outside, there is a south-facing garden with a "sun trap" patio and through the wall is a large paddock, blending onto the fields and fells beyond. Open all year.

Terms £150-£399 includes coal, electricity, linen and fishing rights. For more information and a brochure, contact:

Mrs Belinda Metcalfe, Southolme Farm, Little Smeaton, Northallerton DL6 2HJ Tel: 01609 881302/881052 e-mail: bm@adventuretoys.co.uk

---

Two well equipped holiday cottages in the award-winning Britain in Bloom village of Darley, between Harrogate and Pateley Bridge. Ideal for touring the Dales, with York within easy driving distance; riverside walks, local pub one mile.

Rose Cottage has two bedrooms, one double, one single, open plan lounge with kitchen and dining area. Daffodil Cottage is newly extended and refurbished with a new kitchen with dining area and large lounge. Three bedrooms, one en suite with bath, double and single bed. Further double bedroom and single room, shower room with basin and toilet. Large lawn area. Ample parking. Well behaved pets welcome.

Low Season £250-£320; High Season £350-£420

Southfield Farm Holiday Cottages

Darley, Harrogate
North Yorkshire HG3 2PR
Tel: 01423 780258
www.southfieldcottages.co.uk
info@southfieldcottages.co.uk

Low Bentham, Northallerton

SB

Staithes

SB

Pennysteel Cottage

An old 19th century fisherman's cottage located in the beautiful fishing village of Staithes in North Yorkshire. The oak beamed and wood panelled cottage is set in the heart of the village and retains much of its original character, and has breathtaking views over the harbour from every room and from its sun terrace.

The cottage is situated only 20 yards from a local public house, serving excellent bar meals. The village also boasts two other pubs, a range of cafés and shops, as well as the Captain Cook Museum.

Fully fitted kitchen – including electric hob and cooker, microwave, fridge freezer and dishwasher. Lounge /dining room with TV/DVD/video/CD player, books and games. One double and one single bedroom on the first floor, with twin (attic) bedroom and bathroom on the second floor. Cot and high chair available.

All rooms and the sun terrace overlook the sea

Details from: Chris Wade, 2 Star Row, North Dalton, Driffield, E Yorkshire YO25 9UX
Tel: 01377 219901/ (day) • 01377 217523 (eve) 07801 124264 (anytime)
e-mail: chris.wade@adastra-music.co.uk
www.waterfrontcottages.co.uk

SB

Whitby, York

York Lakeside Lodges
Moor Lane, York YO24 2QU

YORK
LAKESIDE
LODGES

A taste of the countryside, but with all the advantages of the City of York, just two miles away. Stroll in the parkland, relax by the lake (possibly doing a spot of fishing), catch a glimpse of the kingfisher, or go further afield to the North Yorkshire Moors, Yorkshire Dales or the coast.

York Lakeside Lodges is owned and run by the Manasir family who live in the grounds and are at hand for friendly help and advice.

The lodges are situated along one side of the 10-acre lake. Facing south, with beautiful views over the water, they are reached by a private road leading to a parking space beside each lodge.

The two adjoining brick cottages with balconies overlooking the lake have their own cottage garden. All properties are well insulated, double glazed and heated.

Throughout the grounds and in the lodges and cottages wireless internet access is available.

Tel: 01904 702346
e-mail: neil@yorklakesidelodges.co.uk
www.yorklakesidelodges.co.uk

Todmorden

West Yorkshire

SB

Shoebroad Barn
Todmorden • West Yorkshire

Shoebroad Barn is a substantial semi-detached barn conversion enjoying a superb semi-rural setting and commanding wonderful views. The property is within one mile of the town centre and railway station and is convenient for hilltop pubs and local amenities.

The spacious accommodation boasts a grand reception hall with feature staircase and four double bedrooms. Children are most welcome. Open all year. Short breaks available.

Plus adjacent twin bedded Studio Cottage.

Contact Mrs Horsfall • Tel: 01706 817015 • Mobile: 07966 158295
www.shoebroadbarn.co.uk • e-mail: lynne100@live.com

West Yorkshire is a mix of wild moorland and towns and cities with an historic industrial heritage. Spend some time in one of the many fascinating museums of past working life, then stride out over the moors, taking in the dramatic scenery, before a shopping spree or a wonderful afternoon tea. Visit the Rhubarb Triangle near Wakefield early in the year to see the crop being harvested by candlelight. At the model Victorian village for mill workers at Saltaire UNESCO World Heritage Site, Salts Mill has been transformed into the Hockney Gallery, with a restaurant and everything from musical instruments to carpets for shoppers to browse and buy. From there, wander along the banks of the Leeds-Liverpool Canal, so vital for trade in a past age, and watch the Five Rise Locks in action.

Bishop Auckland

Durham

NEW COTTAGE

SB

is a delightful little cottage in a very peaceful location. The accommodation is very cosy and comfortable and all on one level – there are no stairs. Panoramic views from the lounge are a never-ending source of delight – they are

stunning, and made even more beautiful in winter when there is a light dusting of snow. The cottage is accessible for country walks and sightseeing, and being able to start walks from the cottage is a real bonus.

And the sunsets are something else – truly magnificent.

Oil fired central heating is included in price.

Rates: £250 per week, all year round.

Details from Mrs Margaret Partridge.

New Cottage, 'Law One', Hollymoor Farm, Cockfield, Bishop Auckland DL13 5HF
Tel: 01388 718567/ 718260
www.hollymoorfarm.co.uk

enjoyEngland.com
★★★★
SELF CATERING

If you're looking for a few days' break somewhere different, why not go to the city of Durham? Set between the North Pennines and the Durham Heritage Coast, the old medieval heart with its cobbled streets is dominated by the cathedral and castle, a World Heritage Site, and a must for visitors. On the way back to the modern shopping centre, browse through individual boutiques and galleries in the alleys and vennels, then enjoy a stroll along the riverside walks. Stay for longer in County Durham, tour all the heritage sites and enjoy invigorating walks and hikes through the dramatic Pennines countryside and along the clifftop path at the coast. There are paths, trails and tracks for all standards of fitness, whether a family ramble and picnic or a hike along the Pennine Way. High Force, the highest waterfall in England, on the Raby Castle estate, is easily accessible. Include it in a long distance hike or a gentle wander from the car park.

Consett, Lanchester

SB

Derwent Grange Cottages

Five Cottages on a working farm

Five charming cottages situated in beautiful countryside within easy travelling distance of Durham City, Newcastle, Gateshead Metro Centre, Beamish Museum, the Roman Wall and all the tourist attractions of Northumberland and Durham. Local amenities include nearby supermarkets, pubs and restaurants as well as opportunities to fish, play golf, ride, swim, cycle and walk. The locality also would inspire photographers and artists.
We have a laundry available for a small fee.
High chair and cot available on request.
All cottages have shower rooms and kitchens.
All heating and linen are included.
Short Breaks available.

- **Garden** *£300 per week*
Sleeps 5 (two bedrooms – double and 3 single)
- **Dairy** *£300 per week*
sleeps 4 (two bedrooms – Four poster and twin)
- **Forge** *£250 per week*
sleeps 2 (double bedroom plus sofa bed in living room)

- **Stable 1** *£450 per week*
sleeps 5 (two bedrooms - double and 3 single)
- **Stable 2** *£250-£300 per week*
sleeps 4 (family room, double bed and bunk beds)
**Stable 1 and 2 connect, making a
4 bedroom cottage, ideal for families.**

Welcome *to* **Excellence**

2 ★ - 3 ★
SELF CATERING

**BOOK DIRECT THROUGH
HOSEASONS**

**Kay & David Elliot, Derwent Grange Farm, Castleside, Consett DH8 9BN
Tel: 01207 508358 • e-mail: eelliot1@sky.com • www.derwentgrange.co.uk**

SB

Hall Hill Farm

SELF CATERING

Two country cottages, well equipped and comfortable. Situated in an ideal location for Durham City and Beamish Museum. You will have a free pass for the week to visit our own open farm. Please write or telephone for brochure.

Sleep up to four people • Children welcome. Sorry no pets.

Rates: from £180 per week.

**Mrs Ann Darlington, Hall Hill Farm,
Lanchester, Durham DH7 0TA
Tel: 01207 521476 • Tel & Fax: 01388 730300
e-mail: cottages@hallhillfarm.co.uk
www.hallhillfarm.co.uk1207 521476**

Alwinton

Northumberland

SB

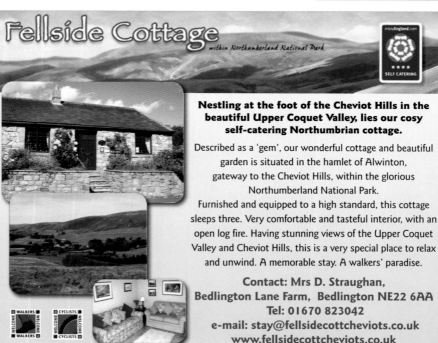

Fellside Cottage
within Northumberland National Park

SELF CATERING

Nestling at the foot of the Cheviot Hills in the beautiful Upper Coquet Valley, lies our cosy self-catering Northumbrian cottage.

Described as a 'gem', our wonderful cottage and beautiful garden is situated in the hamlet of Alwinton, gateway to the Cheviot Hills, within the glorious Northumberland National Park.
Furnished and equipped to a high standard, this cottage sleeps three. Very comfortable and tasteful interior, with an open log fire. Having stunning views of the Upper Coquet Valley and Cheviot Hills, this is a very special place to relax and unwind. A memorable stay. A walkers' paradise.

**Contact: Mrs D. Straughan,
Bedlington Lane Farm, Bedlington NE22 6AA
Tel: 01670 823042
e-mail: stay@fellsidecottcheviots.co.uk
www.fellsidecottcheviots.co.uk**

WALKERS WELCOME   CYCLISTS WELCOME

Visit the FHG website
www.holidayguides.com
for all kinds of holiday
accommodation in Britain

Alnwick

SB

No.1 Crawley
tower cottage
www.crawleytowercottage.co.uk

Peace & Tranquility...
in the very heart of northumberland

Single storey accommodation sleeping 2-3, situated in a very peaceful area of Northumberland with spectacular views of the Cheviot Hills to the west and equally good views in other directions.

Alnwick Garden is only 10 miles away, the coast 15 miles, and for hillwalking, the National Park is only 4 miles.

The cottage has a well equipped kitchen with fridge freezer, washer, hob cooker and microwave. Living room with log burner. One double and one single bedroom. Bathroom with overbath shower.

A conservatory leads out to a very peaceful garden, giving a tranquil setting to relax in. Ample private parking.

**Contact: Mrs N. Birnie,
Crawley Farmhouse, Powburn,
Alnwick NE66 4JA
Tel: 01665 578413
e-mail: crawleyfarmhouse@hotmail.co.uk
www.crawleytowercottage.co.uk**

Crawley Farmhouse

SB

WAREN LEA HALL
Waren Mill, Bamburgh
Luxurious Self-Catering
Holiday Accommodation
for families, parties and friends.

HOLIDAYS AND SHORT BREAKS on the beautiful Northumberland coast.

Standing on the shore of beautiful Budle Bay, an Area of Outstanding Natural Beauty and a Site of Special Scientific Interest for its birdlife, lies spectacular WAREN LEA HALL. This lovely, gracious old Hall, set in 2 ½ acres of shoreline parkland and walled gardens, enjoys breathtaking views across the bay and sea to Lindisfarne. In addition to THE HALL there are two entirely self-contained apartments, GHILLIE'S VIEW and GARDEN COTTAGE.

THE HALL *(for up to 14 guests, with 6 bedrooms)*

Beautifully furnished to complement its Edwardian grandeur, with high ceilings, chandeliers, sash windows, fireplaces and polished wooden floors. Breathtaking views from every room. Large drawing and dining rooms opening on to floodlit terrace; large, fully equipped kitchen/breakfast room. Ground floor twin bedroom and cloakroom/shower room; upstairs five further twin/double/en-suite family bedrooms including en suite master with four-poster; family bathroom. Own private garden and use of walled garden and parkland bordering the shore. ETB Gold Award 2011/12.

GHILLIE'S VIEW *(for up to 10 guests, with 4 bedrooms)*

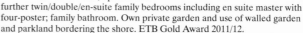

Accommodation is all on one level, with luxurious furnishings throughout. Fully equipped kitchen/dining room, semi-circular drawing room with balcony, and master bedroom with four-poster and en suite shower; all with fine views across the river and bay to Holy Island. Family, double and twin bedrooms, one en suite, and family bathroom. Guests have use of secluded walled garden and parkland bordering the shore. ETB Gold Award 2011/12.

GARDEN COTTAGE *(for up to 4 guests, with 2 bedrooms)*

The terrace wing of Waren Lea Hall, reached through its own entrance from the garden. All the light and sunny rooms are prettily furnished with high quality fabrics, pine furniture and polished wooden floors throughout, and face the lovely gardens which guests can use. The well equipped kitchen/dining room, lounge, double and twin bedrooms, one en suite, and family shower room are all on one level. Guests have use of the secluded walled garden and parkland bordering the shore. ETB Gold Award 2011/12.

For further information please contact the owners:
Carolynn and David Croisdale-Appleby
Abbotsholme, Hervines Road
Amersham, Buckinghamshire HP6 5HS
Tel: 01494 725194 • Mobile: 07901 716136
e-mail: croisdaleappleby@aol.com
www.selfcateringluxury.co.uk

enjoyEngland.com
★★★★★
SELF CATERING

Haltwhistle, Hexham

Milecastle Inn Cottages

These two newly built cottages have excellent views to Hadrian's Wall and are ideally situated next to a traditional pub/restaurant, renowned for its good food and well kept ales. The cottages provide an excellent base for walkers, cyclists and golfers, or indeed anyone visiting the many attractions in the area.

There are a number of quality golf courses within a 20 mile radius, the new Hadrian's Wall Cycle Route follows the wall for 174 miles and passes the cottages and Carlisle, Hexham or Newcastle are all easily accessible for those interested in horse racing.

- *Each sleeps 2 • No children under 12 years*
- *Non-smokers only • Minimum stay 3 nights*

**Contact: Mrs C. Hind,
Milecastle Inn, North Road,
Haltwhistle NE49 9NN • Tel: 01434 321372
e-mail: clarehind@aol.com
www.milecastle-inn.co.uk**

SB

Moorgair Cottage

**Slaley, Hexham NE47 0AN
Tel: 01434 673473
or 07425 160446
Contact: Vicki Ridley
e-mail: g_ridley@lineone.net
www.moorgair.co.uk**

This charming cottage for 4/5 people is attached to the owner's home on a small working farm in rural Northumberland, home of Moorgair Alpacas. The cottage is furnished to a high standard and has every convenience to make your holiday stress free and enjoyable. Cot and high-chair available. Private garden and parking.

From the doorstep there are miles of forest tracks and country lanes for walkers and cyclists, and the cottage is ideally situated to explore Northumberland, Durham and the Scottish Borders. A small shop, post office and two pubs serving food (one with an excellent adventure playground) are within 1½ miles of the cottage.

Hexham

High Dalton Cottage

Cosy and comfortable cottage on a family-run working farm set in 270 acres of beautiful scenery and wildlife.

The cottage has been converted from stables and has two double rooms and one twin, each with en suite bath/shower room. The cottage is in an area of Northumberland's most picturesque and interesting countryside and has private parking and an enclosed garden with patio. The quaint Roman towns of Hexham and Corbridge are nearby.

The award-winning championship golf courses of Slaley Hall and Matfen Hall are a short distance away; other attractions include Newcastle, Kielder Water and Gateshead Metro Centre.

For details contact **Mrs J. Stobbs, High Dalton Farm, Hexham NE46 2LB • tel: 01434 673320 e-mail: stobbsjudy@aol.com**

SB

enjoyEngland.com
★★★★
SELF CATERING

Isaacs Cottage

SB

Sparty Lea, Allendale, Northumbria.

A semi-detached cottage set in the beautiful rolling countryside of Allendale, perfectly placed for exploring Northumberland, Cumbria and the Northern Dales by car. Very comfortably furnished, accommodation comprises sitting room, dining kitchen; one double, one twin and one family bedroom; bathroom and shower room. Full oil-fired central heating and log fires. **Sleeps 7**. Fishing, walking and cycling on the doorstep.

Hannah's & Rose Cottage Allenheads, Northumbria.

Two semi-detached cottages in peaceful rural surroundings within the North Pennines Area of Outstanding Natural Beauty, both traditionally furnished with panoramic views. Centrally heated with open fires; TV/DVD/video; well equipped kitchens; large shared garden. Linen provided. Off-road parking. No smoking. Abundant opportunities for walking, cycling and exploring the region. Allendale is 5 miles away with friendly pubs, tea rooms and craft shops. **Sleeps 6**

Contact:
Mrs H. Robson • Allenheads Farm Hexham, Northumberland NE47 9HT Tel: 01434 685312

Morpeth, Newton-by-the-Sea

SB

Wooler

Rose Cottage • Wooler

Rose Cottage is an old stone cottage in a peaceful hamlet on the edge of the Cheviot Hills, in a wonderful rural setting with magnificent views across the Glendale Valley.

The house is furnished and decorated to a high standard, with a traditional sitting room, a sun room, two bedrooms, one with a double bed, the other with two singles + two Z-beds. Modern kitchen, bathroom; large safe garden and off-road parking; log fire and electric heating.

Rose Cottage is 12 miles from the coast, Holy Island, Bamburgh, beaches, golf courses, castles, bird watching, horse riding and fishing. 16 miles from Alnwick Castle Garden. Horse riding, golf, fishing and bird watching close by. Available April to October.

For details contact:
Mrs Christine Andrews, 1 Littleworth Lane,
Esher KT10 9PF • 01372 464284
e-mail: info@rosecottagewooler.co.uk
www.rosecottagewooler.co.uk

Rambling over the heather-clad Cheviot moorlands, exploring the castles and pele towers built to ward off invading Scots, watching the feast of wildlife on the coast and in the countryside, breathing in the wonderful sea air on a golden sandy beach, you'll find it all in Northumberland. On the coast, a designated Area of Outstanding Natural Beauty, keen walkers can take the Coast Path from the walled Georgian market town of Berwick-on-Tweed to Cresswell, stopping at little fishing villages on the way. Follow the section along Embleton beach from Craster, best known for its traditionally smoked kippers, to get the best views of the ruins of Dunstanburgh Castle. At the lively market town of Alnwick visit the castle, Hogwarts in the Harry Potter films, with its redeveloped gardens, magnificent water features and even a poison garden! Rare and endangered wildlife is found all along the coast and the ultimate destination for enthusiasts is the Farne Islands, with boat trips from the family resort of Seahouses to watch the grey seals and seabirds, including puffins, in the breeding seasons. Wildlife is abundant in the uplands to the west too. In the heather moorlands of the Cheviot Hills there are plenty of opportunities for birdwatching, as well as horse riding, fishing, canoeing and rock climbing, while at Kielder Water and Forest Park watch the red squirrels and ospreys, follow forest trails and mountain bike tracks or watch the stars in the dark night skies. Learn too about the Romans by watching a re-enactment of Roman life at one of the settlements along Hadrian's Wall, or walk along its length from coast to coast. Hexham and Haltwhistle are good bases for a visit, and these and other market towns and villages dotted all over the county make a stay here a very pleasant one.

Macclesfield

Cheshire

SB

The Old Byre
Pye Ash Farm,
Leek Road, Bosley,
Macclesfield

The Old Byre at Pye Ash Farm is particularly well designed to suit two families wishing to spend their holidays together in the countryside.

Set amongst the fields but only half a mile from Bosley Village, with a choice of two pubs, many walks can be taken from the farm, into the fields and woods. Bosley Minns overlooks the reservoir and forms part of the Gritstone Trail. Alton Towers is 15 miles away.

All accommodation is on the ground floor, suitable for the less able visitor. The Cow Shed and the Sheep Shed both sleep four, with well equipped kitchen and shower room; rear porch with washing and drying facilities. Ample parking.

**For further details please contact: Dorothy Gilman,
Woodcroft, Tunstall Road, Bosley, Macclesfield SK11 0PB
Tel: 01260 223293
e-mail: dotgilman@hotmail.co.uk • www.bosley-byre-stay.co.uk**

In Cheshire, just south of Manchester, combine a city break in historic Chester with a day or two at one of relaxing spas either in the city itself or in one of the luxury resorts in the rolling countryside. A round at an on-site golf course offers an alternative way of enjoying the break, and while out in the country, why not visit one of the many gardens open to the public? Chester, with its wonderful array of Roman, medieval and Georgian buildings is a fascinating place to visit. Walk round the most complete example of city walls in the whole country, past the beautiful cathedral, before browsing through the wonderful range of shops, art galleries and museums, making sure you visit The Gallery, a 700 year-old mall with two tiers of boutiques, jewellers and eateries. Explore the history of the area at the Dewa Roman Experience, with reconstructed Roman streets, and take the opportunity to see the Roman, Saxon and medieval remains on view.

Ambleside

Cumbria

• • Betty Fold • •
Hawkshead Hill, Ambleside LA22 0PS

SB

Situated near Hawkshead and Tarn Hows, this large country house in spacious grounds is in the heart of Lake District National Park.

Betty Fold offers self-catering accommodation in a comfortable ground floor apartment with private entrance, sleeps 4. One double en suite and one small twin with dressing room and bathroom. Open-plan kitchen/livingroom with electric cooker, fridge, freezer, microwave, colour TV with Freeview and DVD player. Well behaved pets are welcome.

Terms incl.heat, light, power, bed linen and towels.

015394 36611
e-mail: claire@bettyfold.co.uk
www.bettyfold.co.uk

RAMSTEADS COPPICE,
Outgate, Ambleside LA22 0NH
Mr Evans • 015394 36583

Six timber lodges of varied size and design set in 15 acres of mixed woodland with wild flowers, birds and native wild animals.

There are also 11 acres of rough hill pasture. Three miles south west of Ambleside, it is an ideal centre for walkers, artists, birdwatchers, and country lovers.

No pets • Children welcome • Open March to November

Ambleside, Bowness-on-Windermere

Quaysiders Club • Ambleside

Luxury holiday accommodation, beautifully located by Lake Windermere in the Lake District.

••HIGH CLASS SELF-CATERING APARTMENTS AND HOTEL ROOMS••

•Apartments rented by the week from Saturday to Saturday.
Sleep up to 6.

Bookings can be made direct from our website
www.quaysiders.co.uk

Hotel rooms also available, rented by the night.
En suite facilities, TV, fridge etc.

All guests can make use of leisure spa with whirlpool, sauna and showers; courtyard with BBQ area; laundry room.

01539 433969 • ian@quaysiders.co.uk

SB

Quality Holiday Homes in England's Beautiful Lake District

LAKELOVERS

The biggest and best selection of holiday cottages in the Lake District.
A superb choice of over 400 self-catering holiday cottages,
in the best locations, from quaint country cottages to large lakeside retreats,
Lakelovers have got the perfect holiday cottage for you.
Visit Lakelovers.co.uk or call 015394 88855
to speak to one of our friendly, knowledgeable staff.

**Lakelovers, Belmont House, Lake Road,
Bowness-on-Windermere, Cumbria LA23 3BJ**

Broughton-in-Furness, Eskdale

Woodend Cottages
between the Eskdale and Duddon Valleys

SB

Wi-Fi

Welcome to the peace and tranquillity of the Cumbrian Mountains.

Woodend is located in the Lake District National Park, high on Birker Fell between the Eskdale Valley and the Duddon Valley, conveniently situated for Broughton-in-Furness, Seathwaite and Boot.

Four self-catering cottages offer comfortable holiday accommodation for 2 to 6 people.

•**The Bothy** is a self-contained building standing on its own, offering cosy and comfortable "upside down" self-catering accommodation for two people.

•**The Schoolhouse** is a cosy self-contained building standing privately on its own, facing due south up the fell and offering character studio accommodation for two people.

•**The Buttery** is an annexe to the house, offering self-catering for two people.

•**The Cottage** offers comfortable accommodation for up to six people.

All properties are fully equipped and furnished with care and thought. Bed & Breakfast accommodation is also available. Short breaks available. Broadband internet access. Pet-friendly; dogs welcome.

Visit our website at www.woodendhouse.co.uk   **SHORT BREAKS AVAILABLE**
or phone 01946 723277   **OUT OF SEASON**

SELF CATERING

WALKERS
WELCOME

Situated in the Esk Valley in the west of the Lake District, 3 Randle How is an 18th century cottage located in Holmrook, Cumbria.

The cottage is in a quiet part of the village and is an excellent base for walking, touring or a quiet relaxing rest throughout the year. It has modern facilities while maintaining its traditional style and comfortably accommodates four people.

Two bedrooms, a twin and one double, sitting room and dining room.

Log fires, full central heating • Well equipped kitchen • Parking • £285 - £485 weekly.

A visit to the Roman Fort, Hard Knott or a trip on the Ravenglass and Eskdale Railway, known as La'al Ratty is worthwhile as is a trip to Muncaster Castle to see the gardens and Owl Centre.

Details from Susan Wedley, Randle How,
c/o Long Yocking How, Eskdale Green,
Holmrook CA19 1UA • Tel: 01946 723126
e-mail: jswedley@btinternet.com
www.randlehow.co.uk

Hawkshead

SB

Wi-Fi

hideaways
LAKELAND
COTTAGES

Large enough to offer choice... small enough to care

- Local, friendly agency
- Choice of more than 70 cottages in and around Hawkshead
- Pets Welcome
- Traditional and contemporary cottages
- Short breaks available
- Award winning website, online booking

'Hawkshead – The prettiest village in the Lake District'

The Square, Hawkshead, Cumbria LA22 0NZ | Tel: 015394 42435 | Fax: 015394 36178
Email: bookings@lakeland-hideaways.co.uk | www.lakeland-hideaways.co.uk

Bowness-on-Windermere, Kendal, Keswick

Keswick

SB

SB

Kirkby Lonsdale, Kirkby Stephen

SB

Cragside

Harrison Farm,
Whittington,
Kirkby Lonsdale,
Carnforth,
Lancashire LA6 2NX
Tel: 015242 71415

Near Hutton Roof, three miles from Kirkby Lonsdale and central for touring Lake District and Yorkshire Dales. Coast walks on Hutton Roof Crag, famous limestone pavings.

Property sleeps 8; one room with double and single bed, one with double and cot, third bedroom with three single beds. Bathroom. Sitting room, dining room and kitchen. Electric cooker, microwave, fridge, kettle, iron, immersion heater and TV. Everything supplied but linen. Electricity and coal extra. Parking space. Pets permitted.

*Terms from £250 per week.
SAE brings quick reply.*

Other cottages available, sleeping 2-8.

SB

BLANDSWATH COTTAGE

In a lovely tranquil position on the banks of the River Eden, this old, well established, spacious farm cottage is comfortably furnished and well equipped. Situated on the owners' 100-acre working farm, where visitors are free to roam.

An excellent base for exploring and walking in the Lake District and Yorkshire Dales. Just two miles away is the town of Kirkby Stephen with everyday facilities, restaurants, pubs and tearooms.

- *Free fishing for one person available in season.*
- *Sorry, no pets.*
- *No smoking.*
- *Sleeps six, plus cot.*
- *Short Breaks from £200*

*Contact: Mrs Sandra Watson
Blandswath Farm, Appleby Road
Kirkby Stephen, Cumbria CA17 4PG
Tel: 017683 41842
e-mail: Watson@blandswath.freeserve.co.uk
www.blandswathcottage.co.uk*

Kirkoswald

Lake District, Lamplugh

"Your own country house in the Lakes"
Two luxury holiday houses available to rent in the Lake District.

Routen House

Routen House is a beautiful old farmhouse set in 4 acres in an outstanding position with fabulous views over Ennerdale Lake. Fully modernised while retaining the character of the old farmhouse, it has been furnished to a very high standard. Sleeps 12 plus cot.

Little Parrock is an elegant Victorian Lakeland stone house a short walk from the centre of Grasmere with large rooms and a wealth of period features. Lovely private garden. Fully modernised to a very high standard; real log fires. Sleeps 10 plus cot.

Little Parrock

Both houses are non-smoking but pets are very welcome.

Please contact:

Mrs J. Green • Tel & Fax: 01604 505115

e-mail: joanne@routenhouse.co.uk

www.routenhouse.co.uk • www.littleparrock.co.uk

SB

Felldyke Cottages

"a warm and friendly welcome"

Visiting the Western Lakes? Then why not stay in this lovely 19th century cottage.

Situated on the small hamlet of Felldyke, on the edge of the Lake District national park. Sleeps 4, short breaks can be arranged. Pets are welcome.

Open all year, for you to enjoy the Lake District. Ideally situated for walking, cycling, farming, horse riding, golf and the local beaches.

Contact: Mrs A. Wilson, 2 Folly, Felldyke Cottage, Lamplugh, Cumbria CA14 4SH
Telephone: 01946 861151
e-mail: dockraynook@talk21.com • www.felldykecottageholidays.co.uk

Mungrisdale, Penrith

SB

Copy Hill

Mungrisdale, Penrith

An 18th century farm cottage, overlooking the northern fells, featuring oak beams and open fireplace. Situated in the quiet and unspoilt village of Mungrisdale, eight miles from Keswick and 10 miles from Penrith. An ideal base for touring the Lakes or walking in the hills. Comprises comfortable lounge/dining room, fully equipped kitchen, downstairs cloakroom with shower, three bedrooms (two doubles and one twin), bathroom. Village inn ¼ mile.

Price from £290 to £360 per week including electricity, central heating, colour TV and bed linen. Ample parking. Sorry, no pets. Available all year. Please telephone for details.

Mrs Wilson, High Beckside, Mungrisdale, Penrith CA11 0XR • Tel: 017687 79636 www.mungrisdale.com

SB

Wi-Fi

Morland Hall and three beautifully presented self-catering houses are situated within 15 acres of ancient woods and parkland in the glorious rolling countryside of the Eden Valley in Cumbria. All have been beautifully restored and furnished.

The Hall can sleep up to 20 people in 9 bedrooms (3 en suite); within the estate are 3 very well equipped 4-bedroom cottages sleeping 8/10, 9/10 and 7/8. Each property has own garden and patio. Sleeping a total of 48 in 21 bedrooms, Morland Hall is ideal for weddings, corporate events, as well as holiday lets and short breaks. The properties can be rented individually or together.

THE MORLAND HALL ESTATE
Morland Hall, Morland, Penrith Cumbria CA10 3BB
Tel: 01931 714715 • stay@morland-hall.co.uk • www.morland-hall.co.uk

Penrith

Howscales was originally a 17th century farm. The red sandstone buildings have been converted into four self-contained cottages, retaining many original features.

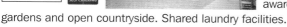

Set around a cobbled courtyard, the cosy, well-equipped cottages for 2-6, are surrounded by award-winning gardens and open countryside. Shared laundry facilities.

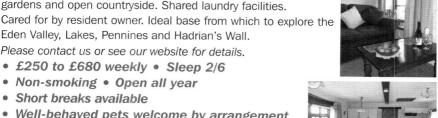

NATIONAL ACCESSIBILITY SCHEME: CATEGORY 2

Cared for by resident owner. Ideal base from which to explore the Eden Valley, Lakes, Pennines and Hadrian's Wall.

Please contact us or see our website for details.

- *£250 to £680 weekly • Sleep 2/6*
- *Non-smoking • Open all year*
- *Short breaks available*
- *Well-behaved pets welcome by arrangement*

Liz Webster, Howscales, Kirkoswald, Penrith CA10 1JG
Tel: 01768 898666 • Fax: 01768 898710
e-mail: liz@howscales.co.uk • www.howscales.co.uk

Your Stepping Stone to the Cumbrian Lake District

Award-winning Carrock Cottages are four renovated stone built cottages set on the fringe of the Lakeland Fells. A quiet rural location near the lovely villages of Hesket Newmarket with its award-winning brewery, Caldbeck and Greystoke. Explore the beauty of the Lake District National Park or head North to historic Carlisle and on to Hadrian's Wall.

Fell walking & other activities close to hand as well as excellent restaurants.

A warm welcome guaranteed.

Accommodation for 1 to 18 people.

On-site games room, home-cooked meal service.

Carrock House, Hutton Roof, Penrith, Cumbria CA11 0XY

Tel: Malcolm or Gillian on 01768 484 111 or Fax: 017684 888 50

www.carrockcottages.co.uk • info@carrockcottages.co.uk

Lancashire

Loudview Barn • Thornley • Ribble Valley

A converted barn enjoying stunning views over fields, fells and mountains. Manchester, Lancaster, the Lakes and Yorkshire Dales are all within an hour's drive; just 15 minutes from the M6. Cyclists and walkers will find quiet country roads, peaceful villages and many ancient rights of way, and a public footpath starts on the doorstep.

The barn consists of two comfortable self-contained units, both of which are furnished to the highest standard, and can be combined to form one single unit for larger groups.

Cloudberry sleeps 4 + baby in one double and one twin (both en suite), and *Windberry* sleeps 6 + baby in one double (en suite), one twin and one room with bunk beds. Both have enclosed gardens and spacious living rooms with exposed roof beams. Linen and towels provided; cot and high chair available.

Contact: **Miss Starkey, Loudview Barn, Rams Clough Farm, Thornley, Preston PR3 2TN • Tel: 01995 61476 e-mail: loudview@yahoo.co.uk • www.loudview.co.uk**

Gizella APARTMENTS

On The Seafront • Luxury Holiday Flats & Flatlets
Mrs G.A. Tamassy, 8 Marine Road West, Morecambe LA3 1BS
Tel: 01524 418249 • mobile: 07901 778260

Mr & Mrs Tamassy welcome you to their luxury holiday flats/ flatlets, overlooking gardens, with views over the Bay to the Lakeland Hills. All modern facilities including <u>en suite</u>. <u>Open all year round</u>. <u>Overnight guests</u> welcome. <u>FREE</u> communal <u>internet box</u> for residents. <u>Contractors welcome.</u> Senior Citizen off-season rates. Sorry - no children, no pets. <u>Non-smoking establishment.</u> Sleep from 1 to 5. <u>Send SAE for confirmation.</u> *Member of Morecambe Bay Warmth of Welcome 3*★★★

<u>www.morecambeholidayflats.com/www.gizellaholidayflats.co.uk</u> • e-mail: gizellaflats@ymail.com

Wi-Fi

Preston, Southport

Knotts Hey Cottages

A warm welcome to the quiet seclusion of Knotts Hey self-catering holiday cottages situated at Banners Farm in the heart of beautiful NW Lancashire. Within easy access of the Lake District, Yorkshire Dales, Forest of Bowland, and the many attractions of the Fylde Coast, the cottages are comfortable, spacious, high standard conversions of former barns with all modern amenities and ample parking.

Knotts Hey Cottage: all accommodation on ground floor • two bedrooms (one en suite king-size, one en suite with three single beds) • spacious open-plan lounge with dining area • fully fitted kitchen area • separate cloakroom• small utility room

Little Knotts Hey Cottage - one bedroom (other facilities as Knotts Hey Cottage)

colour TV • microwave • oil fired central heating • bed linen and towels incl patio garden with furniture • ample parking • sorry no pets • non-smoking

Stanzaker Hall Drive, Banners Farm Courtyard, Preston, Lancashire PR3 0PB • Tel: 01995 640519
e-mail: holidays@brockcottages.co.uk • www.brockcottages.co.uk

---

Sandy Brook Farm
Self-Catering Accommodation

Welcome to our traditional 18th Century barn . The converted barn offers 5 superbly equipped apartments, traditionally furnished with all modern amenities, one apartment having special facilities for the disabled. Apartments sleep 2, 4 or 6.

Please Contact:
Mr W. H. Core, Sandy Brook Farm
52 Wyke Cop Road, Scarisbrick, Southport PR8 5LR
Tel: 01704 880337 • e-mail: sandybrookfarm@gmail.com
www.sandybrookfarm.co.uk

Bude, Crackington Haven

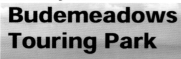
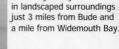

Mild climate, beaches, surf and moorland are all associated with the South West, the region at the southernmost point of the British Isles, but you'll also find gently rolling hills and sleepy villages in the Cotswolds to the north and the Jurassic cliffs and New Forest area in Dorset too, as well as stunning gardens, art galleries, UNESCO World Heritage Sites, miles of walking and cycling trails and bridle paths and, of course, wonderful seafood to enjoy. There is history to explore in Iron Age villages and stone circles, and in the long marine heritage of the area. With medieval villages full of character, historic country pubs and major centres for shopping, and for families, theme parks, farm parks, castles and zoos, as well as over 600 miles of coastline with golden beaches and rocky pools, and ample opportunities for all kinds of water-based activities, this is a ideal holiday destination.

SB

Greenhowe Caravan Park
Great Langdale, English Lakeland.

Greenhowe is a permanent Caravan Park with Self Contained Holiday Accommodation. Subject to availability Holiday Homes may be rented for short or long periods from 1st March until mid-November. The Park is situated in the heart of the Lake District some half a mile from Dungeon Ghyll at the foot of the Langdale Pikes. It is an ideal centre for Climbing, Fell Walking, Riding, Swimming or just a lazy holiday.

Greenhowe Caravan Park
Great Langdale,
Ambleside
Cumbria LA22 9JU
For free colour brochure
Tel: (015394) 37231
Fax: (015394) 37464
www.greenhowe.com

LODGES also available • Please ask about Short Breaks

Three six-berth, modern, well-equipped caravans situated on a quiet family-run farm site with beautiful views over Coniston Water.

Pets are welcome, and pony trekking can be arranged from the farm. A good base for walking and touring the area. We have a good pub 200 yards down the road.

Weekly terms on request.

Showers, toilets, gas cookers, fires and water heaters; electric lighting, fridge, TV, kettle, toaster and microwave.

Mrs E. Johnson, Spoon Hall, Coniston LA21 8AW
Telephone: 015394 41391

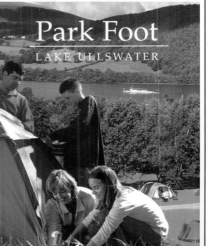

HIGHER TOWN
Dulverton, Somerset TA22 9RX
Tel: 01398 341272

Our farm is situated half-a-mile from open moorland, one mile from the Devon/Somerset border and four miles from Dulverton. 80 acres of the farm is in the Exmoor National Park. We let two caravans which are quarter-of-a-mile apart and do not overlook each other. Both have lovely views, situated in lawns with parking space. Both are 8-berth, with three bedrooms, shower, flush toilet, hot/cold water and colour TV.

The caravans are modern and fully equipped except linen.

We are a walkers's paradise and visitors are welcome to walk over our beef and sheep farm. Riding and fishing nearby.

Price from £180, includes gas and electricity.

Alston Farm Camping & Caravan Site
Malborough, Kingsbridge TQ7 3BJ

SB

Wi-Fi

The family-run site is set in a quiet secluded, sheltered valley adjoining the Salcombe Estuary in amongst Devon's loveliest countryside. Level pitches, ample space and conveniences. Wi-Fi available.

Dish washing and clothes washing facilities. Electric hook-ups, Calor and Gaz stockists. Shop, (high season only), payphone on site. Children and pets welcome.

From £12 per night for two adults and caravan.

Please phone for brochure:
Phil Shepherd.

Tel: 01548 561260

e-mail:
info@alstoncampsite.co.uk

www.alstoncampsite.co.uk

Think of Devon, and wild moorland springs to mind, but this is a county of contrasts, with the wild moors of the Exmoor National Park to the north fringed by dramatic cliffs and combes, golden beaches and picturesque harbours, and busy market towns and sleepy villages near the coast. The award-winning resort of Woolacombe has everything to offer for a traditional family holiday, while Ilfracombe, originally a Victorian resort, provides all kinds of family entertainment including an annual Victorian festival. An experience not to be missed is the cliff railway between the pretty little port of Lynmouth and its twin village of Lynton high on the cliff, with a backdrop of dramatic gorges or combes.

Blandford

Cotswolds

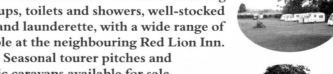

Lower Wick

Hogsdown Farm Camp Site

This site is set between the Cotswold Escarpment and Severn Vale, in open rural countryside. Many local amenities including swimming, golf, riding, fishing. Tourist attractions include Westonbirt Arboretum, Berkeley Castle, Slimbridge Wild Fowl Trust, Jenner Museum and Cotswold Way. Ideal for touring the many picturesque towns and villages on hills and vales and as a stopover for north/south journeys. Inn within walking distance and many inns and hotels within close proximity.

SB

- **Gas and electric hook-ups available** • **Elsan disposal**
- **Toilets and shower** • **washing-up facilities** • **Laundry**
- **Children's play area** • **Storage available all year.**
Pets welcome under control.
Terms from £11.50 to £15.00 tents,
£13.00 caravans and motor homes.

Hogsdown Farm Camp Site, Dursley, Lower Wick GL11 6DB
01453 810224 • www.hogsdownfarm.co.uk

Hayling Island

WELCOME TO HAYLING ISLAND
FAMILY CAMP SITES

SB

Hayling Island is an ideal touring base for Portsmouth, the Isle of Wight and the New Forest, with excellent motorway access. We have safe, clean, award-winning beaches, and windsurfing, sailing, horse riding, golf, tennis and walking to be enjoyed locally. The Oven Campste has a Children's play area, Shop and Café on site, Games Room, Heated Swimming Pool (extra charge applies) open from Easter to September.

The Oven Campsite
Manor Road, Hayling Island PO11 0QX
Tel: 023 9246 4695 Mobile: 077584 10020
Out of Hours: 02392 465850
(leave message if no reply).
e-mail: theovencampsite@talktalk.net
www.haylingcampsites.co.uk

Standard sites £17.50 (including VAT) per night for car/tent or caravan and two people. To book please send £22.50 (£20 deposit and £2.50 booking fee) also SAE if confirmation required

Leominster

Arrow Bank Holiday Park

Nun House Farm, Eardisland
Near Leominster, Herefordshire HR6 9BG

Arrow Bank Holiday Park is a family-run park enjoying peace and tranquillity in a spacious landscaped setting in the picturesque Tudor village of Eardisland. Touring caravans and motor homes are well catered for on a flat, level field with electric hook-up points.

Heated amenity block and Wi-Fi access
Hardstanding seasonal pitches with hook-up available 1st March to 7th January

Arrow Bank Holiday Park offers a superb opportunity to own your dream holiday Home from Home or to hire one of our double glazed 2008 holiday homes with central heating. (Short breaks available).

An ideal touring base with many historic market towns and cathedral cities close by. The beautiful Elan Valley, Brecon Beacons and Shropshire Hills, perfect for walking, bird watching and fishing are easily accessible. From Leominster, follow the A44 west towards Rhayader for approx. 1 mile. As you pass Morrison's, bear right towards Eardisland (approx 4 miles).

Tel & Fax: 01544 388312
enquiries@arrowbankholidaypark.co.uk
www.arrowbankholidaypark.co.uk

Mundesley

Sandy Gulls
Caravan Park Ltd
Cromer Road, Mundesley, Norfolk NR11 8DF

Wi-Fi

Found on the Mundesley cliff tops, this quiet private park, managed by the owning family for over 30 years, offers a warm welcome to all visitors. The touring park has grass and non-turf pitches, all have uninterrupted sea views, electric/TV hook-ups and beautifully refurbished shower rooms. Holiday caravans for sale or hire, which are always the latest models.

Superbly situated for exploring the beauty of North Norfolk including The Broads National Park.

Touring park is for adults only.

Samantha
01263 720513
e-mail: info@sandygulls.co.uk
www.sandygulls.co.uk

Hexham

Greencarts is a working farm situated in Roman Wall country, ideally placed for exploring by car, bike or walking. It has magnificent views of the Tyne Valley. Campsite for 30 tents with facilities, and bunk barn with 12 beds, showers and toilet are now open from Easter until the end of October. Prices for campsite are £5 to £10 per tent, plus £1pp. Bunk barn beds from £10. Linen available. Bed and Breakfast also available from £25 to £40.

Mr & Mrs D Maughan, Greencarts Farm, Humshaugh, Hexham NE46 4BW
Tel/Fax: 01434 681320
e-mail: sandra@greencarts.co.uk.

GREENCARTS FARM
www.greencarts.co.uk

SB

Tuxford

Orchard Park **AA**

Situated in a quiet unspoilt location on the outskirts of the old market town of Tuxford within a mature fruit orchard, Orchard Park offers pitches for touring caravans, tents, trailer tents and small to medium sized motor homes.
Ideally situated for weekend breaks, longer holidays or just an overnight stop. Within a short drive you will find the haunts of Robin Hood, acres of Sherwood Forest, Clumber Park (National Trust) and Rufford Abbey.

Orchard Park Touring Caravan and Camping Park
Marnham Road, Tuxford NG22 0PY
Tel: 01777 870228 • Fax: 01777 870320

Amenities block with free hot showers and hairdryers. Laundry room with coin operated washing machines and tumble dryer. Separate 'access room' designed to disability standards. Electric hook-ups. Play trail for children.

A range of food essentials and Calor Gas exchange is available from reception. Brochure available on request.

Wi-Fi

www.orchardcaravanpark.co.uk

The FHG Directory of Website Addresses
on pages 531-541 is a useful quick reference guide for holiday accommodation with e-mail and/or website details

Lowestoft

Marston

Kirkbymoorside, Pickering

SB

Wi-Fi

You can be assured of a very friendly atmosphere at Wombleton, a small Caravan & Camping Park personally run by the Willoughby family. Wombleton Village is ideally placed just a few miles from the picturesque town of Helmsley, and the surrounding area offers an array of amenities, activities and attractions. The local pub is just one mile away. Our pitches are of a generous size – gravel or grass. Concrete bases for motorhomes. All pitches with electric hook ups. New toilet facilities with a disabled/family room. A good base to explore the North Yorkshire Moors and York and twenty miles from the east coast

Wombleton Caravan & Camping Park
Moorfield Lane, Wombleton,
Kirkbymoorside, North Yorkshire Y062 7RY
Tel/Fax: 01751 431684
e-mail: info@wombletoncaravanpark.co.uk
www.wombletoncaravanpark.co.uk

BLACK BULL CARAVAN PARK

Family Caravan and Camping Park one mile south of Pickering on the A169, behind a public house. The gateway to the North York Moors! Good base for walking, cycling, visiting the coast and numerous other local attractions.

On-site facilities: playground • games room • sports field refurbished amenities with free hot showers • dishwashing and laundry

Touring pitches in open level field with some shelter. Fully serviced and fully equipped holiday caravans also for hire. Double-glazed and heated.

Terms from £115 to £410.
Holiday Caravans for hire,
sleeping six.
Touring pitches available,
from £13 per night

Why not view our website for more photographs?
Malton Road,
Pickering,
North Yorkshire
YO18 8EA

www.blackbullcaravanpark.com
e-mail: enquiries@blackbullcaravanpark.com
Tel: 01751 472528

Whitby

Seaside with cliffs and golden beaches, wild moorland, rolling hills and dales, castles and abbeys, museums, wildlife, lively cities, busy market towns, wonderful food, great shopping, Yorkshire has it all! From gliding to wind surfing to steam trains, there's an activity for everyone. Situated in north east England, and historically divided into North, West and East Ridings, each of the regions in this guide, North, South, East and West, has its own characteristics, but together they still have much in common. There are wide open spaces and trails, both long and short, for walking and horse riding at all levels of experience and fitness. Explore the quiet countryside and villages, or the cities like York, Leeds, Hull and Sheffield with a vast range of entertainment and shops, as well as a fascinating history to discover. All along the often dramatic North Sea coast, with miles of beautiful beaches, lively resorts have all that's required for a traditional family holiday.

Anglesey & Gwynedd

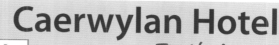

Trearddur Bay, Tywyn

SB

North Wales

Betws-y-Coed, Conwy

In North Wales there are charming towns and villages, castles, stately homes, beautiful gardens, parks, craft centres and museums waiting to be explored, as well as seaside resorts with soft, sandy beaches and rugged stretches of coastline, all with a background of hills and mountains, just the ingredients needed for an active holiday. Betws-y-Coed, North Wales' most popular inland resort, houses The Snowdonia National Visitor Centre with its craft units and thrilling video presentations – always worth a visit. For fun filled family holidays try Llandudno, where you can take the longest cable car ride in Britain, or wander along the Victorian pier. Experience the thrills of the indoor waterpark at Rhyl, meet seals, eels and sharks at the aquarium or take a traditional donkey ride along the beach.

Llanelli

Carmarthenshire

Best Western Diplomat Hotel
Felinfoel, Llanelli SA15 3PJ
Tel: 01554 756156 • Fax: 01554 751649
AA/WTB ★★★

The Diplomat Hotel offers a rare combination of charm and character, with excellent well appointed facilities to ensure your comfort. Explore the Gower Peninsula and the breathtaking West Wales coastline. Salmon & trout fishing, horse riding, golf, and motor racing at Pembrey are all within reach.

e-mail: reservations@diplomat-hotel-wales.com • www.bw-diplomathotel.co.uk

All our 50 bedrooms are stylish and modern, boasting much character and charm. Modern luxury and comfort is integrated with traditional furnishings, allowing relaxation with the familiar comforts of home. All of our rooms include the following: En-suite facilities • Direct-dial telephone Television • Tea & coffee-making facilities Hairdryer • High speed internet access Use of Chasens Health Club and Spa

Our chefs use the finest, freshest ingredients, sourced locally where ever possible, with imaginative presentation to excite the palate. Recently added to the front of the historic mansion, the Atrium is a wonderful fully glassed conservatory, which is comfortably air-conditioned. During the summer, drinks can be enjoyed on the terrace outside the conservatory. We are open to non-residents for morning coffee, lunch, afternoon teas and dinner.

Carmarthenshire is one of the best regions for an activity or leisure break, with everything from mountain biking in the Brechfa Forest to canoeing and kayaking in the challenging stretches of the Teifi river, from walking in the foothills of the Brecon Beacons to a quiet day's fishing for sewin, salmon or trout in some remote river. There are championship courses for golfers, as well as a wide choice offering affordable golf to players of all abilities, and a chance of a day's horse racing at the new venue at Ffos Las. The Millennium Coastal Park is one of the most popular tourist attractions in Britain, with breathtaking views of the Gower Peninsula, and a unique variety of attractions stretching from Pembrey Country Park with its acres of beautiful parkland, and one of the best beaches in the UK, as well as many excellent family activities.

Cardigan

Ceredigion

SB

Wi-Fi

PENBONTBREN

Luxury Bed and Breakfast in West Wales

Penbontbren
Glynarthen, Llandysul, Near Cardigan
Ceredigion SA44 6PE
Tel: 01239 810248
email: contact@penbontbren.com
www.penbontbren.com

Penbontbren Luxury Bed and Breakfast in West Wales is nestled in 32 acres of grounds, surrounded by beautiful countryside with views towards the Preseli mountains, and is only 2 miles from wonderful National Trust beaches. 5 luxury suites are equipped to a 5 star standard, each with spacious sitting room, own garden, king-size bed and sumptuous décor and furnishings. Substantial Welsh breakfasts are prepared from locally sourced ingredients. Pets are welcome by prior arrangement. Luxury self-catering cottage also available.

Come to Ceredigion for spectacular scenery, from the cliffs and golden beaches of the coast to the uplands of the Cambrian Mountains, only some half an hour's drive the sea. This rural county, a centre for Welsh language and culture, is home to the National Library of Wales at Aberystwyth, but the books and manuscripts held there aren't the only attraction for visitors. For an active holiday break there are activity centres for all age groups, sea angling and shore fishing, walking in the mountains and along the coast, challenging mountain bike trails and quiet roads for cycling and all kinds of golf courses from parkland to coastal links. Boat trips take visitors out dolphin-spotting, and many species of bird are to be seen along the coast, including Red Kite. Tresaith, one of the locations most favoured by visitors to Ceredigion, is an almost picture-book seaside village with a wonderful sandy beach, ideal for families, with clean sands, clear waters, and rocks to climb, whilst inland lies the Teifi Valley - offering marvellous angling - and Cenarth's famous falls.

Please note...

Pembrokeshire

There is a genuine welcome to our mixed working family farm. Quietly set in beautiful countryside surrounded by animals and wild life. Comfortable, well appointed accommodation. Bedrooms with tea/coffee tray, radio, TV and en suite facilities. Excellent quality food using home and local produce. Families welcome. Deductions for children and Senior Citizens.

Open January to December. Pretty flowers, lawns in relaxed surroundings. Personal attention. Unrestricted access.

Ideally situated in central Pembrokeshire for coastline walks. Sandy beaches. Bird islands, castles, city of St Davids, Tenby.

Bed and Breakfast • Bed, Breakfast and Evening Dinner. Terms on application.

Mrs M. E. Davies, Cuckoo Mill Farm, Pelcomb Bridge, St David's Road, Haverfordwest SA62 6EA Tel: 01437 762139 www.cuckoomillfarm.co.uk

Cuckoo Mill Farm

symbols 🐕🐴SB&♿️♀Wi-Fi

🐕	*Pets Welcome*	🐴	*Children Welcome*	
SB	*Short Breaks*	♿️	*Suitable for Disabled Guests*	
♀	*Licensed*	**Wi-Fi**	*Wi-Fi available*	

Welcome to Ivybridge

Situated in a quiet part of Goodwick, Ivybridge is a friendly, family-run guest house offering comfortable accommodation just outside of Fishguard, a picturesque area of Pembrokeshire, within easy reach of the Pembrokeshire coastal paths, the historic City of St David's and beautiful beaches.

Try our small heated indoor swimming pool, relax in our conservatory or put your feet up in front of a roaring fire in the bar/lounge area and enjoy the company and atmosphere at Ivybridge.

All rooms are en suite, with Freeview television, hairdryers and hot drink facilities. Wake up to a Full Welsh Breakfast or a Continental Breakfast. Vegetarian guests are welcome and all dietary needs can be catered for. At Ivybridge we offer home cooked evening meals by arrangement using fresh locally sourced ingredients wherever possible (please book before arrival). We serve evening meals between 6.30-7.30 pm. Our guests are more than welcome to bring friends and family to dine with them. We also cater for smaller functions and parties.

For further information
please contact us
Ivybridge, Drim Mill, Dyffryn,
Goodwick SA64 0JT
Tel: 01348 875366 • Fax: 01348 872338
e-mail: info@ivybridgefishguard.co.uk
www.ivybridgefishguard.co.uk

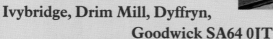

Cymru Wales

★★★

Pembrokeshire's entire coastline is a designated National Park, with sheltered coves and wooded estuaries, a wide choice of award-winning sandy beaches and some of the most dramatic cliffs in Britain. The islands of Skomer, Stokholm and Grasholm are home to thousands of seabirds, and cruise round Skomer is a great opportunity to watch the puffins. Ramsey Island, as well as being an RSPB Reserve boasts the second largest grey seal colony in Britain. You can watch them on a seal safari, or take a boat trip to go whale and dolphin spotting off the coast. Enjoy the wonderful views from the clifftop golf courses, or while walking round the Pembrokeshire Coastal Path. Conditions are ideal for all kinds of water sports including surfing, scuba diving and windsurfing, or try coasteering, a combination of climbing, swimming and leaping round the rocky coast. The sea fishing is superb or just the sample the catch at the annual fish week. There are food and folk music festivals to enjoy, and Pembrokeshire's mild climate, the many delightful towns and villages, gardens, children's attractions and outdoor facilities make this a favourite holiday destination, not just for families but for everyone

Powys

South Wales

As well as being an ideal holiday destination in its own right Swansea Bay is a perfect base for touring the rest of South Wales. Just a short journey from the city you will find the seaside village of Mumbles and the Gower Peninsula. A great place for all sorts of watersports such as sailing and kite surfing, the beaches are perfect for surfing, for beginners and experts alike. Well known for sea fishing, there's plenty of scope for fly fishing and coarse angling as well, or you may prefer extreme hiking along Worms Head or long, leisurely strolls in the secluded coves and inlets along the coast. Cycle along one of the traffic-free routes or use up extra energy on the challenging mountain bike tracks of the Afan Forest Park.

Anglesey & Gwynedd

Glanllyn Lodge

17th century gatehouse lodge lovingly restored with quality furnishings and fittings, comprising one en suite double bedroom, one twin and one single bedroom, luxury bathroom with spa bath, large oak kitchen/diner and a lounge with Sky TV and DVD player.

All rooms are on ground floor level with level entry at front door suitable for wheelchairs. Occupants have access to 16 acres of parkland bordering on Wales' largest natural lake. This parkland is also a touring caravan and camping park from April to September.

There is access to the lake and river for fishing, sailing and canoeing.

Cymru Wales
★★★★★

Megan W. Pugh, Glanllyn, Llanuwchllyn, Bala, LL23 7ST
Tel: 01678 540227
e-mail: info@glanllyn.com • www.glanllyn.com

Tai Gwyliau DWYFACH Cottages

Quality self-catering holiday accommodation

Choose from a 3-bedroom house near the beach in Criccieth or a 2-bedroom cottage on the farm $2\frac{1}{2}$ miles away, set in peaceful countryside with stunning views of Cardigan Bay and Snowdonia. They are superbly equipped, with dishwasher, microwave, washer/dryer, central heating and linen.

S. Edwards, Pen-y-Bryn,
Chwilog, Pwllheli, Gwynedd LL53 6SX
Tel: 01766 810208

e-mail: sulwen.edwards@btconnect.com • www.dwyfach.co.uk

SB

Caernarfon

BRYN BRAS CASTLE
EXCLUSIVE CASTLE APARTMENTS

Enchanting Castle Apartments within a romantic Regency Castle of timeless charm, and a much-loved home. (Grade II* Listed Building of Architectural/Historic interest).
Centrally situated in gentle Snowdonian foothills for enjoying North Wales' magnificent mountains, beaches, resorts, heritage and history.
Many local restaurants and inns nearby.
(Details available in our Information Room).

A delightfully unique selection for 2 persons of self-contained, beautifully appointed, spacious, clean and peaceful accommodation, each with its own distinctive, individual character. Generously and graciously enhanced with antiques/collectables.

32 acres of truly tranquil landscaped gardens, sweeping lawns, woodland walks and panoramic hill-walk overlooking sea, Anglesey and Snowdon. The comfortable, warm and welcoming Castle in serene surroundings is open all year, including for short breaks, offering privacy and relaxation – ideal for couples. Regret children not accepted.
Fully inclusive rents, including breakfast cereals etc., and much, much more...

Please contact Mrs Marita Gray-Parry directly any time for a brochure/booking
Self catering Apartments within the Castle
e.g. 2 persons for 2 nights from £195 incl "Romantic Breaks"
Inclusive Weekly Rents from £500
Llanrug, Near Caernarfon, Gwynedd LL55 4RE
Tel & Fax: (01286) 870210
e-mail: holidays@brynbrascastle.co.uk • www.brynbrascastle.co.uk

NORTH WALES HOLIDAY CHALETS

SB

THE CHALET is set in 200 acres of parkland, 1.5 miles east of Caernarfon, at the edge of the Snowdonia National Park.
• fitted kitchen leading to lounge and dining area • bathroom
• one double bedroom, the other with one single bed and bunk bed. It can accommodate a maximum of five people .
Well behaved pets allowed (max. 2).

Amenities on the park include:
heated outdoor pool, club room, entertainment, bar meals, takeaway food, supermarket, launderette.

Enquiries/bookings:
Mr H. Arfon Jones, 12 Lon Isaf,
Menai Bridge, Anglesey LL59 5LN
Tel/Fax: 01248 712045
email: hajones@northwales-chalet.co.uk
www.northwales-chalet.co.uk

PARC WERNOL PARK

SB

Chwilog, Pwllheli LL53 6SW
01766 810506 • e-mail: catherine@wernol.co.uk

Wi-Fi

• Panoramic views • Peaceful and quiet
• Ideal for touring Lleyn and Snowdonia
• 4 miles Criccieth and Pwllheli • 3 miles beach • Cycle route
• Free coarse fishing lake • Safe children's play area
• Games room • Footpaths • Dog exercise field
• Self-catering holidays
• 1,2 & 3 bedroom cottages
• 2 and 3 bedroom caravans and chalets • Colour brochure
• Personal attention at all times
• A truly Welsh welcome.
• Wi-Fi available

www.wernol.co.uk

Pwllheli, Trearddur Bay

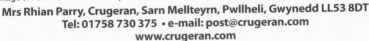

Colwyn Bay, Conwy Valley

North Wales

Conwy

Tal-y-Fan Cottage
& Alltwen Cottage

Tel & Fax: 01492 623737/622053
bookings@glynuchaf.co.uk
www.glyn-uchaf.co.uk

Cymru
Wales
★★★★★

Alltwen and Tal-y-Fan both offer 5 star self-catering holidays. Newly developed and well-appointed, these cottages can accommodate up to four people comfortably. They are located near the sleepy village of Dwygyfylchi, just outside Penmaenmawr, Conwy, with spectacular panoramic views of the sea and mountains.

Off-road parking is provided, and the A55 is within easy reach. They provide an ideal base for exploring Snowdonia and North Wales. Local amenities within a short drive. 2½ miles to Conwy, 5 miles to Llandudno and Colwyn Bay; 3 minutes' walk to village.

Glyn Uchaf Cottages nestle within an extensive country garden and lake, with nature thriving in abundance everywhere. With the most beautiful of sunsets in summertime, Glyn Uchaf is a most unique place to stay. We are open all year round.

Terms from £395
Suitable for disabled access
Pets and children welcome
Short Breaks available • Non-smoking

Mr John Baxter
Glyn Uchaf
Conwy Old Road
Dwygyfylchi
Penmaenmawr
Conwy LL34 6SW

Carmarthenshire

Llandeilo

Maerdy Cottages

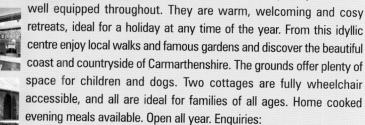

Aberporth

Ceredigion

🐴
🐕
SB

♿
Wi-Fi

Penffynnon Holiday Properties

This small cluster of self-contained properties enjoys a unique and special setting in the quiet holiday village of Aberporth on Cardigan Bay. All visitors are delighted when they first arrive and find out just how close they are to the water's edge - every one of our properties is within 200 yards of the sea. It's hard to imagine a more relaxing holiday.

DOLPHIN COTTAGE (pictured) is all on one level (Access Grade 2) and sleeps 6 in three bedrooms • **MORAWEL** has 5 bedrooms and 4 bathrooms, and sleeps 10 • **CILGWYN** has been converted into two self-contained villas, each with 3 bedrooms • **TY BROC** is a split level house to sleep 8.

All are very well equipped, and prices include bed linen, heating and lighting. Open all year.

Dolphin Cottage

For details contact: **Jann Tucker,
Penffynnon, Aberporth,
Ceredigion SA43 2DA
Tel: 01239 810387
e-mail: jann@aberporth.com
www.aberporth.com**

symbols 🐴🐴SB♿♀Wi-Fi

🐕	Pets Welcome	🐴	Children Welcome
SB	Short Breaks	♿	Suitable for Disabled Guests
♀	Licensed	**Wi-Fi**	Wi-Fi available

Cardigan Bay

Parc Farm
Holiday Cottages

Oakford, Near Llanarth
Ceredigion SA47 0RX

Cardigan Bay and the harbour town of Aberaeron are just 3½ miles away from these comfortable stone cottages situated amidst beautiful farmland and quiet wooded valleys close to the sea.

With lovely gardens to enjoy and relax in, overlooking trout ponds and set in picturesque village in 14 acres of land.

New Quay, 5½ miles away, boasts a sandy beach with slipway water sports, tennis and boat trips for fishing or watching the dolphins offshore. Also many beautiful spots and sandy coves to explore and enjoy. Inland, less than an hour's drive away, lies spectacular mountain scenery. Ideal for walking, cycling, birdwatching and horse riding.

Mr and Mrs Dunn • 01545 580390

Pembrokeshire

Cottage Retreats in Pembrokeshire

Charming, individual cottages situated near sandy beaches, rocky bays and spectacular cliff walks. Traditional stone-built cottages or modern properties, many with central heating and wood-burning stoves. All comfortably furnished, fully equipped and personally supervised. Ideal for watersports, golf, birdwatching, boat trips. Visit art galleries and craft workshops, relax in country pubs and quality restaurants.
Pets and children welcome in most cottages. Sleep 2-8.

**Please contact Carole Rogers on
01348 875318 for a brochure
e-mail: carole.rogers@talktalk.net
www.cottageretreats.net**

St Davids

SB

Ffynnon Ddofn

Ffynnon Ddofn is situated in a quiet lane between St Davids and Fishguard, with panoramic views over 18 miles of coastline.

The cottage is warm, comfortable and very well equipped, with 3 bedrooms sleeping 6, double and twin bedrooms overlooking the garden and adjoining field. Both rooms have new beds and soft furnishings. The third bedroom has pine bunk beds and sea views.

Attractive lounge/diner with exposed natural stone wall and beams, television, DVD and CD players. Bath/shower room, new fitted kitchen with dishwasher, and central heating. Washing machine, tumble dryer, freezer.

There is a large games room with table tennis and snooker, also a barbecue and pleasant, secure garden. Footpath from lane to beach and coast path. Parking beside cottage. Available all year; central heating, electricity and bed linen incl.

For details contact: Mrs B. Rees White, Brickhouse Farm,

Burnham Road, Woodham Mortimer, Maldon, Essex CM9 6SR

Tel: 01245 224611
www.ffynnonddofn.co.uk

St Davids, Whitland

Pembrokeshire's entire coastline is a designated National Park, with sheltered coves and wooded estuaries, a wide choice of award-winning sandy beaches and some of the most dramatic cliffs in Britain. Enjoy the wonderful views from the clifftop golf courses, or while walking round the Pembrokeshire Coastal Path. Conditions are ideal for all kinds of water sports including surfing, scuba diving and windsurfing, or try coasteering, a combination of climbing, swimming and leaping round the rocky coast. The sea fishing is superb or just the sample the catch at the annual fish week. There are food and folk music festivals to enjoy, and Pembrokeshire's mild climate, the many delightful towns and villages, gardens, children's attractions and outdoor facilities make this a favourite holiday destination, not just for families but for everyone

Presteigne

Powys

Whitehall Cottage

SB

Cosy cottage in lovely Border countryside, two miles from Offa's Dyke, ideal centre for touring Mid Wales, its beautiful borderland, South Shropshire and Herefordshire.
- Central heating, washing machine, dishwasher, microwave, colour TV, inglenook fireplace, woodburner, linen included • Power shower over bath
- Two light and airy bedrooms – twin and double • Sleeps 4 plus cot
- Ample parking • Private secure sun-trap garden
- On working farm in peaceful hamlet • Children and pets welcome

MRS R. L. JONES, UPPER HOUSE, KINNERTON,
NEAR PRESTEIGNE LD8 2PE • Tel: 01547 560207

Powys is situated right on England's doorstep and boasts some of most spectacular scenery in Europe. It is ideal for an action-packed holiday with fishing, golf, pony trekking, climbing caving and canoeing readily available, and walkers have a choice of everything from riverside trails to mountain hikes, including The Beacons Way, crossing the beautiful Brecon Beacons National Park, the Offa's Dyke Path running for 177 miles through Border country, often following the ancient earthworks, and Glyndwr's Way which takes in some of the finest landscape features in Wales. At Machynlleth take a ride on the amazing water-balanced cliff railway at the Centre for Alternative Technology, visit the border towns with their Georgian architecture and half-timbered black and white houses to visit, or wander round the wonderful shops in the book town of Hay, famous for its Literary Festival each May.

PENLLWYN LODGES
– MID WALES SELF CATERING HOLIDAYS –

Welcome to our Self Catering Holiday Park ...

Situated in the heart of Montgomeryshire, Mid Wales.

Penllwyn Lodges is the setting for a superb holiday for all seasons.

19 individually architect designed lodges set in 30 acres of unspoilt woodland teeming with an abundance of wildlife, offering the charming beauty of the Shropshire borders to the east and the rugged Welsh mountains and Cardigan Bay to the west.

On your arrival you will be delighted by the welcome given by Noddy the donkey, Tilley the llama, two Kune Kune pigs, Shetland ponies and Sam the parrot.

For the coarse angler we have a large pool stocked with Carp, Tench, Roach, Bream and Rudd and we also have fishing rights along the River Severn.

We have now opened a 9-hole golf course adjacent to Penllwyn Lodges with a pay and play system.
The clubhouse is open all day every day serving breakfasts, lunches and evening restaurant meals.

Well behaved pets are most welcome in specified lodges.

Week and Short Breaks available.

Ideal for those seeking a peaceful and relaxing holiday.

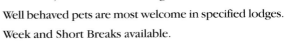

**Phillip, Daphne & Emma Jones,
Penllwyn Lodges
Garthmyl, Powys SY15 6SB
Tel/Fax: 01686 640269
www.penllwynlodges.co.uk
e-mail: daphne.jones@onetel.net**

South Wales

For something different visit the Wye Valley and the Vale of Usk with awesome castles, breathtaking scenery and a rich and colourful history. The area is steeped in industrial heritage, and at Blaenavon World Heritage Site visitors can go underground with a miner and uncover real stories about people from the past. The 13th century castle of Caerphilly is the largest in Wales and home to the ghostly Green Lady who haunts its halls. Many staff at Rhondda Heritage Park claim to have seen a phantom miner, or the ghost of a woman with two young children, and the legendary King Arthur is also reputed to have connections to the valleys. The area is popular for leisurely walks, or serious hikes and there are dedicated paths, challenging bike trails and, of course, plenty of opportunities for a game of golf.

homefromhome.com
Holiday Cottages

Gower's largest & most experienced holiday cottage agency

Tel +44 (0) 1792 360624
enquiries@homefromhome.com
www.homefromhome.com
101 Newton Road, Mumbles, Swansea SA3 4BN

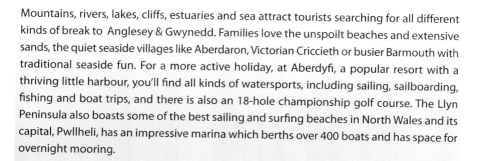

Mountains, rivers, lakes, cliffs, estuaries and sea attract tourists searching for all different kinds of break to Anglesey & Gwynedd. Families love the unspoilt beaches and extensive sands, the quiet seaside villages like Aberdaron, Victorian Criccieth or busier Barmouth with traditional seaside fun. For a more active holiday, at Aberdyfi, a popular resort with a thriving little harbour, you'll find all kinds of watersports, including sailing, sailboarding, fishing and boat trips, and there is also an 18-hole championship golf course. The Llyn Peninsula also boasts some of the best sailing and surfing beaches in North Wales and its capital, Pwllheli, has an impressive marina which berths over 400 boats and has space for overnight mooring.

Colwyn Bay

Cardigan

In North Wales there are charming towns and villages, castles, stately homes, beautiful gardens, parks, craft centres and museums waiting to be explored, as well as seaside resorts with soft, sandy beaches and rugged stretches of coastline, all with a background of hills and mountains, just the ingredients needed for an active holiday. Betws-y-Coed, North Wales' most popular inland resort, houses The Snowdonia National Visitor Centre with its craft units and thrilling video presentations – always worth a visit. For fun filled family holidays try Llandudno, where you can take the longest cable car ride in Britain, or wander along the Victorian pier. Experience the thrills of the indoor waterpark at Rhyl, meet seals, eels and sharks at the aquarium or take a traditional donkey ride along the beach.

Come to Ceredigion for spectacular scenery, from the cliffs and golden beaches of the coast to the uplands of the Cambrian Mountains, only some half an hour's drive the sea. This rural county, a centre for Welsh language and culture, is home to the National Library of Wales at Aberystwyth, but the books and manuscripts held there aren't the only attraction for visitors. For an active holiday break there are activity centres for all age groups, sea angling and shore fishing, walking in the mountains and along the coast, challenging mountain bike trails and quiet roads for cycling and all kinds of golf courses from parkland to coastal links. Boat trips take visitors out dolphin-spotting, and many species of bird are to be seen along the coast, including Red Kite.

Aberdeen, Banff & Moray

Furain Guest House

IDEAL FOR ACCESSING CASTLE AND WHISKY TRAILS AND ROYAL DEESIDE, FISHING, GOLF AND WALKING AVAILABLE LOCALLY.

Furain Guest House, on the A93 8 miles west of Aberdeen centre, is a late Victorian house built from red granite. We have some of the most beautiful countryside in the UK right on our doorstep, offering plenty of scope for walkers. Drum and Crathes Castles are only a few minutes' drive. Golf can be arranged at Peterculter Golf Club, our local course.

Wi-Fi

• 3 Double rooms • 2 Family rooms • 1 Single room • 2 Twin rooms
• Wi-Fi available • Children welcome • Pets by arrangement

**Contact: Mr Reid,
Furain Guest House,
92 North Deeside Road,
Peterculter,
Aberdeen AB14 0QN
Tel: 01224 732189
Fax: 01224 739070
e-mail: furain@btinternet.com
www.furain.co.uk**

Aboyne, Banchory

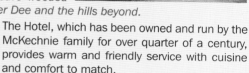

Dominated by the Grampian Highlands to the west, extending through Royal Deeside, and with a long coastline along the Moray Firth and the North Sea, Aberdeenshire, Banff and Moray presents a wonderful combination of countryside, coast and heritage for the holidaymaker to explore. Easily accessible from Aberdeen, with all the attractions of city life, this is an ideal corner of the country for an interesting and relaxing break. Why not follow a tourist trail to see the spectacular scenery and learn more about the area at the same time? A visit to this part of Scotland isn't complete without sampling whisky, the national drink, and what better way than to follow the Malt Whisky Trail, visiting distilleries and a traditional cooperage all the way from Forres through the country towns, woodlands and glens of Speyside to remote Glenlivet on the way to the Grampians.

Argyll & Bute

SB
Wi-Fi

The Argyll Arms Hotel, located on the waterfront of the village of Bunessan, and close to the ferry landing for the famous Isle of Iona, provides accommodation, bar and restaurant facilities on the beautiful Isle of Mull. With spectacular sea and island views, the hotel is the perfect base from which to explore the islands. Island tours available, wildlife watching day tours arranged. The new owners invite you to enjoy their friendly and relaxed Scottish hospitality in comfortable accommodation, value-for-money home cooked style food with many local ingredients, and the unique atmosphere of the Isle of Mull. Single, twin, double and family rooms available, all rooms recently refurbished, all en suite.

Make us your home whilst relaxing on the Isle of Mull.

Check out our website for full up-to-date information.

Open all day 365 days of the year catering for residents and non residents.

From £35.00 single. £60.00 double

Argyll Arms Hotel

Bunessan, Isle of Mull PA67 6DP
Tel: 01681 700240
e-mail: argyllarms@isleofmull.co.uk
www.isleofmull.co.uk

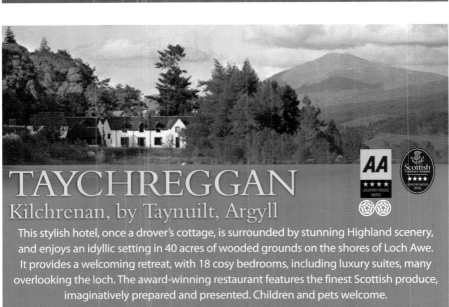

Oban

SB
Wi-Fi

SB

Wi-Fi

Argyll & Bute is a wonderfully unspoilt area, historically the birthplace of Scotland and home to a wealth of fascinating wildlife. Here you may be lucky enough to catch a glimpse of an eagle, a wildcat or an osprey, whales, dolphin, seals, or even a giant octopus. At every step the sea fringed landscape is steeped in history, from prehistoric sculpture at Kilmartin and Knapdale, standing stone circles and Bronze Age cup-and-ring engravings, to the elegant ducal home of the once feared Clan Campbell. On the upper reaches of Loch Caolisport can be found St Columba's Cave, and more recent times are illustrated at the Auchindrain Highland Township south of Inveraray, a friendly little town with plenty to see, including the Jail, Wildlife Park and Maritime Museum. Sample the wonderful seafood and local whiskies, walk along the Atlantic beaches or in the Arrochar Alps, and visit the many beautiful gardens. Bute is the most accessible of the west coast islands, and Rothesay is its main town. Here find out about the island at the Discovery Centre, explore the dungeons and grand hall of Rothesay Castle, and visit the Victorian Gothic splendour of Mount Stuart.

Pubs & Inns

See the Supplement on pages 483-530

Ayr

Ayrshire & Arran

e-mail: *eglintonguesthouse@yahoo.co.uk*
www.eglintonguesthouse.com

SB

Situated within a part of Ayr steeped in history, within a few minutes' walk of the beach, town centre and many other amenities and entertainment for which Ayr is popular. There are sea and fishing trips available from Ayr Harbour, or a cruise "Doon the Water" on the "Waverley"; golf, swimming pool, cycling, tennis, sailing, windsurfing, walking, etc all available nearby; Prestwick Airport only three miles away.

We have family, double and single rooms, all with washbasins, colour TV and tea/coffee making facilities. En suite facilities and cots available on request. We are open all year round.

Bed and Breakfast from £27. Please send for our brochure for further information.

Peter & Julia Clark, Eglinton Guest House, 23 Eglinton Terrace, Ayr KA7 1JJ • Tel/Fax: 01292 264623

Ayrshire and The Isle of Arran in Scotland's south west is flanked by Dumfries and Galloway to the south and the Central Belt to the north. Here the warm waters of the Gulf Stream meet with miles of sandy beaches and a dramatic coastline littered with rocky outcrops and caves, once a favourite with smugglers. As well as long-established seaside resorts like Ayr and Largs, the area is best known for sailing and golf, including three Open Championship courses, and of course, Robert Burns, Scotland's national poet, whose life and works are celebrated at the Burns National Heritage Park at Alloway. The Isle of Arran, as well as being one of Scotland's most accessible islands, is also arguably one of its most truly representative. From the mountainous north to the undulating south it is easy to see how the island became known as "Scotland in miniature", making it a favourite holiday destination for walking, wildlife and simply relaxing.

Ayr

SB

Wi-Fi

Wi-Fi

West Tannacrieff

Fenwick, Kilmarnock KA3 6AZ
Tel: 01560 600258
mobile: 07773 226332
Fax: 01560 600914

Mrs Nancy Cuthbertson

A warm welcome awaits all our guests to our dairy farm, situated in the peaceful Ayrshire countryside. Relax in spacious, well-furnished, en suite rooms with all modern amenities, colour TV and tea/coffee making facilities. Large parking area and garden.

Situated off the M/A77 on the B751 road to Kilmaurs, so easily accessible from Glasgow, Prestwick Airport, and the south. An ideal base for exploring Ayrshire's many tourist attractions.

Enjoy a hearty breakfast with home-made breads and preserves, and home baking for supper. Children welcome. Terms from £30 per person. Brochure available.

e-mail: westtannacrieff@btopenworld.com
www.smoothhound.co.uk/hotels/westtannacrieff.html

South Whittlieburn Farmhouse B&B
and Caravan & Camping, Brisbane Glen, Largs KA30 8SN
Tel: 01475 675881 • Fax: 01475 675080

Superb farmhouse accommodation with lovely scenic views on our working sheep farm in peaceful Brisbane Glen. Ample parking. Only five minutes' drive from the popular tourist resort of Largs and near the ferries to the islands. 40 minutes from Glasgow and Prestwick airports. Warm friendly hospitality, enormous delicious breakfasts. All rooms en suite. *Chosen by "WHICH? TOP TEN BEST BED & BREAKFAST", WELCOME HOST. Nominated for AA LANDLADY OF THE YEAR 2005 and 2006* •

Bed & Breakfast from £31pppn. e-mail: largsbandb@southwhittlieburnfarm.freeserve.co.uk
www.ukcampsite.co.uk • www.SmoothHound.co.uk/hotels/whittlie.html

symbols 🐕🐎SB♿🍷Wi-Fi

🐕	*Pets Welcome*	🐎	*Children Welcome*
SB	*Short Breaks*	♿	*Suitable for Disabled Guests*
🍷	*Licensed*	**Wi-Fi**	*Wi-Fi available*

Borders

Auldgirth

Dumfries & Galloway

Set in 45 acres of woodland, Friars Carse, with its magnificent panelled entrance hall and elegant staircase, offers guests a warm welcome. The 21 en suite bedrooms have remote-control TV, telephone, hairdryer and tea/coffee facilities.

The Whistle Restaurant serves excellent local cuisine. Larger parties catered for in our marquee.

• Private fishing on a mile of the River Nith
• Panelled snooker room
• Free Wi-Fi
• Lifts to all floors
• Close to the border between Scotland and England, 6 miles from Dumfries on the A76

Friars Carse
COUNTRY HOUSE HOTEL
Auldgirth, Dumfries DG2 0SA
Tel: 01387 740388
Fax: 01387 740550

www.friarscarse.co.uk

One of Scotland's most romantic award-winning Hotels, Blackaddie Country House Hotel is set amidst two acres of secluded gardens on the outskirts of Sanquhar in South West Scotland.

The family-run hotel offers comfortable accommodation, excellent facilities, friendly service and great food, combining high standards of personal care with friendly informality.

There are nine comfortable en suite bedrooms in the hotel, and three self-catering River Suites within the grounds.

This area of Scotland is rich in history, with many places of interest just a short way from the hotel.

• Romatic Breaks • Self Catering Lodges •
• Cookery School, Events and Packages •

Blackaddie House Hotel, Sanquhar, Dumfriesshire DG4 6JJ

Tel 01659 50270 • Fax 01659 495935

info@blackaddiehotel.co.uk • www.blackaddiehotel.co.uk

Dumfries & Galloway combines high moorland and sheltered glens, forests, sandy beaches, crags, cliffs and rocky shores, presenting abundant opportunities for hill walking, rambling, fishing for salmon and sea trout, cycling, mountain biking, off-road driving, horse riding, pony trekking and bird watching. Catch a glimpse of a red kite soaring above, or a wild goat or red squirrel in the 300 square miles of the Galloway Forest Park or hunt for sea life in a rocky coastal pool. Golfers can choose from 30 courses, whether the challenging links at Southerness or a local course with spectacular views. Warmed by the influence of the Gulf Stream, touring in this quiet corner of south west Scotland is a pleasure, visiting the dozens of interesting castles, gardens, museums and historic sites. In addition a never-ending succession of music festivals, ceilidhs, village fairs, country dances, classical music concerts and children's entertainment guarantees plenty of scope for enjoyment, and for those whose interest is in the night skies a visit to the Galloway Forest Park, the UK's first designated Dark Sky Park, is a 'must'. Discover the many hidden secrets of this lovely and unspoilt landscape such as the pretty little villages along the coast, including the 'Artists' Town', Kirkcudbright, while those who love 'the written word' must surely visit the book town of Wigtown.

Bathgate

Edinburgh & Lothians

SB

This 17th century farmhouse is situated two miles from M8 Junction 4, which is midway between Glasgow and Edinburgh. This peaceful location overlooks panoramic views of the countryside. All rooms are on the ground floor, ideal for disabled visitors, and have central heating, colour TV and tea/coffee making facilities. We are within easy reach of golf, fishing, cycling (15 mile cycle track runs along back of property).

Scottish TOURIST BOARD ★★★ **B&B**

Ample security parking.
Open January to December.
Children and pets by arrangement
Twin Room from £44–£55,
Family Room £60–£80
**Mrs F. Gibb, Tarrareoch Farm,
Station Road, Armadale,
Near Bathgate EH48 3BJ
Tel: 01501 730404**
nicola@gibb0209.fsnet.co.uk

Visitors to Edinburgh, Scotland's capital, and the surrounding area, the Lothians, will find a wide range of attractions offering something for all ages and interests. Heritage is paramount, with historic and royal connections through the ages centred on Edinburgh Castle, down the Royal Mile to the Palace of Holyroodhouse, and its new neighbour, the Scottish Parliament building. Stroll through the Georgian New Town, browsing through some of the many shops on the way, or a wander through the Royal Botanic Gardens. Imagine sailing on the Royal Yacht Britannia, now berthed at Leith, or travel on a journey with our planet through time and space at Our Dynamic Earth. The Edinburgh Festival in August is part of the city's tradition and visitors flock to enjoy the performing arts, theatre, ballet, cinema and music, and of course "The Tattoo" itself. At the Festival Fringe there is a wide variety of shows and impromptu acts, and jazz and book festivals too.

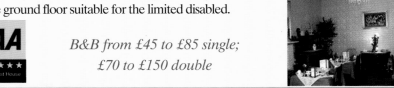

Musselburgh

Visitors to Edinburgh, Scotland's capital, and the surrounding area, the Lothians, will find a wide range of attractions offering something for all ages and interests. Outside the city East Lothian has beautiful countryside and a dramatic coastline, where once thriving fishing villages like North Berwick and Dunbar now cater for visitors who delight in their traditional seaside charm. You can step back in time with a visit to Rosslyn, Chapel or Borthwick and Crichton Castles in Midlothian, and to Mary Queen of Scots' birthplace at Linlithgow Palace in East Lothian. Outdoors, seize the chance to brush up on your golf swing at one of the historic links or more recent parkland courses in the area, or pay a visit to the Scottish Seabird Centre at North Berwick.

symbols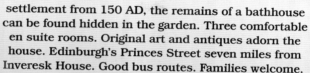

🐕 Pets Welcome		🐎 Children Welcome	
SB Short Breaks		♿ Suitable for Disabled Guests	
♈ Licensed		Wi-Fi Wi-Fi available	

Lower Largo

Fife

The Crusoe Hotel

Main Street, Lower Largo, Fife KY8 6BT
Tel: 01333 320759 • Fax: 01333 320865
e-mail: relax@crusoehotel.co.uk
www.crusoehotel.co.uk

There can be few hotels with a more dramatic location than The Crusoe Hotel in Lower Largo. This family-run hotel is situated at the water's edge with most bedrooms having superb views over the sea or harbour. Combined with the wonderful character of the hotel's bar, restaurant, meeting rooms and bedrooms it makes The Crusoe the ideal destination for your short break, golf holiday or just a great evening out.

The hotel offers a range of single, double or twin rooms as well as two suites, all en suite, with remote-control TV, hairdryer, trouser press, tea and coffee making facilities and telephone. The Hotel is well known locally for both its lively bar and its excellent meals.

Ideally situated for a golfing break, only 12 miles from St Andrews, and surrounded by many of the finest courses in Scotland, the hotel is situated in

The East Neuk of Fife - a coastal paradise with a string of fishing villages and harbour towns.

Edinburgh is easily accessible by train, with a 40 minute journey from the nearby railway station. Dundee is less than 45 minutes' drive north and Stirling and Perth all easily accessed by main roads.

The Kingdom of Fife - and more particularly the coastal university town of St Andrews – is renowned worldwide as the home of golf, where not only the famous links, but parkland and heathland courses number among more than 40 available for golfers to choose from. The south of this small, self-contained former county has been dominated by industry and the Forth Road and Rail Bridges, the imposing road and rail links with Edinburgh and the south, but the sandy beaches and traditional fishing villages at places like Elie, Crail, Pittenweem, and Aberdour are major attractions for holidaymakers. At North Queensferry families will love the excitement of Deep Sea World with its Underwater Safari and seal sanctuary. The historic associations of centres like Dunfermline, Scotland's former capital, the restored medieval village of Culross and the Palace of Falkland make these just some of many fascinating places to visit.

Kilsyth

Glasgow & District

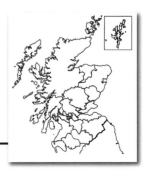

In one of Europe's most dynamic cultural centres, there's so much to see and do – from the City of Glasgow itself, alive with heritage, architecture, entertainment and nightlife, to the charm of the bustling towns, scenic villages and countryside of the surrounding districts. James Watt, Adam Smith, Charles Rennie Mackintosh, Lord Kelvin and a host of others have all played a major part in Greater Glasgow's past. Today the area has a wealth of attractions which recall their works. Entertainment and sport feature in an exciting year round calendar that encompasses opera and theatre, music of all kinds, Scottish ceilidhs and top sporting events. Established as one of the UK's top shopping centres, Glasgow is home to a multitude of shops, from boutiques and specialist stores, to the High Street favourites, and shopping malls. Out in the easily accessible countryside, follow the famous River Clyde from New Lanark, the site of the historic 18th century mills established by Robert Owen.

Highlands

Aviemore

A family-run Bed and Breakfast, situated in a quiet cul-de-sac in the centre of Aviemore

Pat & Alan Finlayson, Craig-na-gower Avenue, Aviemore, Inverness-shire PH22 1RW

Wi-Fi

Ideal base for a holiday, whether it is fishing, skiing, sailing, birdwatching, climbing or any other outdoor pursuit. One double, one family and one twin, all en suite, with TV, radio, hairdryers, controllable electric heating, and a host of other extras. Luxurious guest lounge with blazing log fire. Purpose-built drying room and secure storage. Pick-up/drop-off service to and from the station. Private off-road parking. Packed lunches available. Well behaved dogs by prior arrangement. Wi-Fi. Self-catering accommodation also available.

Tel: 01479 810717 • e-mail: enquiry@eriskay-aviemore.co.uk
www.eriskay-aviemore.co.uk

Cairngorm Guest House

Cairngorm Guest House
Main Street, Aviemore PH22 1RP
Tel: 01479 810 630
e-mail: enquiries@cairngormguesthouse.com
www.cairngormguesthouse.com

Ideally situated in Aviemore, in the Cairngorm National Park, a perfect base to explore the Scottish Highlands or to enjoy the abundance of outdoor pursuits which the immediate area has to offer.

Cairngorm House is a 12 bedroomed guest house located in the village of Aviemore on the main road, with all the amenities - Bars and Restaurants, Rail and Bus links 5 to 10 minutes' walk away.

The bedrooms are all en suite, and each has television and hairdryer, and tea coffee making facilities. Five rooms are on the ground floor. A superb breakfast is served in the beautiful Victorian dining room with stove fire, or in the bright, sunny conservatory. A vegetarian option is available. High chair available if required.

There is ample private parking and extensive grounds in which to relax.

Culloden, Fort William

Fort William

Glencoe

Wi-Fi

•We are a family-run guest house situated in the Highland village of Ballachulish. Set on the shores of Loch Leven and only one mile from the majesty of Glencoe, Ballachulish makes an ideal centre for exploring much of Scotland's natural beauty. Attractions in and around Glencoe, Fort William, Oban, Skye, Mull, Loch Ness, Loch Lomond and many others are easily accessible.

Imposing craggy mountains, beautiful lochs, waterfalls and forestry can all be found locally and wildlife such as seals, dolphins, otters, deer, pine-martens and eagles thrive.There are a multitude of beautiful and interesting walks, from strolls to view historic Glencoe or around the Lochan trails to mainland Britain's most challenging mountain ridge - Glencoe's Aonach Eagach (The Notched Ridge).

•All of our rooms have en suite facilities, colour TV, DVD player, hospitality tray and individually controlled room heaters.

•We have a comfortable guest lounge, snack bar, separate dining room, drying room, bike store and large car park.

•Free Wi-Fi internet access available.

•Easy to find, next door to the Tourist Information Centre.

•B&B from £20.

**Mike and Christine Richardson
Strathassynt Guest House, Loanfern,
Ballachulish, Near Glencoe PH49 4JB
Tel: 01855 811261
e-mail: info@strathassynt.com
www.strathassynt.com**

Gairloch, Glenshiel

Kingussie

Plockton, Spean Bridge

Apart from the stunning and varied scenery, the major attraction of The Scottish Highlands is that there is so much to see and do, whatever the season. Stretching from Fort William in the south, to Wick in the far north, and with access links radiating out from the busy city of Inverness, there is a wealth of visitor attractions and facilities. Perhaps the most famous is Loch Ness, home of the legendary monster, and a good starting point for a sail down the Caledonian Canal, through the unspoiled scenery of the Great Glen to Fort William. Just to the south lies Ben Nevis, Glencoe and a whole range of outdoor sporting activities from fishing and sailing to skiing. In the Cairngorm National Park it's possible to glimpse an osprey or capercaillie while walking, climbing, skiing or cycling, or just enjoying the stunning mountain scenery.

SCOTLAND

Board - Highlands 423

Thurso

The family-run Northern Sands Hotel is situated on the shores of the beautiful Dunnet Bay Sands, only three miles away from mainland Britain's most northerly point of Dunnet Head. We are conveniently situated for ferries to the Orkney Isles at Gills Bay and Scrabster. The Castle of Mey and John O' Groats are also close by.

The Hotel has 9 comfortable en suite rooms, and public and lounge bars as well as our restaurant, which is known for being one of the finest in the north, featuring finest local produce cooked fresh for you.

The Northern Sands Hotel
Dunnet, Caithness KW14 8XD
Tel: 01847 851270 • Fax: 01847 851626
www.northernsands.co.uk
e-mail: info@northernsands.co.uk

Sharvedda · www.sharvedda.co.uk

Our spacious lounge has panoramic views over Strathy Bay where seals, dolphins, porpoises and whales are regular visitors, or browse through a wide selection of maps, books and information on the surrounding area to help plan the next day's activities.

Sharvedda offers one double and twin bedroom en suite and a twin room with private bathroom across the corridor. All rooms are on the ground floor, finished to a high standard and centrally heated. Generous hospitality trays and complimentary toiletries, hairdryer, radio alarm clock and electric blanket are provided.

The house is totally non-smoking and we are unable to allow any pets.

Meals are served in the conservatory with outstanding views of Dunnet Head and the Orkney Islands. Our tempting breakfast menu offers a full Scottish Breakfast or local specialities. Evening meals can be provided if booked in advance.

Strathy Point, Strathy, Thurso KW14 7RY
TEL: 01641 541311 • patsy@sharvedda.co.uk

Lanarkshire

🐴
🐕
SB

Wi-Fi

WALSTON MANSION FARMHOUSE

Welcome to Walston Mansion Farmhouse, well known for its real home-from-home atmosphere, where guests return year after year. There is a hearty breakfast menu and delicious evening meals, using home produced meat, eggs, organic vegetables and freshly baked bread. All room have TV/video and tea/coffee making; there is a children's toy cupboard and lots of small animals to see. Pets by arrangement. In lovely walking area and an ideal touring base for the Scottish Borders and Clyde Valley; Edinburgh 24 miles, Glasgow 30 miles. Terms from £24 standard, £26 en suite.

For details contact: Margaret Kirby, Walston, Carnwath, By Biggar ML11 8NF
Tel: 01899 810338 • Fax: 01899 810334
e-mail: margaret.kirby@walstonmansion.co.uk • www.walstonmansion.co.uk

symbols 🐕🐴 SB ♿ ♇ Wi-Fi

🐕	*Pets Welcome*	🐴	*Children Welcome*
SB	*Short Breaks*	♿	*Suitable for Disabled Guests*
♇	*Licensed*	Wi-Fi	*Wi-Fi available*

A modern farmhouse bungalow on Dykecroft Farm, set in lovely surroundings in a rural area on the B7086 (old A726) and within easy reach of the M74, making it the ideal stop between north and south; also convenient for Glasgow and Prestwick airports. Centrally situated for touring Glasgow, Edinburgh, Ayr, Stirling and New Lanark - all within one hour's drive. Nearby is Strathclyde Country Park with all watersports activities; other sporting facilities within two miles include sports centre, golf, fishing, quad bikes, rifle and clay pigeon shooting, and swimming. Guests will enjoy the open fires in our TV lounge and the good breakfasts; TV and tea making facilities in all rooms. A warm and friendly welcome awaits all guests.

SB

Dykecroft Farm

Boghead, Kirkmuirhill,
Lesmahagow ML11 0JQ
e-mail: Dykecroft.bandb@tiscali.co.uk

Tel & Fax: 01555 892226
www.Dykecroftfarm.co.uk

Scottish
TOURIST BOARD
★★
B&B

Perth & Kinross

Set just outside the village of Crianlarich, Inverardran House is sited in an elevated position with views across Strathfillan to Ben Challum. This property offers excellent fishing, walking and touring prospects.
We can offer you Bed and Breakfast accommodation for up to nine people in two double rooms and one twin (all en suite) and one triple room with a private bathroom. Tea/coffee making facilities in the rooms. Self-catering cottage also available.
Open all year • Prices from £25 to £28 per person per night based on two sharing, £8 surcharge for a single person. Discounts for longer stays.
Packed lunches on request.

John and Janice Christie, Inverardran House, Crianlarich FK20 8QS
Tel: 01838 300240 • e-mail: janice@inverardran.demon.co.uk
www.inverardran.demon.co.uk

The wonderful variety of landscape in Perthshire ensures not only that touring is a delight, but that all kinds of activities from canyoning to climbing, walking to white water rafting are available right in the centre of Scotland within easy reach of Glasgow and Edinburgh. From the southern fringes of the Cairngorm National Park and the 'gateway to the Highlands' at Pitlochry, with its Festival Theatre, through the long, narrow glens and alongside the tranquil lochs to the lowlands of the south, Perth & Kinross offers opportunities for a relaxing scenic break or action-packed adventure. Pass by Britain's tallest hedge near Blairgowrie in the fruit-growing lowlands, and explore the cluster of little resort towns including Crieff, Comrie, Dunkeld, Aberfeldy, and Pitlochry, which have grown up along the Highland Boundary Fault separating north from south.

Stirling & The Trossachs

At the heart of Scotland, Stirling, Loch Lomond and the Trossachs combines history and scenic beauty, and endless opportunities for walking, cycling and boating, all within an hour of Edinburgh and Glasgow. Stirling Castle, magnificently restored to tell the story of this former seat of Scottish monarchs, provides a panoramic view from Ben Lomond across the Trossachs and over Bannockburn and other battlegrounds so important in Scotland's history. A walk through the medieval Old Town of Stirling, Scotland's newest city, is the ideal starting point for touring the area, then explore the wild glens and sparkling lochs in Loch Lomond and The Trossachs National Park, and perhaps take a steamer trip down Loch Katrine.

Whatever your fitness, there are walks suitable for everyone, cycle routes, challenging mountain bike trails, golf and wildlife. The amazing Falkirk Wheel linking the Forth and Clyde and Union Canals is a sight and experience not to be missed, while villages and small towns such as Drymen, Killearn, Fintry and Kippen offer hospitality and interesting outings less than an hour from Glasgow, yet feels worlds apart from the bustle of city life.

Scottish Islands

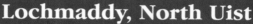

REDBURN HOUSE
Lochmaddy, North Uist

Redburn House is a Bed and Breakfast establishment in Lochmaddy, the main township of the wonderful Hebridean Isle of North Uist. Redburn House offers four en suite Bed and Breakfast rooms, a self-catering cottage (the Boat House), a self-catering annexe (the Studio) and a large self-catering Apartment.

Redburn House has recently undergone extensive renovation which has transformed it into the warm, cosy, clean and modern guesthouse it is now.

It is ideally located close to the post office, pub, Arts Centre, Sailing Club, Outdoor Centre, shop, Tourist Information Centre and Ferry Terminal.

**Contact Maggie at
info@redburnhouse.com
Tel/Fax: 01876 500301 or
Redburn House,
Lochmaddy, Isle of North Uist,
Western Isles HS6 5AA
www.redburnhouse.com**

So many islands are waiting to be visited off the Scottish mainland, each with a mystery and magic of its own. To the north lie the Orkney and Shetland Isles, with their strong connections to the Vikings whose influence is still seen and heard today. To the west, exposed to the Atlantic, lie the Inner and Outer Hebrides, including the islands of Skye, Islay, Mull and Tiree, Lewis, Harris and Barra, each with its own culture, traditions and heritage. Everywhere there's evidence of settlement going back to prehistoric times, including awe-inspiring standing stones and circles and chambered cairns. Some islands have mountains to climb, but most are low-lying, ideal for exploring on foot and for cycling and bird watching, while the Atlantic waves have proved a great attraction to surfers from all over the world.

Westray

Aberdeen, Banff & Moray

Newseat & Kirklea

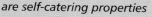

SB

both within five miles of the fishing town of Fraserburgh, are self-catering properties available from April to October. Both houses have good garden areas and ample parking in quiet surroundings.

Newseat (★) sleeps four and has four rooms and a bathroom, all situated on the one level.

Kirklea (★★★) which sleeps six, is a two-storey Victorian house set in its own grounds. The ground floor has a utility room, kitchen/diner, dining room and lounge, and three bedrooms are situated on the first floor along with the bath/ shower room.

Terms per week from £180 for Newseat and from £320 for Kirklea, both fully inclusive of gas and electricity. All bed and table linen and towels are provided.

Contact: Mrs E.M. Pittendrigh, Kirkton, Tyrie, Fraserburgh AB43 7DQ
Tel: 01346 541231
e-mail: pittendrigh@supanet.com

On the Victorian Heritage Trail follow in the footsteps of Queen Victoria to Royal Deeside to reach the best-known castle of all, Balmoral, visiting many of her favourite towns and viewpoints on the way, taking in Crathie Church, still attended by the Royal Family. Golfers have 45 inland courses to choose from, as well as the links courses along the coast. The countryside is ideal for mountain-biking, and there's a network of trails on the on the hills and in the forests of the Glenlivet estate, and all kinds of snow sports are available at Glenshee and the Lecht. Aberdeen, a university city of sparkling granite buildings, has museums, art galleries, theatres, concerts and films, shopping from designer-wear to Scottish crafts, as well as beaches, golf and fishing.

Johnshaven

Angus & Dundee

Brawliemuir Holiday Cottages Kincardineshire

Two delightful stone-built cottages situated in a lovely country setting yet only three miles from the sea. Both cottages have central heating and are fully equipped to a high standard. Towels and bed linen included. This is a great base for exploring the Angus Glens, the Mearns countryside, the Castle Trail and the granite city of Aberdeen. Golf, fishing, horse riding, hill walking and a great beach are all nearby.

No smoking. Pets welcome. Available all year from £280 to £485 per week

Telephone Carole Duvall on 01561 362453 or e-mail for further information.

e-mail: carole@the-duvalls.com • www.brawliemuircottages.co.uk

SB

The former Pictish stronghold of Angus stretches from the sand and pebble beaches and rugged cliffs of the North Sea coast inland into the deep, narrow glens at the foothills of the Cairngorm National Park, perfect countryside for walking or for climbing, with ten 'Munros' mountains over 3000 feet, to choose from. The rivers are well known for salmon and trout fishing, alternatively sea anglers can charter a boat, or simply fish from the beach. The area is a golfers' dream, with a wide choice of courses, from classic links like Carnoustie to the heathland at Edzell in the north and parkland courses nearer the lively coastal city of Dundee. Visit the ancient port of Arbroath during the Sea Fest, celebrating its maritime heritage, and taste a traditional 'smokie'. The more recent past is commemorated in Dundee at Discovery Point, now the home of the RRS Discovery, the ship that took Captain Scott on his ill-fated journey to the Antarctic.

Appin

Argyll & Bute

ARDTUR COTTAGES

Two adjacent cottages in secluded surroundings on promontory between Port

Appin and Castle Stalker. Ideal for hill walking, climbing, pony trekking, boating and fly-fishing. (Glencoe and Ben Nevis half-hour drive). Tennis court by arrangement. Direct access across the field to sea (Loch Linnhe). First cottage is suitable for up to 8 people in one double and three twin-bedded rooms, large dining/sittingroom/kitchenette and two bathrooms. Second cottage is suitable for 6 people in one double and two twin-bedded rooms, dining/sittingroom/ kitchenette and bathroom. Everything provided except linen. Shops one mile; sea 200 yards. Pets allowed. Car essential, parking. Open March/October. Terms from £250 to £420 weekly.

SAE, please for details to Mrs J. Pery, Ardtur, Appin PA38 4DD
(01631 730223 or 01626 834172)
e-mail: pery@btinternet.com • www.ardturcottages.com

Argyll & Bute is a wonderfully unspoilt area, historically the birthplace of Scotland and home to a wealth of fascinating wildlife. Here you may be lucky enough to catch a glimpse of an eagle, a wildcat or an osprey, whales, dolphin, seals, or even a giant octopus. At every step the sea fringed landscape is steeped in history, from prehistoric sculpture at Kilmartin and Knapdale, standing stone circles and Bronze Age cup-and-ring engravings, to the elegant ducal home of the once feared Clan Campbell. On the upper reaches of Loch Caolisport can be found St Columba's Cave, and more recent times are illustrated at the Auchindrain Highland Township south of Inveraray, a friendly little town with plenty to see, including the Jail, Wildlife Park and Maritime Museum. Sample the wonderful seafood and local whiskies, walk along the Atlantic beaches or in the Arrochar Alps, and visit the many beautiful gardens.

Bridge of Awe, Dalmally

ROSNEATH CASTLE PARK
SO NEAR... YET SO FAR AWAY

Rosneath Castle Park has everything to offer if you are looking for a relaxing holiday. No more than an hour's drive from Glasgow, the 57 acres that the park occupies along the shore of Gareloch offer the perfect opportunity to relax and discover another world, and another you.

Thistle Awarded Luxury Self-Catering Holiday Homes with superb views. In a beautiful setting with first class facilities including an adventure playground, boat house, fun club, restaurant and bar, there's no end to the reasons why you would 'wish you were here'.

**Rosneath Castle Park, Rosneath,
Near Helensburgh, Argyll G84 0QS
Tel: (01436) 831208
Fax: (01436) 831978
enquiries@rosneathcastle.demon.co.uk
www.rosneathcastle.co.uk**

Inveraray

Halftown Cottages • St Catherine's •Argyll

SB

Wi-Fi

In the heart of the West Highlands.
55 miles from Glasgow and across Loch Fyne from Inveraray.
Two radically modernised 18thC farm cottages.
Wholly secluded woodland site just above the loch.
A real 'chill out' place for humans and animals.
Extensive woodland, lochside and hillside walking.
Nearby top class restaurants. Extensive day touring. Beach BBQs.

Tel: 01369 860750 or book direct on
www.argyllcottages.com

19th century Minard Castle beside Loch Fyne is a peaceful location for a quiet break. Stroll in the grounds, walk by the loch, explore the woods, or tour this scenic area with lochs, hills, gardens, castles and historic sites.

SB

THE LODGE • a comfortable bungalow with two bedrooms, livingroom, kitchen and bathroom. Ample parking space, small private garden and view through trees to the loch, sleeps 4-6.

• Well equipped; central heating, hot water, electricity, linen and towels included.
• Terms £170 to £390 per week. Open all year.

Minard Castle
SELF-CATERING
Minard, Inveraray PA32 8YB
Tel & Fax: 01546 886272
reinoldgayre@minardcastle.com
www.minardcastle.com

Isle of Seil, Loch Crinan

Kilbride Cottage

Situated on beautiful Seil Island with wonderful views of surrounding countryside. These lovingly restored cottages (one detached and one attached to the main croft house) retain their traditional character while incorporating all modern facilities. The cottages are near to each other and ideal for two families on holiday together. Seil is one of the most peaceful and tranquil spots in the West Highlands, with easy access to neighbouring Isles of Luing and Easdale. Oban, the hub for trips to Mull and Iona, is half an hour's drive away over the famous 18th century "Bridge Over The Atlantic". Wonderful area for hillwalking, cycling, fishing and bird watching. Short breaks from £45 per day.

kilbRide cRoft

Balvicar, Isle of Seil, Argyll PA34 4RD
Contact: Mary & Brian Phillips
Tel: 01852 300475
e-mail: kilbridecroft@aol.com
www.kilbridecroft.co.uk

Croft Cottage

Duntrune Castle Holiday Cottages

Five traditional self-catering cottages set in the spacious grounds of 12th century Duntrune Castle, which guards the entrance to Loch Crinan. All have been attractively modernised and accommodate two to five persons.

The estate comprises 5000 acres and five miles of coastline. Without leaving our land, you can enjoy easy or testing walks, sea or river fishing, and watching the abundant wildlife. Nearby are several riding establishments, a bicycle-hire firm, and a number of excellent restaurants.

Prices from £300 to £550 per week. Pets are welcome.

For further details please contact:
Robin Malcolm, Duntrune Castle,
Kilmartin, Argyll PA31 8QQ
01546 510283 • www.duntrune.com

Scottish
TOURIST BOARD
★★★
SELF CATERING

---

symbols 🐕🎠 SB ♿ ⚲ Wi-Fi

🐕	*Pets Welcome*	🎠	*Children Welcome*
SB	*Short Breaks*	♿	*Suitable for Disabled Guests*
⚲	*Licensed*	**Wi-Fi**	*Wi-Fi available*

The Exclusive Highland Estate of
ELLARY
and lovely
CASTLE SWEEN

SB

Wi-Fi

- Peace • Seclusion
- Variety of interests
- Freedom • History
- Outstanding scenery

This 15,000 acre Highland Estate lies in one of the most beautiful and unspoilt areas of Scotland and has a wealth of ancient historical associations within its bounds. There is St Columba's Cave, one of the first places of Christian Worship in Britain, also Castle Sween, the oldest ruined castle in Scotland, and Kilmory Chapel where there is a fascinating collection of Celtic slabs. There is a wide range of accommodation, from small groups of cottages, many of the traditional stone-built estate type, to modern holiday chalets and super luxury caravans at Castle Sween.

Most of the cottages accommodate up to six, but one will take six/eight.
All units fully equipped except linen.
Ellary is beautiful at all times of the year and is suitable for windsurfing, fishing, swimming, sailing and the observation of a wide variety of wildlife; there are paths and tracks throughout the estate for the visitor who prefers to explore on foot, and guests will find farmers and estate workers most helpful in their approach.
For further details, brochure and booking forms, please apply to:

ELLARY ESTATE OFFICE, by LOCHGILPHEAD, ARGYLL PA31 8PA

Tel: 01880 770232/770209
or 01546 850223
info@ellary.com
www.ellary.com

SB
Wi-Fi

Inchmurrin Island

SELF-CATERING HOLIDAYS

Inchmurrin is the largest island on Loch Lomond and offers a unique experience. Three self-catering apartments, sleeping from four to six persons, and a detached cedar clad cottage sleeping eight, are available.

The well appointed apartments overlook the garden, jetties and the loch beyond. Inchmurrin is the ideal base for watersports and is situated on a working farm.

Terms from £410 to £900 per week, £285 to £600 per half week.

A ferry service is provided for guests, and jetties are available for customers with their own boats. Come and stay and have the freedom to roam and explore anywhere on the island.

e-mail: scotts@inchmurrin-lochlomond.com
www.inchmurrin-lochlomond.com
Inchmurrin Island,
Loch Lomond G63 0JY
Tel: 01389 850245 • Fax: 01389 850513

Rothesay (Isle of Bute)

Taynuilt

Argyll & Bute is a wonderfully unspoilt area, historically the birthplace of Scotland and home to a wealth of fascinating wildlife. Here you may be lucky enough to catch a glimpse of an eagle, a wildcat or an osprey, whales, dolphin, seals, or even a giant octopus. At every step the sea fringed landscape is steeped in history, from prehistoric sculpture at Kilmartin and Knapdale, standing stone circles and Bronze Age cup-and-ring engravings, to the elegant ducal home of the once feared Clan Campbell. On the upper reaches of Loch Caolisport can be found St Columba's Cave, and more recent times are illustrated at the Auchindrain Highland Township south of Inveraray, a friendly little town with plenty to see, including the Jail, Wildlife Park and Maritime Museum. Sample the wonderful seafood and local whiskies, walk along the Atlantic beaches or in the Arrochar Alps, and visit the many beautiful gardens. Bute is the most accessible of the west coast islands, and Rothesay is its main town. Here find out about the island at the Discovery Centre, explore the dungeons and grand hall of Rothesay Castle, and visit the Victorian gothic splendour of Mount Stuart nearby.

Ayrshire & Arran

Borders

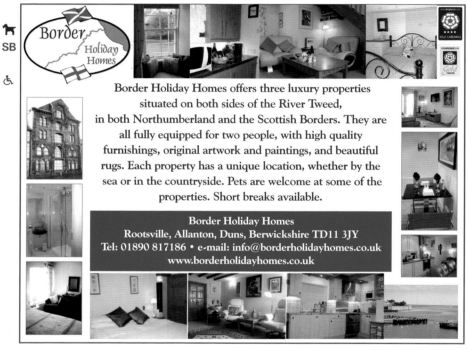

Border Holiday Homes offers three luxury properties situated on both sides of the River Tweed, in both Northumberland and the Scottish Borders. They are all fully equipped for two people, with high quality furnishings, original artwork and paintings, and beautiful rugs. Each property has a unique location, whether by the sea or in the countryside. Pets are welcome at some of the properties. Short breaks available.

Border Holiday Homes
Rootsville, Allanton, Duns, Berwickshire TD11 3JY
Tel: 01890 817186 • e-mail: info@borderholidayhomes.co.uk
www.borderholidayhomes.co.uk

Crossed by the River Tweed, which provides some of the best fishing in Scotland, the Scottish Borders stretch from the rolling hills and moorland in the west, through gentler valleys and agricultural plains, to the rocky Berwickshire coastline with its secluded coves and picturesque fishing villages. This variety of landscape has led to numerous opportunities for walking, horse riding and cycling, fishing and golf, as well as surfing, diving and birdwatching on the coast. Friendly towns, long known for their textiles, and charming villages are there to be discovered, while castles, abbeys, stately homes and museums illustrate the exciting and often bloody history of the area. It's this history which is commemorated in the Common Ridings and other local festivals, creating a colourful pageant much enjoyed by visitors and native Borderers alike.

Kelso, Melrose

SB

Wi-Fi

Relax in your south-facing conservatory and enjoy the splendid view over the large secluded garden to the Cheviots. Nestle before a log fire in your clean, cosy, well equipped 4-Star cottage for two within the peace of Burnbrae.

Within 40 minutes' drive of Edinburgh, fishing villages, superb coastal scenery, Borders towns, Cheviot and Ettrick Hills. Ideal for visiting a wealth of abbeys, gardens and stately homes. Fishing, walking, cycling, horse-riding and several golf courses nearby.

Just 5km from Kelso with splendid square and abbey ruins.

Terms £260 - £430 per week

• *All on one level* • *Entirely non-smoking*
• *Free broadband wi-fi* • *Dogs welcome in one cottage only* • *Helpful proprietors live on site*

Burnbrae Holidays • Burnbrae Mill • Nenthorn • Kelso TD5 7RY
Tel: 01573 225570
e-mail: fhg@burnbraehol.co.uk • www.burnbraehol.co.uk

...Simply Scottish Holiday Cottages

Welcome to
Melrose Self-Catering Cottages

Selected quality self-catering holiday accommodation in Melrose, all different but with a common theme ... welcoming, comfortable, enviable locations and value for money.
Each cottage has been personally selected, inspected and has met our demanding standards!
Visit our website to view individual cottages... you'll be impressed!

Pavilion Cottage • Sleeps 8

Old Mill House, Newstead • Sleeps 7

Hoebridge Stable Cottage • Sleeps 4

Glendevon, Melrose• Sleeps 7

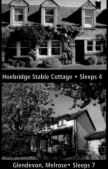

Melrose Self-Catering Cottages
Phone/Fax: 01896 820388
e-mail: info@melroseselfcatering.co.uk
www.melroseselfcatering.co.uk

Swallow Cottage • Sleeps 6

Castle Douglas

Dumfries & Galloway

Dumfries & Galloway combines high moorland and sheltered glens, forests, sandy beaches, crags, cliffs and rocky shores, presenting abundant opportunities for hill walking, rambling, fishing for salmon and sea trout, cycling, mountain biking, off-road driving, horse riding, pony trekking and bird watching. Catch a glimpse of a red kite soaring above, or a wild goat or red squirrel in the 300 square miles of the Galloway Forest Park or hunt for sea life in a rocky coastal pool. Golfers can choose from 30 courses, whether the challenging links at Southerness or a local course with spectacular views. Warmed by the influence of the Gulf Stream, touring in this quiet corner of south west Scotland is a pleasure, visiting the dozens of interesting castles, gardens, museums and historic sites.

Castle Douglas, Dalbeattie

Cloud Cuckoo Lodge

An enchanting and peaceful "dark skies" holiday cabin ... with a difference!

A very well appointed and lavishly equipped log cabin with a touch of luxury • Nestling amongst trees in spectacular Galloway countryside in South West Scotland, visited daily by bird life and red squirrels • Sleeps 6 • Three bedrooms, two double (one en suite) and one twin • Bathroom • Log burner • Washer/dryer • Barbecue • All linen, fuel, use of bicycles included • Easy reach of market towns and Solway coast beaches • Pets by arrangement.

Contact John & Lesley Wykes, Cuckoo Stone
St John's Town of Dalry, Castle Douglas DG7 3UA
Tel: 01644 430375
e-mail: enquiries@cloudcuckoolodge.co.uk
www.cloudcuckoolodge.co.uk

BAREND HOLIDAY VILLAGE   SANDYHILLS, DALBEATTIE DG5 4NU

Escape to the beautiful South West Colvend coast, the perfect base for walking, touring and cycling in Dumfries & Galloway, which is Scotland in miniature, and only one hour's drive from England. Our chalets, situated only a short walk from Sandyhills beach, are well equipped and centrally heated for all year comfort. Pets welcome or pet-free. Their decks overlook our loch or Colvend 18-hole golf course, and the surrounding countryside teems with wildlife - red squirrels, badgers and deer are our neighbours.

On-site boules courts, bar, restaurant, sauna and indoor pool. Wifi internet access available.

3 days minimum: any day of entry, prices include linen and swimming. From £260 for four for 3 days.

Tel: 01387 780663
www.barendholidayvillage.co.uk

Barend HOLIDAY VILLAGE

Quote FHG for 5% off new bookings

Gelston, Portpatrick

Rose Cottage
Gelston
Castle Douglas
Kirkcudbrightshire
DG7 1SH
Tel: 01556 502513

Dating back to 1760 and located in a quiet backwater, this holiday cottage borders a stream and waterfall and the large garden has a gated area for younger children to play in. Secluded sandy beaches a short drive away, water sports, birdwatching, walking, golf and fishing in the area. Shop, pub 2½ miles. Living room with open fire • Fully equipped kitchen • Sun room • Utility room. 4 bedrooms: 2 double, 2 twin. 2 bathrooms, each with shower over bath and toilet. Enclosed courtyard with sitting-out area and furniture. BBQ. Ample parking. No smoking.

Dunskey Holiday Cottages

SB

are well equipped, traditional, comfortable country cottages, for those who love to experience the peace and tranquillity of glorious countryside by the sea. The picturesque harbour village of Portpatrick with its good pubs, restaurants, shops, etc is only 1½ miles away and Dunskey's own Glen Walks are located very close to the holiday cottages.

Blair Cottage sleeps 4

This cosy, single storey cottage sits in a tranquil garden at the head of Dunskey Glen, one mile from Portpatrick. Sittingroom with dining table; open fire, central heating. Colour TV and video. One bedroom with double bed and one twin-bedded room. Well equipped kitchen. Night store heaters. Fenced garden with picnic table.

Glen Cottage sleeps 5

Situated above two small bays at the foot of Dunskey Glen, the ideal holiday home for a family who like the seclusion of the countryside, with the sea very near by. Two large bedrooms; one with a double bed, the other with three single beds. Sittingroom with log fire, colour TV and video. Well equipped kitchen with eating area. Bathroom with shaver point, shower. Night store heaters throughout.

Mrs Orr Ewing, Dunskey House, Portpatrick DG9 8TJ
Tel: 01776 810211 • info@dunskey.com • www.dunskey.com

Thornhill

Warmed by the influence of the Gulf Stream, touring in this quiet corner of south west Scotland is a pleasure, visiting the dozens of interesting castles, gardens, museums and historic sites. In addition a never-ending succession of music festivals, ceilidhs, village fairs, country dances, classical music concerts and children's entertainment guarantees plenty of scope for enjoyment, and for those whose interest is in the night skies a visit to the Galloway Forest Park, the UK's first designated Dark Sky Park, is a 'must'. Discover the many hidden secrets of this lovely and unspoilt landscape such as the pretty little villages along the coast, including the 'Artists' Town', Kirkcudbright, while those who love 'the written word' must surely visit the book town of Wigtown.

symbols 🐴 🐎 SB ♿ ⚲ Wi-Fi

🐴	*Pets Welcome*	🐎	*Children Welcome*
SB	*Short Breaks*	♿	*Suitable for Disabled Guests*
⚲	*Licensed*	**Wi-Fi**	*Wi-Fi available*

Loch Lomond

Dunbartonshire

The Gardeners Cottages
Arden, Loch Lomond

SB

Secluded in the wooded grounds of Arden House by the shores of Loch Lomond is the row of Gardeners Cottages, built as one side of a magnificent Victorian walled garden.
Linnhe and **Lomond** are ideal for families or friends (sleeping 4 to 5 each), and **Luss** is a perfect hideaway for two. Only 6 miles from the picturesque village of Luss and world famous Loch Lomond Golf Courses. The cottages are warm, comfortable and full of character, situated amidst breathtaking scenery.

Wi-Fi

The Gardeners Cottages, Loch Lomond G83 8RD
Tel/Fax 01389 850601
amacleod@gardeners-cottages.com
www.gardeners-cottages.com

The Lorn Mill Cottages

SB

Relax, unwind and recharge at The Lorn Mill - three peaceful and pretty cottages within an 18th century water mill. Tucked away in a secluded country estate overlooking Loch Lomond, the cottages provide a unique four seasons location in which to enjoy this gorgeous area of Scotland. Tennis court with stunning views. Perfect for couples.

We look forward to welcoming you.

ASSC

The Lorn Mill Cottages
Gartocharn,
Loch Lomond
Dunbartonshire G83 8LX

www.lornmill.com
e-mail: gavmac@globalnet.co.uk
Tel: 44 (0) 1389 753074

Lasswade

Edinburgh & Lothians

SB

Quality self-catering accommodation in an historic rural setting.
Seven properties including three new lodge cottages set within spacious grounds on the edge of a nature reserve, yet only 9 miles from Edinburgh centre. Nearby golf, fishing, riding, dri-skiing, walks and many historic buildings including Rosslyn Chapel. Great base for Edinburgh with the city's Princes Street only a 20 minute drive, Lothians, Borders and Fife within driving distance. Village shops, pubs one mile.

All properties have well equipped kitchens, linen provided, private safe gardens with patio and private parking. Electric heating is included in price and there is a tennis court on site for use by visitors.
Available all year. Sleep 4-7.

**Mrs Young,
Gorton House, Hawthornden,
Lasswade EH18 1EH
0131 440 4332 • Fax: 0131 440 1779
e-mail: info@gorton.plus.com • www.gorton.plus.com**

Visitors to Edinburgh, Scotland's capital, and the surrounding area, the Lothians, will find a wide range of attractions offering something for all ages and interests. Heritage is paramount, with historic and royal connections through the ages centred on Edinburgh Castle, the Palace of Holyroodhouse and the Scottish Parliament building. Outside the city East Lothian has beautiful countryside and a dramatic coastline, where once thriving fishing villages like North Berwick and Dunbar now cater for visitors who delight in their traditional seaside charm. You can step back in time with a visit to Rosslyn, Chapel or Borthwick and Crichton Castles in Midlothian, and to Mary Queen of Scots' birthplace at Linlithgow Palace in East Lothian. Outdoors, seize the chance to brush up on your golf swing at one of the historic links or more recent parkland courses in the area, or pay a visit to the Scottish Seabird Centre at North Berwick.

Colinsburgh

Fife

Cottage to let in a conservation village in the attractive East Neuk of Fife, 3 miles from Elie and 11 from St Andrews.
Easy reach of sandy beaches, coastal walks and numerous golf courses.
Two bedrooms, lounge, kitchen/diner and a walled rear garden. Sleeps 4/5, pets welcome. Prices from £275 per week.

SB

For further details, telephone
01788 890942 or see
www.eastneukcottage.co.uk

The Kingdom of Fife - and more particularly the coastal university town of St Andrews – is renowned worldwide as the home of golf, where not only the famous links, but parkland and heathland courses number among more than 40 available for golfers to choose from. The south of this small, self-contained former county has been dominated by industry and the Forth Road and Rail Bridges, the imposing road and rail links with Edinburgh and the south, but the sandy beaches and traditional fishing villages at places like Elie, Crail, Pittenweem, and Aberdour are major attractions for holidaymakers. They can be explored by following the Fife Coastal Path, stretching from to Crail to North Queensferry, where families will love the excitement of Deep Sea World with its Underwater Safari and seal sanctuary. The historic associations of centres like Dunfermline, Scotland's former capital, the restored medieval village of Culross and the Palace of Falkland make these just some of many fascinating places to visit.

Please note...

All the information in this book is given in good faith in the belief that it is correct. However, the publishers cannot guarantee the facts given in these pages, neither are they responsible for changes in policy, ownership or terms that may take place after the date of going to press. Readers should always satisfy themselves that the facilities they require are available and that the terms, if quoted, still apply.

Highlands

Tyndrum
Boat of Garten

Completely renovated, well furnished self-catering accommodation retaining the original pine panelling in the lounge.

Set in a rural village, Boat of Garten, in beautiful Strathspey, six miles from Aviemore, an ideal base for touring. Fishing is available locally on the River Spey, just two minutes away, with attractive riverside picnic spots. The famous Osprey nest is nearby, at Loch Garten RSPB Reserve. Local steam train journeys, good golf and water sports; skiing at Cairngorm in season. Shop and pub half a mile.

Large lounge, attractive dining/sitting room, spacious fully fitted dining kitchen, shower room. First floor: bathroom, one double and one twin room, both with washbasin, and one single bedroom. Colour TV with Sky digital; dishwasher, microwave, washer/dryer and deep freeze. Electricity, bed linen and towels inclusive. Parking. Large garden.

Contact: Mrs N.C. Clark, Dochlaggie, Boat of Garten PH24 3BU
Tel: 01479 831242 • e-mail: dochlaggie99@aol.com

Invermoriston
❖ Holidays

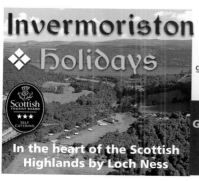

In the heart of the Scottish Highlands by Loch Ness

Invermoriston Holidays offer a peacefully secluded yet central location in spectacular scenery only a few hundred metres from Loch Ness. Offering home-from-home comfort and privacy, all have private patio area with barbecue and garden furniture. Games room, spacious play area, aerial glide and swings. Dogs are welcome in a selection of holiday chalets. Pay telephone and launderette on site. Sleep 2-4.

SB

Wi-Fi

Invermoriston Holiday Chalets
Glenmoriston, By Loch Ness, Highlands IV63 7YF
Tel: 01320 351254 Fax: 01320 351343
E-mail: info@invermoriston-holidays.co.uk
www.invermoriston-holidays.co.uk

Great Glen Holidays
Self Catering - Riding - Fishing

Eight timber chalets situated in woodland with spectacular mountain scenery. These spacious two-bedroom lodges are attractively furnished, with linen provided. On a working Highland farm, with riding, fishing and walking. Ideal for family holidays and an excellent base for touring; four miles from town. Sleep 4-5. Prices from £320 to £550 per week.

**Great Glen Chalets
Torlundy, Fort William PH33 6SW
Tel: 01397 703015
e-mail: chris.carver@btconnect.com
www.fortwilliam-chalets.co.uk**

Alvie Holiday Cottages
Kincraig, Inverness-shire

Situated amongst farm fields and woodland on a 13,000 acre Highland Estate. Located within the Cairngorm National Park, four miles south of Aviemore, Alvie can provide peace and quiet or an unsurpassed opportunity for recreation and activities. For details call **01540 651255** or see our website at

www.alvie-estate.co.uk

e-mail: info@alvie-estate.co.uk

Traditional cottages with superb views of the Cairngorms!

Spean Bridge, Ullapool

SB

Invergloy,
Spean Bridge
Inverness-shire
PH34 4DY

Tel: 01397 712684

Riverside Lodges
...the ultimate Highland location

Set in 12 acres of grounds, just three uniquely designed lodges sleeping six comfortably. Private beach with free fishing, spectacular river gorge, specimen trees and plants. Ideal for all outdoor pursuits, or for just relaxing. Tariff from £460-£780 per week; discounts for small parties/long stay. Pets welcome. Linen included.
Open all year. Proprietors: Steve & Marilyn Dennis.

enquiries@riversidelodge.org.uk • www.riversidelodge.org.uk

Two high quality self-catering apartments set in a stunning location on the banks of Loch Broom near Ullapool. Both are fully equipped, and each has its own separate access.

Broomview, on the ground floor, sleeps up to 5 comfortably in two double rooms, one en suite, and a single room; lounge with panoramic views; kitchen-diner; family bathroom. Rates £330-£430.

Sunset sleeps 3 in a double and a single room; kitchen-diner; shower room; lounge overlooking loch.

All bed linen included; oil-fired central heating; electric coin meter. Ample parking. No pets. Rates £220-£330.

Idyllic location for birdwatching, climbing, walking, fishing, photography, or just relaxing. A short drive away is the fishing village of Ullapool with its ferry terminal to the Western Isles.

Mrs Linda Renwick,
Spindrift, Keppoch Farm, Dundonnell,
By Garve, Ross-shire IV23 2QR
Tel & Fax: 01854 633269 (Quote FHG)
e-mail: linda@lochbroomcottages.co.uk
www.lochbroomcottages.co.uk

Perth & Kinross

LOCH TAY LODGES

Acharn, By Aberfeldy

This stone-built terrace houses six self catering lodges - three lodges sleep up to 4, two lodges sleep up to 6, one sleeps up to 8. They are fully equipped with colour television, washing machine, microwave, electric cooker & oven, and fridge. Bed linen, duvets and towels are all provided, electric blankets are also available. A separate drying area is available to hang up wet clothes or store bicycles. On the loch side 150 yards from the lodges there is access to a boat house to store sail boards, diving equipment and the like. A "starter pack' of groceries can be ordered from the village shop and will be delivered to your lodge prior to your arrival. Each lodge has own enclosed garden. Cots and highchairs available. Rates £240-£650.

Tel: 01887 830209
Fax: 01887 830802
e-mail: remony@btinternet.com
www.lochtaylodges.co.uk

SB

Altamount Leisure
Blairgowrie, Perthshire
SELF-CATERING ACCOMMODATION
01250 873512
www.altamountleisure.co.uk

Creiff, Dunkeld

Appreciate the countryside while cycling along the quiet roads, or experience the thrills of mountain biking. Enjoy a round of golf on any of Perthshire's 40 courses, including those at Gleneagles by Auchterarder. Water is an important element in the Perthshire landscape, and angling and sailing are two of the most popular activities on offer. Visit the romantic island on Loch Leven in lowland Kinross where Mary Queen of Scots was imprisoned. Also a nature reserve the loch is an amazing sight in autumn with the arrival of thousands of migrating geese. The historic city of Perth on the banks of the river Tay has plenty of shops with High Street names as well as specialist outlets selling everything from Scottish crafts to local pearls.

Fearnan, Killiecrankie

Hawthorn Cottage

Hawthorn Cottage is a comfortable 18th century cottage on the fringe of Fearnan village, Lochtayside, sleeping four plus cot. Sitting room with TV/DVD, hi-fi, books and board games. All-electric kitchen/diner with washing machine, tumble dryer, fridge, freezer, microwave etc. Bathroom with electric shower. Central heating. Enclosed garden with garden furniture, barbecue. Four-acre paddock for exercising pets, which are welcome by arrangement. Rates from £265-£370 per week

Hawthorn Cottage, Fearnan, Aberfeldy, Perthshire PH15 2PG
For further information please contact: Fraser MacLean,
Clach An Tuirc, Fearnan, By Aberfeldy, Perthshire PH15 2PG
Tel: 01887 830615 (enquiries are preferred by telephone first)
www.cottageguide.co.uk/hawthorn-cottage

Atholl Cottage • Killiecrankie • Perthshire

Atholl Cottage is situated between Pitlochry and Blair Atholl. It offers high quality self-catering accommodation in peaceful surroundings.

One twin room, one double bedroom + single bed • sitting room with Sky Freeview/DVD • well equipped kitchen with dining area • bathroom

Easy access to the A9 gives visitors the opportunity to explore some splendid and historic countryside. Golfing, hill walking, fishing, mountain bike riding and bird watching are all available locally. Pitlochry lies five miles to the south and offers a wide range of facilities, including interesting shops, good restaurants and bars, and the famous Pitlochry Festival Theatre. Atholl Cottage is about 4 miles south of the retail experience at House of Bruar.

Dogs are welcome at Atholl Cottage by prior arrangement.

**Joan Troup, Dalnasgadh, Killiecrankie,
Pitlochry, Perthshire PH16 5LN**
Tel: 01796 470017 • Fax: 01796 472183
e-mail: info@athollcottage.co.uk
www.athollcottage.co.uk

Muthill, Perth

The wonderful variety of landscape in Perthshire ensures not only that touring is a delight, but that all kinds of activities from canyoning to climbing, walking to white water rafting are available right in the centre of Scotland within easy reach of Glasgow and Edinburgh. From the southern fringes of the Cairngorm National Park and the 'gateway to the Highlands' at Pitlochry, with its Festival Theatre, through the long, narrow glens and alongside the tranquil lochs to the lowlands of the south, Perth & Kinross offers opportunities for a relaxing scenic break or action-packed adventure. Walk through the Big Tree Country and don't miss the giant Douglas fir near Dunkeld, where you can also view nesting opsreys at Loch of the Lowes. Pass by Britain's tallest hedge near Blairgowrie in the fruit-growing lowlands, and explore the cluster of little resort towns including Crieff, Comrie, Dunkeld, Aberfeldy, and Pitlochry, which have grown up along the Highland Boundary Fault separating north from south.

Pub & Inns

See the Supplement on pages 483-530

Alva

Stirling & The Trossachs

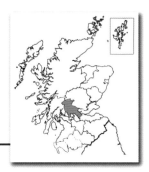

A walk through the medieval Old Town of Stirling, Scotland's newest city, is the ideal starting point for touring the area, then explore the wild glens and sparkling lochs in Loch Lomond and The Trossachs National Park, and perhaps take a steamer trip down Loch Katrine. Whatever your fitness, there are walks suitable for everyone, cycle routes, challenging mountain bike trails, golf and wildlife. The amazing Falkirk Wheel linking the Forth and Clyde and Union Canals is a sight and experience not to be missed, while villages and small towns such as Drymen, Killearn, Fintry and Kippen offer hospitality and interesting outings less than an hour from Glasgow, yet feels worlds apart from the bustle of city life.

Scottish Islands

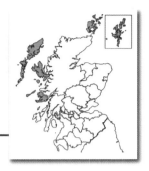

Modern stone-built house in own grounds situated at the head of Northbay with a panoramic view of the bay and islands. The front of the house is south-east facing and is a sun trap for relaxation (weather permitting). It is near to the church and Heathbank Hotel.

Small bedroom on ground floor, bathroom with electric shower, kitchen, sitting room/dining area with coal fire. Upstairs - two large double bedrooms, one with additional single bed.

Electricity is included in the price; bed linen is provided.

Colour TV, fridge/freezer, electric fires, microwave; double glazing throughout.

WEEKLY RENTAL: April £250 • May/September £250 • June £350 • July/August £500

3 Northbay Inn

Isle of Barra HS9 5XY • Tel: 01871 890 274

Contact: Mr Alexander MacInnes
49B Howden Hall Rd, Edinburgh EH16 6TY
Tel: 0131 664 6373 • Mobile 07717 222295
e-mail: macinnesalexander@yahoo.co.uk

So many islands are waiting to be visited off the Scottish mainland, each with a mystery and magic of its own. To the north lie the Orkney and Shetland Isles, with their strong connections to the Vikings whose influence is still seen and heard today. To the west, exposed to the Atlantic, lie the Inner and Outer Hebrides, including the islands of Skye, Islay, Mull and Tiree, Lewis, Harris and Barra, each with its own culture, traditions and heritage. Everywhere there's evidence of settlement going back to prehistoric times, including awe-inspiring standing stones and circles and chambered cairns. Some islands have mountains to climb, but most are low-lying, ideal for exploring on foot and for cycling and bird watching, while the Atlantic waves have proved a great attraction to surfers from all over the world.!.

info@visit-the-hebrides.co.uk

The Hebrides - timeless, miles of magnificent white sandy beaches, rugged mountains and peatlands, ever-changing skies and endless seascapes - a haven for photographers and artists.

Romance, peace and tranquillity....

Isn't it time you visited?

Ħannabreck
Dounby
Orkney Isles

Charming, recently refurbished old-style Orkney cottage. Two-bedroomed with old fashioned box beds. Bathroom with bath and level access shower. Living room has an open fire to burn peat, combined kitchen with dishwasher, washing machine/dryer. The flagstone and wooden floors are heated by ground source heat extracted from the surrounding land. Situated in quiet bird and wildlife conservation area. Many archaeological and historical sites nearby. Free local trout fishing. Internet access available.

Contact: Mrs P. Norquoy, Bigging, Dounby, Orkney Isles KW17 2HR • Tel: 01856 771340 e-mail: enquiries@lochlandchalets.co.uk www.hannabreck.co.uk

Irresistible Orkney

Hostel, Caravan and Camping Accommodation

Warbeth Beach overlooking the Hoy Hills

Point of Ness Caravan & Camping Site, Stromness

Stromness is a small picturesque town with impressive views of the hills of Hoy.
The site is one mile from the harbour in a quiet, shoreline location.
Many leisure activities are available close by, including fishing, sea angling, golf and a
swimming & fitness centre.
Contact: stromnesscashoffice@orkney.gov.uk or leisure.culture@orkney.gov.uk
www.orkney.gov.uk • Tel: 01856 850262

Birsay Outdoor Centre / Caravan & Camping Site

A new campsite located on the 3-Star hostel site in the picturesque north west of Orkney.

Hoy Centre

Four Star hostel accommodation with en suite facilities.
Ideal base for exploring Hoy's magnificent scenery and natural environment.

Rackwick Hostel

Rackwick is considered one of the most beautiful places in Orkney with towering cliffs and
steep heathery hills. This cosy hostel has spectacular views over Rackwick's cliffs and beach.
For Birsay, Hoy and Rackwick contact leisure.culture@orkney.gov.uk
Tel: 01856 873535 • www.hostelsorkney.co.uk

The Pickaquoy Centre and Camping Park, Kirkwall
Tel: 01856 879900

the pickaquoy centre

A 4-Star touring park with the latest in park amenities is situated at the Pickaquoy Centre
complex, an impressive leisure facility offering a range of activities for all the family.
Within walking distance of the St Magnus Cathedral and Kirkwall town centre.

e-mail: enquiries@pickaquoy.com
www.pickaquoy.co.uk

ORKNEY
ISLANDS COUNCIL

Port Ban Holiday Park

Kilberry, Tarbert, Argyll PA29 6YD
Tel: 01880 770224
www.portban.com
e-mail: portban@aol.com

Beautiful, remote, secluded, coastal park enjoying fantastic sunsets over the Paps of Jura. Many sports facilities including Games Hall, Putting Green, Football Pitch, Tennis Court, Crazy Golf, Bowling Green and also Bikes for Hire.
Sandy beaches and rock pools.
Organised events during school holidays including children's club, sports competitions and ceilidhs.

Ideal for wildlife enthusiasts – dolphins, seals, birds of prey, wildflowers etc.
Shop selling gifts and basic groceries.
Cafe selling snacks, homemade cakes and freshly ground coffees.
Standard and Luxury caravans for hire from £200 -£455 per week.

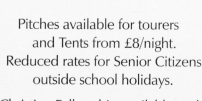

Pitches available for tourers and Tents from £8/night. Reduced rates for Senior Citizens outside school holidays.

Christian Fellowship available and Services held during School Holidays.

Kinlochleven

Newton Stewart

Almost a botanical garden, Linnhe is recognised as one of the best and most beautful Lochside parks in Britain. Magnificent gardens contrast with the wild, dramatic scenery of Loch Eil and the

mountains beyond. Superb amenities, launderette, shop & bakery, and free fishing on private shoreline with its own jetty all help give Linnhe its Five Star grading. Linnhe Lochside Holidays is ideally situated for

ay trips with Oban, Skye, Mull, Inverness and the airngorms all within easy driving distance.

- **Holiday Caravans from £240 per week**
- **Touring pitches from £16 per night**
- **Tent pitches from £12 per night**
- **Pets welcome**
- **Tourer playground, pet exercise area**
- **Motorhome waste and water facilities**
- **Recycling on park**
- **Colour brochure sent with pleasure.**

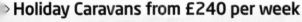

www.linnhe-lochside-holidays.co.uk/brochure
Tel: 01397 772 376 to check availability

John O'Groats, Laide

Roy Bridge

Welcome to Bunroy Park Caravan & Camping Site

....a haven of peace in the heart of the Highlands, set in 9 acres of secluded parkland, surrounded by breathtaking scenery, and within easy reach of Ben Nevis and Fort William, an ideal base for exploring, walking, cycling, fishing or just relaxing.

SB

• toilet/shower block • electric hook-ups
• laundry room • fridge & freezer
• short walk to two hotels, shop, Post Office and railway station.

Also available: 8 well equipped self-catering lodges with one/two bedrooms

**Alex & Flora Macdonald, Bunroy Park, Roy Bridge, Fort William PH31 4AG • Phone: 01397 712332
e mail : info@bunroycamping.co.uk • www.bunroycamping.co.uk**

Abington

symbols 🐕🐴 SB ♿ ♀ Wi-Fi

🐕 Pets Welcome		🐴 Children Welcome	
SB Short Breaks		♿ Suitable for Disabled Guests	
♀ Licensed		Wi-Fi Wi-Fi available	

Largo Leisure Parks

For Living Life to the Full

Our holiday parks are ideally suited for those seeking a tranq retreat with beautiful scenery, whilst enjoying the many a varied attractions of the Kingdom of Fife and Perthshire areas Scotland.

Holiday homes are perfect for getting away from it all. Our parks offer atmosphere to relax and enjoy the long holiday or short break.

Sauchope Links Park is situated on the shoreline, near the eastern most ti Fife in a beautiful, unspoilt position close to the historic town of Crail. This aw winning park with stunning views makes the perfect holiday destination.

Letham Feus Park is situated only 3 miles from Lundin Links with its championship course and beautiful sandy beach. The park is blessed with breathtaking views over Forth Estuary to the South and beautiful woodland to the north. Letham Feus i perfect place to take that well earned break.

Braidhaugh Park is situated on the banks of the River Earn amid the s surroundings of Crieff. The park is an ideal base from which to explore not the beautiful surroundings of Perthshire, but also the magnificent scenic gran of Central Scotland.

Loch Tay Highland Lodges Holiday Park is beautifully situated on a well established acre Highland Estate nestling on the shores of Loch Tay in Perthshire. It is the perfect all round holiday destination for those who love pure relaxation or for those energetic types love the great outdoors.

Sauchope Links Holiday Park, Crail, Fife KY1
Tel: 01333 450 460 info@sauchope.

Letham Feus Holiday Park, Cupar Rd by Lundin Links KY8
Tel: 01333 351 900 info@lethamfeus.

Braidhaugh Holiday Park, South Bridgend, Crieff PH7
Tel: 01764 652951 info@braidhaugh

Loch Tay Highland Lodges, Milton Morenish Estate by
Perthshire FK21 8TY Tel: 01567 82
info@lochtay-vacations.co.uk www.lochtay-vacations

Largo Leisure Parks

www.largoleisure.co.uk

Isle of Barra
Static Caravan for Hire

- One double bedroom
- Two rooms with single beds in each
- Living room • Kitchen with gas cooker
- Instant running hot and cold water • Gas heater
- Shower room • WC • Bed linen, utensils etc. provided.

Located at 12 Eoligarry, Isle of Barra HS9 5YD
Price from £200 per week.

Contact: Mr D. Maclean
Tel: 01871 890 723 or 0141 954 2101
email: barraaccommodation@hotmail.com

Ireland

Creveen Lodge

Immaculately run small hill farm overlooking Kenmare Bay in a striking area of County Kerry. Reception is found at the Lodge, which also offers guests a comfortable sitting room, while a separate block has well-equipped and immaculately maintained toilets and showers, plus a communal room with a large fridge, freezer and ironing facilities. The park is carefully tended, with bins and picnic tables informally placed, plus a children's play area with slides and swings.

There are 20 pitches in total, 16 for tents and 4 for caravans, with an area of hardstanding for motor caravans. Electrical connections are available. Fishing, bicycle hire, water sports and horse riding available nearby. SAE please, for replies.

Mrs M. Moriarty, Creveen Lodge, Healy Pass Road, Lauragh
Tel: 00 353 64 66 83131
e-mail: info@creveenlodge.com • www.creveenlodge.com

Pubs & Inns

A selection of inns, pubs and hostelries offering food, refreshment and traditional good cheer; many also provide comfortable overnight accommodation.

🛏 Accommodation available
🍽 Food available
🅿 Parking

Wi-Fi Wi-Fi available
🐕 Pets welcome
🎠 Children welcome

Kintbury

The Dundas Arms

53 Station Road, Kintbury RG17 9UT
Tel: 01488 658263 • Fax: 01488 658568

Set in an Area of Outstanding Natural Beauty on the banks of the Kennet and Avon Canal, this welcoming inn has provided sustenance for the hungry and thirsty traveller since the end of the 18th century.

Accommodation is available in five en suite bedrooms situated on the ground floor, all with patio doors leading to the terrace overlooking the River Kennet.

The restaurant provides a comfortable setting for enjoying the finest local produce prepared with flair and imagination; in the more relaxed atmosphere of the bar, diners can choose from an extensive blackboard menu.

Bed and Full English Breakfast
from £80 single, £90 double.

e-mail: info@dundasarms.co.uk
www.dundasarms.co.uk

Aylesbury

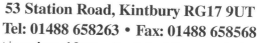

The Five Arrows

Waddesdon, Near Aylesbury, Buckinghamshire HP18 0JE
Tel: 01296 651727 • Fax: 01296 655716
e-mail: five.arrows@nationaltrust.org.uk • www.thefivearrows.co.uk

This charming small country hotel and restaurant stands at the gates of Waddesdon Manor. It was originally built by Baron Ferdinand de Rothschild to house the craftsmen and architects working on the Manor. There are nine en suite bedrooms and two suites. The bar and restaurant are open seven days a week. Lunch or dinner is a relaxed, informal experience, and on fine days may be enjoyed in the pretty courtyard and garden. It has a reputation for imaginative modern European food, with a wine list featuring a wide range of Rothschild wines.

Open for breakfast, morning coffee, lunch, afternoon tea and dinner
Sunday lunches are served from 12 noon to 3.30pm • Children welcome

Newport (Pembrokeshire)

TREWERN ARMS HOTEL

Nevern, Newport, Pembrokeshire SA42 0NB
Tel: 01239 820395 • Fax: 01239 820173

Cymru
Wales

★★★★

Inn

AA

★★★★
INN

www.trewernarms.com
e-mail: info@trewern-arms-pembrokeshire.co.uk

Set deep in a forested and secluded valley on the banks of the River Nevern, this picturesque, 16th century hostelry has a warmth of welcome that is immediately apparent in the interestingly-shaped Brew House Bar with its original flagstone floors, stone walls, old settles and beams decorated with an accumulated collection of bric-a-brac. Bar meals are served here from a popular grill area. By contrast, the Lounge Bar is furnished on cottage lines and the fine restaurant has received many accolades from far and wide for its culinary delights.

The tranquil village of Nevern is ideally placed for Pembrokeshire's historic sites and uncrowded, sandy beaches and the accommodation offered at this recommended retreat is in the multi-starred class.

Milton Keynes

DIFFERENT DRUMMER HOTEL
High Street, Stony Stratford,
Milton Keynes, Bucks MK11 1AH
Tel: 01908 564733 • Fax: 01908 260646
info@hoteldifferentdrummer.co.uk
www.hoteldifferentdrummer.co.uk

Wi-Fi

Known as 'The Swan with Two Necks' until 1982, this historic coaching inn has been transformed into a superbly furnished hotel, while maintaining its olde worlde charm. Guest rooms are en suite, with colour TV and satellite channels, free Wi-Fi access, and tea/coffee making facilities. The premises boasts an oak-panelled fine dining restaurant serving Italian and seafood dishes. There is also a modern and chic wine bar and restaurant, The Vine, which serves European and British fare, and an extensive selection of international wines.

SMALL HOTEL

Ely

THE ANCHOR INN
Sutton Gault, Near Ely, Cambridgeshire CB6 2BD

The 17th Century Anchor Inn offers modern British cuisine with an emphasis on seasonal and traditional ingredients; superb wine list. We have four guest bedrooms offering a variety of accommodation to suit every need. The Anchor is ideally situated for exploring East Anglia; it is only 7 miles from Ely and is less than half an hour from Cambridge. Newmarket and its racecourse are within easy reach.

AA
★★★★
Restaurant with Rooms

Tel: 01353 778537
Fax: 01353 776180
e-mail: anchorinn@popmail.bta.com
www.anchor-inn-restaurant.co.uk

RESTAURANT WITH ROOMS
★★★★

Eaton

The Plough
AT EATON

**Macclesfield Road, Eaton,
Near Congleton, Cheshire CW12 2NH
Tel: 01260 280207 • Fax: 01260 298458**

Traditional oak beams and blazing log fires in winter reflect the warm and friendly atmosphere of this half-timbered former coaching inn which dates from the 17th century.

The heart of the 'Plough' is the kitchen where food skilfully prepared is calculated to satisfy the most discerning palate. Luncheons and dinners are served seven days a week with traditional roasts on Sundays.

In peaceful, rolling countryside near the Cheshire/Staffordshire border, this is a tranquil place in which to stay and the hostelry has elegantly colour-co-ordinated guest rooms, all with spacious bathrooms, LCD colour television, direct-dial telephone and tea and coffee-making facilities amongst their impressive appointments. Wireless internet access available.

**e-mail: theploughinn@hotmail.co.uk
www.theploughinnateaton.co.uk**

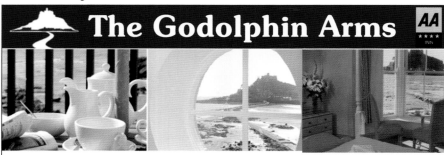

Cumberland Inn   Tel: 01434 381875

Townfoot, Alston, Cumbria CA9 3HX
stay@cumberlandinnalston.com
www.cumberlandinnalston.com

A comfy retreat in the secluded North Pennines. Within reach of the Lake District National Park. Real beer, real fires and real hospitality await your arrival.
Home-made hearty fare available all day to revive flagging spirits.
Our 5 recently refurbished rooms are all en suite.
An ideal base for walking, cycling and golfing.

The Black Cock Inn

The Black Cock Inn stands at the heart of the attractive little town of Broughton-in-Furness, within easy reach of some of the Lake District's finest scenery. This much-loved village inn is full of history, charm and atmosphere. This 16th century Inn with its low beamed ceiling boasts a suntrap courtyard garden during the summer and a roaring log fire during the winter months, giving it a wonderful traditional ambience.

Princes Street,
Broughton-in-Furness
Cumbria LA20 6HQ
Tel: 01229 716529
theblackcockinn20@gmail.com
www.blackcockinncumbria.co.uk

There's always a selection of real ales and lagers on offer in the bar which is open from morning 'til night, every day.

The inn has five comfortable and very well appointed en suite guest bedrooms.

There is excellent walking country in the area, with plenty of history and natural features to discover, and Broughton itself is well worth taking time to explore.

 Accommodation available

 Food available

 Parking

Wi-Fi Wi-Fi available

 Pets welcome

 Children welcome

Brampton

Welcome to...

The Blacksmith's Arms offers all the hospitality and comforts of a traditional country inn. Enjoy tasty meals served in the bar lounges, or linger over dinner in the well appointed restaurant. The inn is personally managed by the proprietors, Anne and Donald Jackson, who guarantee the hospitality one would expect from a family concern. Guests are assured of a pleasant and comfortable stay. There are eight lovely bedrooms, all en suite.

Peacefully situated in the beautiful village of Talkin, the inn is convenient for the Borders, Hadrian's Wall and the Lake District.
There is a good golf course, walking and other country pursuits nearby.

The Blacksmiths Arms
Talkin Village, Brampton, Cumbria CA8 1LE
Tel: 016977 3452 • Fax: 016977 3396
e-mail: blacksmithsarmstalkin@yahoo.co.uk
www.blacksmithstalkin.co.uk

The Boot Inn

Caroline & Sean welcome you to Boot Inn, dating in parts from 1570, and situated in the centre of the tiny village of Boot in Eskdale. This stunning valley offers superb walks for all abilities from a riverside stroll to an assault on Scafell straight from our door.

In the restaurant, the bar or the conservatory, we offer a comprehensive menu and a daily Chef's Specials board. All our food is homemade using local produce wherever possible as we are very aware of the impact of 'food miles', including free range eggs from local farms, Bewley's beef and Cumberland Sausages, and local cheeses . We specialise in traditional hearty home cooking and baking.

There are 9 comfortable en suite rooms, a lovely beer garden with separate children's play areas and wonderful fell views.

Pet-friendly.

Special Breaks regularly available on our website.

The Boot Inn, Boot, Eskdale, Cumbria CA19 1TG
Tel: 019467 23224
e-mail: enquiries@bootinn.co.uk
www.bootinn.co.uk

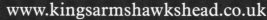

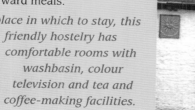

Ulverston

The Stan Laurel Inn

Situated just 30 minutes from M6 (junction 36) is the bustling historic market town of Ulverston with its wonderful cobbled streets and yards. An ideal base to explore the South Lakes area, with Windermere, Kendal, Bowness, Coniston and Morecambe Bay all within easy reach of the town. The coast is only two miles away, and the area offers plenty of nice walks.

The inn is named after Stan Laurel (of Laurel and Hardy fame), who was born and lived in Ulverston before moving to America. Also situated in the town is the world famous Laurel and Hardy museum, well worth a visit while you are here.

We are located close to the town centre and offer six changing cask ales, good quality home-cooked food, and comfortable accommodation. Three bedrooms, two en suite.

Good service, good food, good beer... what more could you ask for!

Stan Laurel Inn, 31 The Ellers, Ulverston LA12 0AB
Tel: 01229 582814 • e-mail: thestanlaurel@aol.com

Further information on menus and pictures can be viewed on our website: **www.thestanlaurel.co.uk**

The Bridge Inn
Santon Bridge

The Bridge Inn, once a coach halt, is now a fine, comfortable, award-winning country inn, offering hospitality to all travellers and visitors.

◆The Inn has an excellent reputation for good food, with "real" food served in the Dalesman Bar, or in the Eskdale Room.

◆We serve an excellent selection of Jennings real ales.

◆ Weddings and other private and business functions catered for in our function room.

◆ Licensed for civil ceremonies, partnerships, naming ceremonies and renewal of vows.

◆16 bedrooms. ◆Dogs welcome. ◆Free Wi-Fi

10 minute drive to "Britain's favourite view – Wastwater"

This unspoiled area of the Lake District offers superb walking and climbing.

Features in the 'Good Beer & Pub Guide' 2011

Bridge Inn
Santon Bridge, Wasdale
Cumbria CA19 1UX
Tel: 019467 26221 • Fax: 019467 26026
info@santonbridgeinn.com
www.santonbridgeinn.com

Nestling in a peaceful setting in the Gilpin Valley, The Wild Boar benefits from beautiful surrounding countryside, including its own private 72 acres of woodland, and many other Lake District attractions close by.

A special venue for many an occasion, whether that be a romantic or adventurous break, family get-together, intimate business meeting or as one of our very valued frequent diners.

After undergoing a refurbishment The Wild Boar now offers individually designed bedrooms, Grill and Smokehouse with an open kitchen and chef's table.

THE WILD BOAR
INN, GRILL & SMOKEHOUSE
NEAR WINDERMERE
CUMBRIA LA23 3NF
RESERVATIONS: 08458 504 604
www.wildboarinn.co.uk

English Lakes Hotels Resorts & Venues

Ashbourne

Dog & Partridge
Country Inn
With rooms in the grounds

HOTEL ★★

enjoyEngland.com

Short Breaks & Offers available throughout the year

Mary and Martin Stelfox welcome you to this family-run 17th century Inn and Motel set in five acres, five miles from Alton Towers and close to Dovedale and Ashbourne. We specialise in family breaks, and special diets and vegetarians are catered for.

Children and pets welcome.

Accommodation at the Dog and Partridge is purpose-built and situated in the grounds with own parking directly outside.

Most rooms have en suite facilities and all have flat screen TV with Freeview, DVD player, tea/coffee making facilities, clock radio, direct telephone, ample heating and hot water. Family suites available.

Free Wi-Fi internet access. Hot tub and private garden.

Ideal for touring Stoke Potteries, Derbyshire Dales and Staffordshire Moorlands. Open Christmas and New Year. Restaurant open all day, non-residents welcome.

e-mail: info@dogandpartridge.co.uk
Tel: 01335 343183 • www.dogandpartridge.co.uk
Swinscoe, Ashbourne DE6 2HS

Hope Valley

Dartmoor, Dittisham

Mark and Judy Harrison
welcome you to

THE ROYAL OAK INN
Dunsford, Devon

The Royal Oak is a traditional village pub in the heart of the beautiful Devon village of Dunsford. It's a family-run place with a warm, friendly atmosphere and something for everyone.

Real ales from all over Britain. The kitchen serves generous portions of home-cooked good food with regular well-known specials.

The Royal Oak has a walled courtyard and a large Beer Garden with beautiful views across Dunsford and the Teign Valley

Dogs on leads are welcome and there are lots of animals to visit, great for children with our own play area. Plenty of off-road parking.

Quiet newly refurbished en suite bedrooms are available in the tastefully converted 400 year old granite and cob cob barn located to the rear of the Inn. All non-smoking. Each room has its own front door which opens out onto a pretty, walled courtyard. Ideal base for touring Dartmoor, Exeter and the coast

The Royal Oak Inn
Dunsford, Near Exeter, Devon EX6 7DA

TEL: 01647 252256 • e-mail:mark@troid.co.uk • www.royaloakd.com

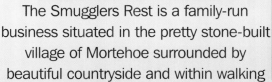

The Smugglers Rest is a family-run business situated in the pretty stone-built village of Mortehoe surrounded by beautiful countryside and within walking distance of the beaches and coves of the North Devon coast.

The luxury accommodation ranges from twin rooms through to the family suites. All rooms are en suite and have tea & coffee making facilities.

Treat yourselves and your pets to beautiful coastal walks and golden beaches, before you sample our delicious home-cooked meals, real ales and warm, year round hospitality.

The Smugglers Rest

**North Morte Road, Mortehoe,
North Devon EX34 7DR
Tel/Fax: 01271 870891
thesmugglersrest@gmail.com
www.thesmugglersrest.co.uk**

Chelmsford

Moreton-in-Marsh

Parkend

The Fountain Inn & Lodge

Parkend, Royal Forest of Dean, Gloucestershire GL15 4JD

Traditional village inn, well known locally for its excellent meals and real ales.

A Forest Fayre menu offers such delicious main courses as Lamb Shank in Redcurrant and Rosemary Sauce, and locally made sausages, together with a large selection of curries, vegetarian dishes, and other daily specials.

Centrally situated in one of England's foremost wooded areas, the inn makes an ideal base for sightseeing, or for exploring some of the many peaceful forest walks nearby.

All bedrooms (including two specially adapted for the less able) are en suite, decorated and furnished to an excellent standard, and have television and tea/coffee making facilities.

Tel: 01594 562189 • Fax: 01594 564438
e-mail: thefountaininn@aol.com • www.thefountaininnandlodge.com

Fordingbridge

Three Lions
Stuckton, near Fordingbridge, Hampshire SP6 2HF
Tel: 01425 652489 • Fax: 01425 656144

A place to relax in a beautiful setting and come and go as you please without the formality of a hotel.
All bedrooms are en suite, overlooking the gardens and beyond to the forest. Hot tub and Sauna.
Ground floor accommodation with ease of access for less mobile guests.

Local attractions include the New Forest, the Dorset and Hampshire coastline with coastal walks and sandy beaches, and the cathedral cities of Salisbury and Winchester.
Family activities nearby include a leisure pool centre, Marwell Zoo, Paulton's Fun Park and Beaulieu Car Museum.
Three times Hampshire 'Restaurant of the Year', Good Food Guide.

www.thethreelionsrestaurant.co.uk

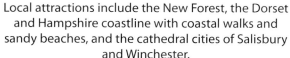

New Forest

Wi-Fi

Tyrrells Ford Country Inn
Avon, Near Ringwood,
New Forest BH23 7BH
Tel: 01425 672646 • Fax: 01425 672262
e-mail: info@tyrrellsford.co.uk
www.tyrrellsford.co.uk

This elegant and handsomely furnished 18th Century Country House is
set in 8 acres of beautiful grounds on the edge of the New Forest.
The public and private rooms exhibit a wealth of fine panelling,
especially in Tyrrells Bar and the sumptuous Tattersalls Restaurant
where the worth of the chef inspired à la carte and table d'hôte cuisine
is proclaimed far and wide. Guest rooms are charming, all have
en suite facilities, colour TV, radio alarm, direct-dial telephone and
tea and coffee making facilities. There are prime opportunities for golf,
fishing, riding and walking in the vicinity and the delightful and diverse
attractions of Bournemouth may be reached in 15 minutes.

A jewel of a hotel well worth a visit.

Leominster

The New Inn
**Market Square, Pembridge,
Leominster,
Herefordshire HR6 9DZ
Tel: 01544 388427**

The last battle of the Wars of the Roses was fought just a few miles from here
at Mortimers Cross, and the treaty which gave England's crown to the Yorkist
leader is believed to have been signed in the courtroom of this fourteenth
century inn. Two ghosts are said to haunt the Inn: one a girl who appears only
to women; the other a red-coated soldier armed with a sword.

*A varied and interesting menu is offered at most reasonable prices in
the bar, which has a log fire to warm it on chillier days, and the
attractive lounge area is a popular venue for cosy evening dinners.*

The Rob Roy

**Dock Road, Tweedmouth
Berwick-upon-Tweed
Northumberland TD15 2BE
Tel & Fax: 01289 306428**

Your hosts Ian and Linda Woods extend to you the warmest welcome to this family-run Northumberland B&B.

Situated in Tweedmouth, in historic Berwick-upon-Tweed, the Rob Roy is a guest house in the classic, welcoming Northumberland style.

Within easy walking distance of Berwick-upon-Tweed town centre and also Spittal beach and promenade.

Perfect for Northumberland holidays and visitors keen to explore the open country, historic sites and remarkable coastline of this beautiful county.

The five bedrooms, three double rooms, one twin room, and a family room, all have en suite facilities and are comfortable and stylishly furnished with television, tea and coffee making facilities, alarm clocks and hairdryers. Free Wi-Fi is also available.

The guest lounge with real fire and stone walls is the perfect place to relax and can also be used for a private function or business meeting.

The fully licensed bar is well stocked with real ales and a selection of wines, while the popular beer garden is a great way to enjoy a drink whilst taking in the views of the River Tweed as it joins the North Sea.

Prices start from £60 per night for a double or twin room, £75 for the family room and £45 for single occupancy.

Prices include breakfast, chosen from a full English selection or alternatives. Lunches and dinners are also available at the Rob Roy in our Harbour Lights Restaurant, serving the best of fresh produce locally sourced wherever possible.

www.robroyberwick.co.uk • e-mail: therobroy@hotmail.co.uk

The Anglers Arms

A Legend in the very Heart of Northumberland

This traditional Coaching Inn is situated only 6 miles from Morpeth, beside picturesque Weldon Bridge on the River Coquet. Bedrooms are cosy and welcoming, with a touch of olde worlde charm. Be prepared for a hearty Northumbrian breakfast!

Meals can be be enjoyed in the friendly bar, or outdoors on sunny summer days; alternatively dine in style and sophistication in the à la carte Pullman Railway Carriage restaurant. Ideal for exploring both coast and country, the Inn also caters for fishermen, with its own one-mile stretch of the River Coquet available free to residents.

The Anglers Arms
Weldon Bridge,
Longframlington,
Northumberland NE65 8AX
Tel: 01665 570271/570655
info@anglersarms.fsnet.co.uk
www.anglersarms.com

The Black Bull Hotel

2 High Street, Wooler NE71 6BY
Tel & Fax: 01668 281309
e-mail: theblackbullhotel@hotmail.com
www.theblackbullhotel.co.uk

17thC coaching inn situated on the main street of Wooler, a wonderful base for walking, riding, golf and fishing.

The hotel is fully licensed and serves good home-made food each lunchtime and evening.

All rooms en suite, with hairdryers, tea/coffee making facilities and Freeview TV. Wifi available. Gym for use of guests.

Accommodation available		**Wi-Fi** Wi-Fi available
Food available		Pets welcome
Parking		Children welcome

Wi-Fi

Main Street, Seahouses, Northumberland NE68 7RD
Tel: 01665 720200 • Fax: 01665 721383

A former farmhouse dating from 1745, the inn stands overlooking the harbour in the village of Seahouses.

The Olde Ship, first licensed in 1812, has been in the same family for over 100 years and is now a fully residential hotel.

All guest rooms, including three with four-poster beds, and executive suites with lounges and sea views, are en suite, with television, refreshment facilities, direct-dial telephone and Wi-Fi.

The bars and corridors bulge at the seams with nautical memorabilia. Good home cooking features locally caught seafood, along with soups, puddings and casseroles.

www.seahouses.co.uk
e-mail: theoldeship@seahouses.co.uk

The Talbot

15th Century Coaching Inn
at Mells, Near Frome BA11 3PN

Set in the enchanting Somerset village of Mells, the historic Talbot Inn offers beautiful en suite accommodation, an award-winning restaurant and all the charm of a traditional English inn.

Close to some of the country's most popular attractions, including Bath, Longleat, Cheddar and Wells, the Talbot Inn is the perfect base for exploring this charming corner of England.

Traditional comforts and modern convenience combine to make the Talbot Inn the ideal place for a relaxing weekend break or a base for exploring the beautiful countryside and historic towns and villages around Somerset and Bath. An ideal area for walkers, cyclists and golfers.

All our rooms are named after characters from the history of Mells - from Little Jack Horner to the poet Siegfried Sassoon, and offer supreme comfort and thoughtful amenities.

Dining here offers an award-winning à la carte menu of traditional English food with a delicate French influence, sourced from the best local ingredients. The informal restaurant offers a backdrop of extremes, with low oak beams and ceiling hops the alternative to a front room that would grace any country house hotel.

On sunny days, enjoy al fresco dining in the garden area. Our overnight guests are served a freshly cooked English breakfast, whilst the Talbot's Sunday lunch has become a Mells institution.

Tel: 01373 812254
enquiries@talbotinn.com
www.talbotinn.com

The Bull Inn

Woolpit • Bury St Edmunds

The Bull Inn at Woolpit, near Bury St Edmunds, is a traditional Suffolk Country family-run Pub, offering a warm welcome, very comfortable accommodation and excellent service, together with good traditional food and ales and a fine selection of wines.

In the centre of a pretty village just off the A14 between Bury St. Edmunds and Stowmarket, The Bull Inn is within easy reach of all parts of this beautiful county, and offers an ideal base for touring East Anglia.

Whether you want to pop in for a quick drink, enjoy a leisurely lunch or dinner, or stay a while in one of the comfortable en suite bedrooms, you will be most welcome.

The Bull Inn offers a choice of accommodation, either singles, doubles or family rooms. All our rooms offer en suite facilities, tea/coffee making facilities and TV.

The Bull Inn & Restaurant
The Street, Woolpit, Bury St Edmunds IP30 9SA
Tel: 01359 240393 • e-mail: info@bullinnwoolpit.co.uk
www.bullinnwoolpit.co.uk

Gomshall

Alfriston

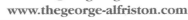

Hindon

The Lamb Inn

High Street, Hindon
Wiltshire SP3 6DP
Tel: 01747 820573 • Fax: 01747 820605
www.lambathindon.co.uk

The fascinating history of this ancient inn is related in its brochure, which reveals among other intriguing facts that it was once the headquarters of a notorious smuggler. No such unlawful goings-on today – just good old-fashioned hospitality in the finest traditions of English inn-keeping. Charmingly furnished single, double and four-poster bedrooms provide overnight guests with cosy country-style accommodation, and the needs of the inner man (or woman!) will be amply satisfied by the varied, good quality meals served in the bar and restaurant. Real ales can be enjoyed in the friendly bar, where crackling log fires bestow charm and atmosphere as well as warmth.

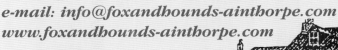

Wi-Fi

Skipton

Dolgellau

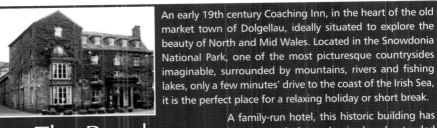
Accommodation available		**Wi-Fi** Wi-Fi available
Food available		Pets welcome
Parking		Children welcome

Hay-on-Wye

Wi-Fi

BASKERVILLE ARMS HOTEL

Delightfully placed in the upper reaches of the Wye Valley with the Black Mountains and Brecon Beacons on the doorstep, this comfortable retreat could not be better placed for lovers of both lush and wild unspoilt scenery. Hay-on-Wye, the 'town of books' is only 1.2 miles away with its narrow streets, antique shops and over 30 bookshops.

Run by resident proprietors, June and David, the hotel provides tasty, home-cooked food in bar and restaurant, using the best local produce.

Cymru Wales ★★★

With so many pursuits to enjoy in the area, this little hotel is a fine holiday base and well-appointed en suite bedrooms serve the purpose excellently. Totally non-smoking.

Single from £55, Double/Twin from £79.
See website for Special Rate Breaks.

Clyro, Near Hay-on-Wye, Herefordshire HR3 5RZ
Tel: 01497 820670
e-mail: info@baskervillearms.co.uk
www.baskervillearms.co.uk

Llanymynech, Powys SY22 6EJ

Set in the historic village of Llanymynech, this former coaching inn has been renovated and upgraded to a very high standard. There are 5 superb bedrooms, all en suite, with tea/coffee making facilities and colour TV.

High quality home-cooked cuisine using local produce is served in the conservatory or more formal restaurant.

Situated in an area of outstanding natural beauty on the English/Welsh border, the hotel is an ideal base for walking on the nearby Offa's Dyke Trail and for exploring this historic area.

Tel: 01691 830582 • Fax: 01691 839009
e-mail: catelou@tesco.net • www.bradfordarmshotel.com

Craignure Inn is a small characteristic old drovers' inn providing excellent service, food and accommodation whether you're looking for a longer holiday, full of fun outdoor wildlife activities, or simply a relaxing short break for you and your family, partner or friend.

The main attractions of the island, Torosay Castle and its gardens, and Duart

Castle with its Clan Maclean history, are at your doorstep. If you are lucky you might just see dolphins in Craignure Bay and otters just across the road by the rocks on the seashore. The Inn is open all year and prides itself on its friendly staff and warm welcome. It is favoured by locals and visitors alike.

There are three letting rooms, all en suite, with colour television and tea/coffee making facilities. The bar has a wide range of malts, fine wines, a large fire for the cooler evenings, outdoor seating and a cosy lounge.

There is an extensive bar menu with many wholesome, home cooked offerings using local produce such as Highland Beef, Hebridean Lamb, Mussels, Mull Cheddar and Smoked Trout.

We have regular live entertainment and welcome well behaved dogs. We provide information on local walks, trips and tours. Bus tours leave from Craignure, making it a great base for those without their own transport.

Craignure Inn
Isle of Mull, Argyll PA65 6AY
Tel: 016808 12305
craignureinn@btconnect.com
www.craignure-inn.co.uk

Portpatrick

THE **Harbour House** HOTEL

**53 Main Street,
Portpatrick
DG9 8JW**

**Tel: 01776 810456
Fax: 01776 810488**

Photo by southrhinswebdesign.com

Julie and Steve Reynolds, owners of the Harbour House Hotel, take pride in offering personal attention and the warmest hospitality.

Choose from the extensive menu of home-cooked Scottish country-style food, either in the bar or in the non-smoking bistro. All bedrooms have en suite or private bathrooms, and most enjoy sea views. The newly refurbished bar is the perfect place for a morning coffee, a lunchtime snack or a cosy evening with a well-conditioned pint or a malt whisky from the extensive selection. Portpatrick is an ideal base for the many leisure opportunities the area has to offer, as well as for visiting Port Logan Botanic Gardens.

www.theharbourhousehotel.co.uk

Thurso

This former 19th century coaching inn on the John O'Groats peninsula is set in six acres of parkland, close to the Queen Mother's former Highland home, the Castle of Mey.

Fully modernised, the hotel has eight centrally heated en suite bedrooms with colour television and tea making facilities; the spacious Pentland Suite offers a double and family room with en suite bathroom.

Locally caught salmon, crab and other fine Highland produce feature on the varied table d'hôte and grill menus available in the Garden Room, while lighter meals and snacks can be enjoyed in the cosy Pentland Lounge.

A warm Highland welcome awaits you.

**www.castlearms.co.uk
Tel & Fax: 01847 851244
e-mail: castlearms.mey@btinternet.com**

THE CASTLE ARMS
HOTEL
Mey, By Thurso,
Caithness KW14 8XH

THE FERRY BOAT INN &

THE FRIGATE

We welcome you to The Ferry Boat Inn on the shorefront in Ullapool. All of our 9 bedrooms are en suite and we offer Bar Meals or fine dining in our beautiful Restaurant.

**Ferry Boat Inn
Shore Street
Ullapool IV26 2UJ
Tel: 01854 612 366
www.ferryboat-inn.com**

THE FRIGATE CAFÉ & BISTRO

High quality licensed Bistro, Café, Outside Caterers, Deli, Bakery and Take Away

Frigate Café, Shore Street, Ullapool, IV26 2UJ
Tel: 01854 612 969
www.ullapoolcatering.co.uk

DIRECTORY OF WEBSITE AND E-MAIL ADDRESSES

A quick-reference guide to holiday accommodation with an e-mail address and/or website, conveniently arranged by country and county, with full contact details.

•LONDON

Hotel
Athena Hotel, 110-114 Sussex Gardens, Hyde Park, LONDON W2 1UA
Tel: 020 7706 3866
• e-mail: stay@athenahotellondon.co.uk
• website: www.athenahotel.co.uk

B & B
Hanwell B & B, 110a Grove Avenue, Hanwell, LONDON W7 3ES
Tel: 020 8567 5015
• e-mail: tassanimation@aol.com
• website: www.ealing-hanwell-bed-and-breakfast.co.uk/new/index

Hotel
Queens Hotel, 33 Anson Road, Tufnell Park, LONDON N7 0RB
Tel: 020 7607 4725
• e-mail:stay@queenshotellondon.co.uk
• website: www.queenshotellondon.co.uk

•BERKSHIRE

Touring Campsite
Wellington Country Park, Odiham Road, Riseley, Near READING, Berkshire RG7 1SP
Tel : 0118 932 6444
• e-mail: info@wellington-country-park.co.uk
• website: www.wellington-country-park.co.uk

•CAMBRIDGESHIRE

Guest House
Hamden Guest House, 89 High Street, Cherry Hinton, CAMBRIDGE, Cambridgeshire CB1 9LU
Tel: 01223 413263
• e-mail: info@hamdenguesthouse.co.uk
• website: www.hamdenguesthouse.co.uk

•CHESHIRE

Farmhouse B & B
Astle Farm East, Chelford, MACCLESFIELD, Cheshire SK10 4TA
Tel: 01625 861270
• e-mail: stubg@aol.com
• website: www.astlefarmeast.co.uk

•CORNWALL

Self-Catering
Penrose Burden Holiday Cottages, St Breward, BODMIN, Cornwall PL30 4LZ
Tel : 01208 850277
• website: www.penroseburden.co.uk

Self-Catering
Mr P. Watson, Creekside Holiday Houses, Restronguet, FALMOUTH, Cornwall TR11 5ST
Tel: 01326 372722
• website: www.creeksideholidayhouses.co.uk

Self-Catering
Fowey Harbour Cottages c/o WJB Hill & Son, 3 Fore Street, FOWEY, Cornwall PL23 1AH
Tel: 01726 832211
• e-mail: hillandson@talk21.com
• website: www.foweyharbourcottages.co.uk

Self-Catering / Caravan
Mrs A. E. Moore, Hollyvagg Farm, Lewannick, LAUNCESTON, Cornwall PL15 7QH
Tel: 01566 782309
• website: www.hollyvaggfarm.co.uk

Self-Catering
Butterdon Mill Holiday Homes, Merrymeet, LISKEARD, Cornwall PL14 3LS
Tel: 01579 342636
• e-mail: butterdonmillst@btconnect.com
• website: www.bmhh.co.uk

Self-Catering

Celia Hutchinson, Caradon Country Cottages, East Taphouse, LISKEARD, Cornwall PL14 4NH
Tel: 01579 320355
• e-mail: celia@caradoncottages.co.uk
• website: www.caradoncottages.co.uk

Self- Catering

Mr Lowman, Cutkive Wood Holiday Lodges, St Ive, LISKEARD, Cornwall PL14 3ND
Tel: 01579 362216
• e-mail: holidays@cutkivewood.co.uk
• website: www.cutkivewood.co.uk

Self-Catering

Valleybrook Holidays, Peakswater, Lansallos, LOOE, Cornwall PL13 2QE
Tel: 01503 220493
• e-mail: admin@valleybrookholidays.com
• website: www.valleybrookholidays.com

Guest House

Mrs Dewolfreys, Dewolf Guest House, 100 Henver Road, NEWQUAY, Cornwall TR7 3BL
Tel: 01637 874746
• e-mail: holidays@dewolfguesthouse.com
• website: www.dewolfguesthouse.com

Caravan / Camping

Quarryfield Caravan & Camping Park, Crantock, NEWQUAY, Cornwall
Contact: Mrs A Winn, Tretherras, Newquay, Cornwall TR7 2RE
Tel: 01637 872792
• e-mail: quarryfield@crantockcaravans.orangehome.co.uk
• website: www.quarryfield.co.uk

B&B

Bolankan Cottage B & B, Crows-an-Wra, St Buryan, PENZANCE, Cornwall TR19 6HU
Tel: 01736 810168
• e-mail: bolankancottage@talktalk.net
• website: www.bolankan-cottage.co.uk

Caravan / Camping

Globe Vale Holiday Park, Radnor, REDRUTH, Cornwall TR16 4BH
Tel: 01209 891183
• e-mail: info@globevale.co.uk
• website: www.globevale.co.uk

Guest House

Mr S Hope, Dalswinton House, ST MAWGAN-IN-PYDAR, Cornwall TR8 4EZ
Tel: 01637 860385
• e-mail: dalswintonhouse@btconnect.com
• website: www.dalswinton.com

Self-Catering

Maymear Cottage, ST TUDY
Contact: Ruth Reeves, Polstraul, Trewalder, Delabole, Cornwall PL33 9ET
Tel: 01840 213120
• e-mail: ruth.reeves@hotmail.co.uk
• website: www.maymear.co.uk

Self-Catering

The Garden House, Port Isaac, Near WADEBRIDGE, Cornwall
Contact: Mr D Oldham, Trevella, Treveighan, St Teath, Cornwall PL30 3JN
Tel: 01208 850529
• e-mail: david.trevella@btconnect.com
• website: www.trevellacornwall.co.uk

•CUMBRIA

Guest House / Self- Catering

Cuckoo's Nest & Smallwood House, Compston Road, AMBLESIDE, Cumbria LA22 9DJ
Tel: 015394 32330
• e-mail: enq@cottagesambleside.co.uk
  enq@smallwoodhotel.co.uk
• website: www.cottagesambleside.co.uk
  www.smallwoodhotel.co.uk

Caravan Park

Greenhowe Caravan Park, Great Langdale, AMBLESIDE, Cumbria LA22 9JU
Tel: 015394 37231
•website: www.greenhowe.com

Self-Catering

Lakelovers, Belmont House, Lake Road, BOWNESS-ON-WINDERMERE LA23 3BJ
Tel: 015394 88855
• website: www.lakelovers.co.uk

Hotel

The Borrowdale Gates Hotel, GRANGE-IN-BORROWDALE, Keswick, Cumbria CA12 5UQ
Tel: 017687 77204
• e-mail: hotel@borrowdale-gates.com
• website: www.borrowdale-gates.com

Self-Catering

3 Randle Howe, Eskdale, HOLMROOK.
Contact: Susan Wedley, Long Hocking How, Eskdale Green, Holmrook CA19 1UA
Tel: 01946 723126
• e-mail jswedley@btinternet.com
• www.randlehow.co.uk

Self-Catering

Mrs Almond, Irton House Farm, Isel, Near
KESWICK, Cumbria CA13 9ST
Tel: 017687 76380
* e-mail: joan@irtonhousefarm.co.uk
* website: www.irtonhousefarm.com

Self-Catering

Mr D Williamson, Derwent Water Marina,
Portinscale, KESWICK, Cumbria CA12 5RF
Tel: 017687 72912
* e-mail: info@derwentwatermarina.co.uk
* website: www.derwentwatermarina.co.uk

Inn

Horse and Farrier Inn, Threlkeld, KESWICK,
Cumbria CA12 4SQ
Tel: 017687 79688
* e-mail: info@horseandfarrier.com
* website: www.horseandfarrier.com

Self-Catering

Mrs S.J. Bottom, Crossfield Cottages,
KIRKOSWALD, Penrith, Cumbria CA10 1EU
Tel: 01768 898711
* e-mail: info@crossfieldcottages.co.uk
* website: www.crossfieldcottages.co.uk

•DERBYSHIRE

Self-Catering Holiday Cottages

Mark Redfern, Paddock House Farm Holiday
Cottages, Peak District National Park,
Alstonefield, ASHBOURNE, Derbyshire
DE6 2FT
Tel: 01335 310282 / 07977 569618
* e-mail: info@paddockhousefarm.co.uk
* website: www.paddockhousefarm.co.uk

Caravan

Golden Valley Caravan Park, Coach Road,
RIPLEY, Derbyshire DE55 4ES
Tel: 01773 513881
* e-mail:
enquiries@goldenvalleycaravanpark.co.uk
* website: www.goldenvalleycaravanpark.co.uk

•DEVON

Hotel

Fairwater Head Hotel, Hawkchurch, Near
AXMINSTER, Devon EX13 5TX
Tel: 01297 678349
* e-mail: info@fairwaterheadhotel.co.uk
* website: www.fairwaterheadhotel.co.uk

Farm B & B

Mrs J Ley, West Barton, Alverdiscott, Near
BARNSTABLE, Devon EX31 3PT
Tel: 01271 858230
* e-mail: ela@andrews78.freeserve.co.uk

Self-Catering / B&B

Lake House Cottages and B&B, Lake
Villa, BRADWORTHY, Devon EX22 7SQ
Tel : 01409 241962
* email: lesley@lakevilla.co.uk
* website: www.lakevilla.co.uk

Guest House

Woodlands Guest House, Parkham Road,
BRIXHAM, South Devon TQ5 9BU
Tel: 01803 852040
* e-mail: woodlandsbrixham@btinternet.com
* website: www.woodlandsbrixham.co.uk

Self-Catering

Linda & Jim Watt, Northcote Manor
Farm Holiday Cottages, Kentisbury,
COMBE MARTIN, Devon EX31 4NB
Tel: 01271 882376
* e-mail: info@northcotemanorfarm.co.uk
* website: www.northcotemanorfarm.co.uk

Self-Catering

G Davidson Richmond, Clooneavin,
Clooneavin Path, LYNMOUTH, Devon
EX35 6EE
Tel: 01598 753334
* e-mail: relax@clooneavinholidays.co.uk
* website: www.clooneavinholidays.co.uk

B & B

Merritt House, 7 Queens Road,
PAIGNTON, Devon TQ4 6AT
* e-mail: bookings@merritthouse.co.uk
* website: www.merritthouse.co.uk

Visit the FHG website
www.holidayguides.com
for all kinds of holiday accommodation in Britain

Guest House
A J Hill, Beaumont, Castle Hill, SEATON,
Devon EX12 2QW
Tel: 01297 20832
• e-mail: tony@lymebay.demon.co.uk
• website:
www.smoothhound.co.uk/hotels/beaumon1.html

Caravans / Camping
Salcombe Regis Camping & Caravan
Park, SIDMOUTH, Devon EX10 0JH
Tel: 01395 514303
• e-mail: contact@salcombe-regis.co.uk
• website: www.salcombe-regis.co.uk

Self-Catering / Camping
Dartmoor Country Holidays, Magpie Leisure
Park, Bedford Bridge, Horrabridge,
Yelverton, TAVISTOCK, Devon PL20 7RY
Tel: 01822 852651
• website: www.dartmoorcountryholidays.co.uk

Caravan / Camping Park
Harford Bridge Holiday Park, Peter Tavy,
TAVISTOCK, Devon PL19 9LS
Tel: 01822 810349
• email: enquiry@harfordbridge.co.uk
• website: www.harfordbridge.co.uk

Holiday Park
Langstone Manor Holiday Park,
Moortown, TAVISTOCK,
Devon PL19 9JZ
Tel: 01822 613371
• e-mail: web@langstonemanor.co.uk
• website: www.langstonemanor.co.uk

B&B
Sampford Manor, Sampford Spiney,
Yelverton, TAVISTOCK, Devon PL20 6LH
Tel: 01822 853442
• e-mail:
manor@sampford-spiney.fsnet.co.uk
• website:
www.sampford-spiney.fsnet.co.uk

Caravan & Camping
North Morte Farm Caravan & Camping Park,
Mortehoe, WOOLACOMBE, Devon EX34 7EG
Tel: 01271 870381
• e-mail: info@northmortefarm.co.uk
• website: www.northmortefarm.co.uk

Holiday Park
Woolacombe Bay Holiday Parks,
WOOLACOMBE, Devon
Tel: 0844 770 0384
• website: www.woolacombe.com

•DORSET

Self-Catering
Bournemouth Holiday Apartments, 15
Florence Road, BOURNEMOUTH, Dorset
BH5 1HF
Tel: 01202 304925
• e-mail: mikelyn_lambert@btinternet.com
• website: www.selfcateringbournemouth.co.uk

Guest House
Southbourne Grove Hotel, 96 Southbourne
Road, BOURNEMOUTH, Dorset BH6 3QQ
Tel: 01202 420503
• e-mail: neil@pack1462.freeserve.co.uk
• website: www.southbournegrovehotel.co.uk

Self-Catering
C. Hammond, Stourcliffe Court, 56
Stourcliffe Avenue, Southbourne,
BOURNEMOUTH, Dorset BH6 3PX
Tel: 01202 420698
• e-mail: rjhammond1@hotmail.co.uk
• website: www.stourcliffecourt.co.uk

Self-Catering Cottage / Farmhouse B & B
Mrs S. E. Norman, Frogmore Farm,
Chideock, BRIDPORT, Dorset DT6 6HT
Tel: 01308 456159
• e-mail: bookings@frogmorefarm.com
• website: www.frogmorefarm.com

B&B
Nethercroft, Winterbourne Abbas,
DORCHESTER, Dorset DT2 9LU
Tel: 01305 889337
• e-mail: val.bradbeer@btconnect.com
• website: www.nethercroft.com

Self-Catering
Josephine Pearse, Tamarisk Farm Cottages,
Beach Road, West Bexington,
DORCHESTER, Dorset DT2 9DF
Tel: 01308 897784
• e-mail: holidays@tamariskfarm.com
• website: www.tamariskfarm.com/holidays

Farmhouse B&B / Caravan & Camping
Luckford Wood Farmhouse, Church
Lane, East Stoke, Wareham, Near
LULWORTH, Dorset BH20 6AW
Tel: 01929 463098 / 07737 742615
• e-mail: luckfordleisure@hotmail.co.uk
• website: www.luckfordleisure.co.uk

Self-Catering
Westover Farm Cottages, Wootton Fitzpaine,
Near LYME REGIS, Dorset DT6 6NE
Tel: 01297 560451/561395
• e-mail: wfcottages@aol.com
• website: www.westoverfarmcottages.co.uk

Hotel
The Knoll House, STUDLAND BAY,
Dorset BH19 3AW
Tel: 01929 450450
* e-mail: **info@knollhouse.co.uk**
* website: **www.knollhouse.co.uk**

Hotel
Manor House Hotel, STUDLAND, Dorset
BH19 3AU
Tel: 01929 450288
* e-mail: **info@themanorhousehotel.com**
* website: **www.themanorhousehotel.com**

Inn B&B
The White Swan, The Square, 31 High
Street, SWANAGE BN19 2LJ
Tel: 01929 423804
* e-mail: **info@whiteswanswanage.co.uk**
* website: **www.whiteswanswanage.co.uk**

•GLOUCESTERSHIRE

Self-Catering
Two Springbank, 37 Hopton Road, Cam,
DURSLEY, Gloucs GL11 5PD
Contact: Mrs F A Jones, 32 Everlands, Cam,
Dursley, Gloucs G11 5NL
Tel: 01453 543047
* e-mail: **info@twospringbank.co.uk**
* website: **www.twospringbank.co.uk**

B & B
Mrs A Rhoton, Hyde Crest, Cirencester Road,
Minchinhampton, STROUD, Gloucs GL6 8PE
Tel: 01453 731631
* e-mail: **stay@hydecrest.co.uk**
* website: **www.hydecrest.co.uk**

•HAMPSHIRE

Holiday Park
Downton Holiday Park, Shorefield Road,
Milford-on-Sea, LYMINGTON, Hampshire
SO41 0LH
Tel: 01425 476131 / 01590 642515
* e-mail: **info@downtonholidaypark.co.uk**
* website: **www.downtonholidaypark.co.uk**

•KENT

Self-Catering
Cottage Farm Self-Catering
Accommodation, Cackets Lane, Cudham,
Near SEVENOAKS, Kent TN14 7QG
Tel: 01959 534048
* e-mail: **cottagefarmaccommodation@googlemail.com**
* website: **www.cottagefarmgardens.com**

•LANCASHIRE

Guest House
Parr Hall Farm, Parr Lane, Eccleston,
Chorley, PRESTON, Lancs PR7 5SL
Tel: 01257 451917
* e-mail: **enquiries@parrhallfarm.com**
* website: **www.parrhallfarm.com**

•LINCOLNSHIRE

Self-Catering
Grange Farm Cottages, Waltham Road,
BARNOLDBY-LE-BECK, N.E. Lincolnshire
DN37 0AR
Tel: 01472 822216
* e-mail: **sueuk4000@netscape.net**
* website: **www.grangefarmcottages.com**

Self-catering
Paul & Flora Bennett, Brackenborough
Hall Coach House Holidays, LOUTH,
Lincolnshire LN11 0NS
Tel: 01507 603193
* e-mail:
paulandflora@brackenboroughhall.com
* website: **www.brackenboroughhall.com**

•NORFOLK

Holiday Park
Castaways Holiday Park, Paston Road,
BACTON-ON-SEA, Norfolk NR12 0JB
Tel : 01692 650436
* e-mail: **info@castawaysholidaypark.net**
* website: **www.castawaysholidaypark.net**

Self-catering
Scarning Dale, Dale Road, Scarning,
DEREHAM, Norfolk NR19 2QN
Tel: 01362 687269
* e-mail: **jean@scarningdale.co.uk**
* website: **www.scarningdale.co.uk**

Holiday Park
Waveney Valley Holiday Park, Airstation
Lane, Rushall, DISS, Norfolk IP21 4QF
Tel: 01379 741228
* e-mail: **waveneyvalleyhp@aol.com**
* website: **www.caravanparksnorfolk.co.uk**

Self-Catering
Blue Riband Holidays, HEMSBY,
Great Yarmouth, Norfolk NR29 4HA
Tel: 01493 730445
* website: **www.BlueRibandHolidays.co.uk**

Self-Catering
Winterton Valley Holidays, Edward Road,
WINTERTON-ON-SEA, Norfolk NR29 4BX
Contact:15 Kingston Avenue, Caister-on-
Sea, Norfolk NR30 5ET
Tel: 01493 377175
• e-mail: info@wintertonvalleyholidays.co.uk
• website: www.wintertonvalleyholidays.co.uk

•NORTHUMBERLAND

Self-Catering
Bank House Holiday Cottages,
GUYZANCE, Northumberland NE65 9AP
Tel: 07957 100615
• e-mail:
info@bankhouseholidaycottages.co.uk
• website:
www.bankhouseholidaycottages.co.uk

•NOTTINGHAMSHIRE

Caravan & Camping Park
Orchard Park, Marnham Road, Tuxford,
NEWARK, Nottinghamshire NG22 0PY
Tel: 01777 870228
• e-mail: info@orchardcaravanpark.co.uk
• website: www.orchardcaravanpark.co.uk

•OXFORDSHIRE

B&B
Middle Fell, Moreton Road, Aston Upthorpe,
DIDCOT, Oxfordshire OX11 9ER
Tel: 01235 850207
• e-mail: middlefell@ic24.net
• website: www.middlefell.co.uk

B & B / Guest House
June Collier, Colliers, 55 Nethercote Road,
Tackley, KIDLINGTON, Oxfordshire OX5 3AT
Tel: 01869 331255 / 07790 338225
• e-mail: junecollier@btinternet.com
• website: www.colliersbnb.co.uk

Guest House
The Bungalow, Cherwell Farm, Mill
Lane, Old Mawston, OXFORD OX3 0QF
Tel: 01865 557171
• e-mail: ros.bungalowbb@btinternet.com
• website:
www.cherwellfarm-oxford-accom.co.uk

•SHROPSHIRE

Hotel
Longmynd Hotel, Cunnery Rd, CHURCH
STRETTON, Shropshire SY6 6AG
Tel: 01694 722244
• e-mail: info@longmynd.co.uk
• website: www.longmynd.co.uk

Self-Catering
Clive & Cynthia Prior, Mocktree Barns
Holiday Cottages, Leintwardine, LUDLOW,
Shropshire SY7 0LY
Tel: 01547 540441
• e-mail: mocktreebarns@care4free.net
• website: www.mocktreeholidays.co.uk

Self-Catering
Jane Cronin, Sutton Court Farm Cottages,
Sutton Court Farm, Little Sutton, LUDLOW,
Shropshire SY8 2AJ
Tel: 01584 861305
• e-mail: enquiries@suttoncourtfarm.co.uk
• website: www.suttoncourtfarm.co.uk

•SOMERSET

Farm / Guest House / Self-Catering
Jackie Bishop, Toghill House Farm, Freezing
Hill, Wick, Near BATH, Somerset BS30 5RT
Tel: 01225 891261
• e-mail:
accommodation@toghillhousefarm.co.uk
• website: www.toghillhousefarm.co.uk

Self-Catering
Westward Rise Holiday Park, South Road,
BREAN, Burnham-on-Sea, Somerset TA8 2RD
Tel: 01278 751310
• e-mail: info@westwardrise.com
• website: www.westwardrise.com

Self-Catering / Holiday Park / Touring Pitches
Mary Randle, St Audries Bay Holiday Club,
West Quantoxhead, MINEHEAD, Somerset
TA4 4DY
Tel: 01984 632515
• e-mail: info@staudriesbay.co.uk
• website: www.staudriesbay.co.uk

B & B
The Old Mill, Netherclay, Bishop's Hull,
TAUNTON, Somerset TA1 5AB
Tel: 01823 289732
• website: www.theoldmillbandb.co.uk /
www.bandbtaunton.co.uk

Farm / Guest House

G. Clark, Yew Tree Farm, THEALE,
Near Wedmore, Somerset BS28 4SN
Tel: 01934 712475
* e-mail: enquiries@yewtreefarmbandb.co.uk
* website: www.yewtreefarmbandb.co.uk

B & B

Mrs S Crane, Birdwood House, Bath Road,
WELLS, Somerset BA5 3EW
Tel: 01749 679250
* e-mail: info@birdwood-bandb.co.uk
* website: www.birdwood-bandb.co.uk

•STAFFORDSHIRE

Self-Catering

T.A. Mycock, Rosewood Cottage, Lower
Berkhamsytch, Bottom House, Near LEEK,
Staffordshire ST13 7QP
Tel: 01538 308213
* website: www.rosewoodcottage.co.uk

•SUFFOLK

Self-Catering

Kessingland Cottages, Rider Haggard Lane,
KESSINGLAND, Suffolk.
Contact: S. Mahmood, 156 Bromley Road,
Beckenham, Kent BR3 6PG
Tel: 020 8650 0539
* e-mail: jeeptrek@kjti.co.uk
* website: www.k-cottage.co.uk

Holiday Park

Broadland Holiday Village, Oulton
Broad, LOWESTOFT, Suffolk NR33 9JY
Tel: 01502 573033
* e-mail: info@broadlandvillage.co.uk
* website: www.broadlandvillage.co.uk

•EAST SUSSEX

Hotel

Grand Hotel, 1 Grand Parade, St Leonards,
HASTINGS, East Sussex TN37 6AQ
Tel: 01424 428510
* e-mail: info@grandhotelhastings.co.uk
* website: www.grandhotelhastings.co.uk

Self-Catering

"Pekes", CHIDDINGLY, East Sussex
Contact: Eva Morris, 124 Elm Park
Mansions, Park Walk, London SW10 0AR
Tel: 020 7352 8088
* e-mail: pekes.afa@virgin.net
* website: www.pekesmanor.com

Guest House / Self-Catering

Longleys Farm Cottage, Harebeating Lane,
HAILSHAM, East Sussex BN27 1ER
Tel: 01323 841227
* website: www.longleysfarmcottage.co.uk

• WEST SUSSEX

Guest Accommodation

St Andrews Lodge, Chichester Road,
SELSEY, West Sussex PO20 0LX
Tel: 01243 606899
* e-mail: info@standrewslodge.co.uk
* website: www.standrewslodge.co.uk

•WARWICKSHIRE

Guest House

John & Julia Downie, Holly Tree
Cottage, Pathlow, STRATFORD-UPON-
AVON, Warwickshire CV37 0ES
Tel: 01789 204461
* e-mail: john@hollytree-cottage.co.uk
* website: www.hollytree-cottage.co.uk

•NORTH YORKSHIRE

Self-Catering

Rudding Holiday Park, Follifoot,
HARROGATE, North Yorkshire HG3 1JH
Tel: 01423 870439
* e-mail: stay@ruddingpark.com
* website: www.ruddingholidaypark.co.uk

Self-Catering

Southfield Farm Holiday Cottages,
Darley, HARROGATE, North Yorkshire
HG3 2PR
Tel: 01423 780258
* e-mail: info@southfieldcottages.co.uk
* website: www.southfieldcottages.co.uk

Farmhouse B & B

Mrs Julie Clarke, Middle Farm, Woodale,
Coverdale, LEYBURN, North Yorkshire
DL8 4TY • Tel: 01969 640271
* e-mail: j-a-clarke@hotmail.co.uk
* www.yorkshirenet.co.uk/stayat/middlefarm/
index.htm

Self-Catering

East Farm Country Cottages, SCALBY
NABS, Scarborough, N.Yorkshire
YO13 0SL
Tel: 01723 353635
* e-mail: joeastfarmcottages@hotmail.co.uk
* www.eastfarmcountrycottages.co.uk

Guest House / Self-Catering
Sue & Tony Hewitt, Harmony Country Lodge,
80 Limestone Road, Burniston,
SCARBOROUGH, North Yorkshire YO13 0DG
Tel: 01723 870276
• e-mail: mail@harmonylodge.net
• website: www.harmonycountrylodge.co.uk

Self-Catering
2 Hollies Cottages, Stainforth, SETTLE,
N.Yorkshire
Contact : Bridge Cottage, Stainforth,
Near Settle BD24 9PG
Tel: 01729 822649
• e-mail: vivmills30@hotmail.com
• website: www.stainforth-holiday-cottage-settle.co.uk

B & B
Beck Hall, Cove Road, Malham,
SKIPTON, N.Yorkshire BD23 4DL
Tel: 01729 830332
• e-mail: alice@beckhallmalham.com
• website: www.beckhallmalham.com

Hotel
The Coniston Hotel, Coniston Cold,
SKIPTON, North Yorkshire BD23 4EA
Tel: 01756 748080
• e-mail: info@theconistonhotel.com
• website: www.theconistonhotel.com

Self-Catering
York Lakeside Lodges Ltd, Moor Lane,
YORK, North Yorkshire YO24 2QU
Tel: 01904 702346
• e-mail: neil@yorklakesidelodges.co.uk
• website: www.yorklakesidelodges.co.uk

WALES

•ANGLESEY & GWYNEDD

Self-Catering
Crugeran Farm Holidays, ABERSOCH
Contact : Mrs R Parry, Crugeran, Sarn
Mellteyrn, Pwllheli, Gwynedd LL53 8DT
Tel: 01758 730375
• e-mail: post@crugeran.com
• website: www.crugeran.com

Self-Catering / Caravan & Camping Park
Bryn Gloch Caravan and Camping Park,
Betws Garmon, CAERNARFON, Gwynedd
LL54 7YY Tel: 01286 650216
• e-mail: eurig@bryngloch.co.uk
• website: www.campwales.co.uk

Self-Catering Chalet
Chalet at Glan Gwna Holiday Park, Caethro,
CAERNARFON, Gwynedd
Contact: Mr H A Jones, Menai Bridge,
Caernarfon, Gwynedd LL59 5LN
Tel: 01248 712045
• e-mail: hajones@northwales-chalet.co.uk
• website: www.northwales-chalet.co.uk

Motel
The Beach Motel, Lon St Ffraid,
Trearddur Bay, HOLYHEAD, Anglesey
LL65 2YT
• e-mail: info@thebeachmotel.co.uk
• website: www.thebeachmotel.co.uk

Guest House
Cefn Uchaf Farm Guesthouse,
Garndolbenmaen, PORTHMADOG
LL51 9PJ Tel: 01766 530239
• e-mail: enquiries@cefnuchaf.co.uk
• website: www.cefnuchaf.com

Self-Catering
Parc Wernol, Chwilog Fawr, Chwilog,
PWLLHELI, Criccieth, Gwynedd LL53 6SW
Tel: 01766 810506
• e-mail: catherine@wernol.co.uk
• website: www.wernol.co.uk

•NORTH WALES

Self-Catering
Bron-Y-Wendon & Nant-Y-Glyn Holiday
Parks, Wern Road,Llanddulas, COLWYN
BAY, North Wales LL22 8HG
Tel: 01492 512903/512282
• e-mail: stay@northwales-holidays.co.uk
• website: www.northwales-holidays.co.uk

• PEMBROKESHIRE

Self-Catering
Llanteglos Estate, Llanteg, Near
AMROTH, Pembs SA67 8PU
• e-mail: llanteglosestate@supanet.com
• website: www.llanteglos-estate.com

Self-Catering
Timberhill Farm, BROAD HAVEN,
Pembrokeshire SA62 3LZ
Contact: Mrs L Ashton, 10 St Leonards
Road, Thames Ditton, Surrey KT7 0RJ
Tel: 02083 986349
• e-mail: lejash@aol.com
• website: www.33timberhill.com

Self-Catering
Quality Cottages, Cerbid, Solva,
HAVERFORDWEST, Pembrokeshire SA62 6YE
Tel: 01348 837871
• e-mail: reserve@qualitycottages.co.uk
• website: www.qualitycottages.co.uk

Golf Club / Resort
Newport Links Golf Club & Resort,
NEWPORT, Pembrokeshire SA42 0NR
Tel: 012239 820244
• e-mail: newportgc@lineone.net
• website: www.newportlinks.co.uk

Self-Catering
Ffynnon Ddofn, Llanon, Llanrhian, Near ST
DAVIDS, Pembrokeshire.
Contact: Mrs B. Rees White, Brick House
Farm, Burnham Road, Woodham Mortimer,
Maldon, Essex CM9 6SR. Tel: 01245 224611
• e-mail: daisypops@madasafish.com
• website: www.ffynnonddofn.co.uk

• POWYS

Self-Catering
Old Stables Cottage & Old Dairy, Lane Farm,
Paincastle, Builth Wells, HAY-ON-WYE,
Powys LD2 3JS
Tel: 01497 851 605
• e-mail: lanefarm@onetel.com
• website: www.lane-farm.co.uk

• SOUTH WALES

Campsite
Mr G. Watkins, Wernddu Caravan Park, Old
Ross Road, ABERGAVENNY,
Monmouthshire NP7 8NG
Tel:01873 856223
• e-mail: info@wernddu-golf-club.co.uk
• website: www.wernddu-golf-club.co.uk

SCOTLAND

• ANGUS & DUNDEE

Golf Club
Edzell Golf Club, High Street, EDZELL,
Brechin, Angus DD9 7TF
Tel: 01356 648462
• e-mail: secretary@edzellgolfclub.com
• website: www.edzellgolfclub.com

• ARGYLL & BUTE

Self-Catering
Appin House Lodges, APPIN, Argyll
PA38 4BN
Tel: 01631 730207
• e-mail: denys@appinhouse.co.uk
• website: www.appinhouse.co.uk

Self-Catering
Blarghour Farm Cottages, Blarghour Farm,
By Dalmally, INVERARAY, Argyll PA33 1BW
Tel: 01866 833246
• e-mail: blarghour@btconnect.com
• website: www.self-catering-argyll.co.uk

Self-Catering
Prospect House S/C Apartments & House,
ROTHESAY
Contact: Mrs A. Shaw, 21 Battery Place,
Rothesay, Isle of Bute PA20 9DU
Tel: 01700 503526
• e-mail: janmckirdy@aol.com
• website: www.prospecthouse-bute.co.uk

Hotel
Falls of Lora Hotel, Connel Ferry, By OBAN,
Argyll PA37 1PB
Tel: 01631 710483
• e-mail: enquiries@fallsoflora.com
• website: www.fallsoflora.com

• BORDERS

B & B
Hundalee House, JEDBURGH,
Roxburghshire TD8 6PA
Tel: 01835 863011
• e-mail: sheila.whittaker@btinternet.com
www.accommodation-scotland.org

B & B
The Garden House, Whitmuir, SELKIRK,
Borders TD7 4PZ
Tel: 01750 721728
* e-mail: whitmuir@btconnect.com
* website: www.whitmuirfarm.co.uk

• DUMFRIES & GALLOWAY

Self-Catering
Barend Holiday Village, Barend Farmhouse,
SANDYHILLS, Dalbeattie, Dumfries &
Galloway DG5 4NU
Tel: 01387 780663
* e-mail: info@barendholidayvillage.co.uk
* website: www.barendholidayvillage.co.uk

Self-Catering
Ae Farm Cottages, Gubhill Farm, Ae,
DUMFRIES, Dumfriesshire DG1 1RL
Tel: 01387 860648
* e-mail: gill@gubhill.co.uk
* website: www.aefarmcottages.co.uk

Self-Catering
Rusko Holidays, GATEHOUSE OF FLEET,
Castle Douglas, Dumfriesshire DG7 2BS
Tel: 01557 814215
* e-mail: info@ruskoholidays.co.uk
* website: www.ruskoholidays.co.uk

Hotel
Corsewall Lighthouse Hotel, Kirkcolm,
STRANRAER, Dumfries & Galloway
DG9 0QG Tel: 01776 853220
* e-mail info@lighthousehotel.co.uk
* website: www.lighthousehotel.co.uk

• EDINBURGH & LOTHIANS

Self-Catering
Mrs C. M. Kilpatrick, Slipperfield House,
WEST LINTON, Peeblesshire EH46 7AA
Tel: 01968 660401
* e-mail: cottages@slipperfield.com
* website: www.slipperfield.com

• FIFE

Guest House
The Spindrift Guest House, Pittenweem
Road, ANSTRUTHER, Fife KY10 3DT
Tel: 01333 310573
* e-mail: info@thespindrift.co.uk
* website: www.thespindrift.co.uk

• HIGHLANDS

Self-Catering
Frank & Juliet Spencer-Nairn, Culligran
Cottages, Struy, Near BEAULY, Inverness-
shire IV4 7JX . Tel: 01463 761285
* e-mail: info@culligrancottages.co.uk
* website: www.culligrancottages.co.uk

Hotel
The Clan MacDuff Hotel, Achintore Road,
FORT WILLIAM, Inverness-shire PH33 6RW
Tel: 01397 702341
* e-mail: reception@clanmacduff.co.uk
* website: www.clanmacduff.co.uk

Caravan Park
A.J.Davis, Gruinard Bay Caravan Park,
LAIDE, Ross-shire IV22 2ND
Tel: 01445 731225
* e-mail: gruinard@ecosse.net
* website: www.gruinard.scotshost.co.uk

Hotel
Whitebridge Hotel, Whitebridge, LOCH
NESS, Inverness-shire IV2 6UN
Tel: 01456 486226
* e-mail: info@whitebridgehotel.co.uk
* website: www.whitebridgehotel.co.uk

B & B / Self-Catering
Mondhuie Chalets & B&B, NETHY
BRIDGE, Inverness-shire PH25 3DF
Tel: 01479 821062
* e-mail: david@mondhuie.com
* website: www.mondhuie.com

B & B
Bruach Ard, POOLEWE
Tel: 01445 781765
* e-mail: dgeorge@globalnet.co.uk
* website: www.davidgeorge.co.uk

Self Catering
Broomview & Sunset Cottages, Rhiroy,
Lochbroom, By Garve, ULLAPOOL IV23 2QR
Contact: Mrs L Renwick, Spindrift, Keppoch
Farm, Dundonnell, Ross-shire IV23 2QR
Tel: 01854 633269
* e-mail: linda@lochbroomcottages.co.uk
* website: www.lochbroomcottages.co.uk

• LANARKSHIRE

Self-Catering
Carmichael Country Cottages, By BIGGAR,
Lanarkshire ML12 6PG
Tel: 01899 308336
* e-mail: information@carmichael.co.uk
* website: www.carmichael.co.uk

•PERTH & KINROSS

Self-Catering
Laighwood Holidays, Laighwood,
DUNKELD, Perthshire PH8 0HB
Tel: 01350 724241
• e-mail: holidays@laighwood.co.uk
• website: www.laighwood.co.uk

Self-Catering
Atholl Cottage, Killiecrankie, PITLOCHRY,
Perthshire PH16 5LR
Contact: Mrs Joan Troup, Dalnasgadh,
Killiecrankie, Pitlochry, Perthshire PH16 5LN
Tel: 01796 470017
• e-mail: info@athollcottage.co.uk
• website: www.athollcottage.co.uk

•ORKNEY

Caravan & Camping
Point of Ness, STROMNESS, Orkney
Tel: 01856 873535
• e-mail: recreation@orkney.gov.uk
• website: www.orkney.gov.uk

NORTHERN IRELAND

Caravan Park
Six Mile Water Carvan Park, Lough
Road, ANTRIM BT41 4DG
Tel: 028 9446 4963
• e-mail: sixmilewater@antrim.gov.uk
• website: www.antrim.gov.uk/caravanpark

**Please mention this
FHG Guide when enquiring about
accommodation
featured in these pages**

INTERNET & Wi-Fi Access

ZONE

All the properties below provide Internet or WiFi access for their visitors.

•CORNWALL

PORT ISAAC • *Self-catering*

The Garden House. Contact Mr D. Oldham, Trevella, Treveighan, Bodmin PL30 3JN
Tel: 01208 850529
e-mail: david.trevella@btconnect.com
website: www.trevellacornwall.co.uk

Wi-Fi internet access up to 4MB. Broadband powerline networking. Available in lounge/dining room. Free.

•CUMBRIA

CARLISLE • *Guest House*

Cornerways Guest House, 107 Warwick Road, Carlisle CA1 1EA
Tel: 01228 521733
e-mail: info@cornerwaysbandb.co.uk
website: www.cornerwaysbandb.co.uk

Wi Fi available in all bedrooms and public areas, free of charge. Broadband (high speed). Secure network.

KESWICK • *Self-catering Cottages*

Irton House Farm, Isel, Cockermouth CA13 9ST
Tel: 017687 76380
e-mail: joan@irtonhousefarm.co.uk
website: www.irtonhousefarm.com

Wi Fi available.

•DERBYSHIRE

ASHBOURNE • *Self-catering*

Paddock House Farm Holiday Cottages, Alstonefield, Ashbourne DE6 2FT
Tel: 01335 310282
e-mail: info@paddockhousefarm.co.uk
website: www.paddockhousefarm.co.uk

Wi Fi available.

•DORSET

BOURNEMOUTH • *Self-catering*

Bournemouth Holiday Apartments, 6 Forest Edge Drive, Bournemouth BH5 1HF
Tel: 01202 304925
e-mail: mikelyn-lambert@btinternet.com.
website: www.selfcateringbournemouth.co.uk

Wi-Fi access points on all floors throughout.

MIDDLEMARSH/SHERBORNE • *Self-catering*

White Horse Farm, Middle Marsh, Sherborne DT9 5QN
Tel: 01963 210222
e-mail: enquiries@whitehorsefarm.co.uk
website: www.whitehorsefarm.co.uk

Wi-Fi access in all properties.

•LINCOLNSHIRE

BARNOLDBY-LE-BECK • *Self-catering*

Grange Farm Holiday Cottages, Waltham Road, Barnoldby-le-Beck DN37 0AR
Tel: 01472 822216.
e-mail: sueuk4000@netscape-net
website: www.grangefarmcottages.com

Wi-Fi connection available in every room. £10 per stay.

•NORTHUMBERLAND

HEXHAM • *B&B*

Coach House B&B, South View/Tavern House, Bardon Mill, Hexham NE47 7HZ
Tel: 01434 344779
e-mail: mail@bardonmillcoachhouse.co.uk
website: www.bardonmillcoachhouse.co.uk

Free Wi-Fi available at breakfast time in the dining room; computer available for guests' use.

Please mention this FHG Guide when enquiring about accommodation featured in these pages

•OXFORDSHIRE

DIDCOT • *B&B*

Middle Fell B&B, Moreton Road, Aston
Upthorpe, Didcot OX11 9ER
Tel: 01235 850207 or 07833 920678
e-mail: middlefell@ic24.net
website: www.middlefell.co.uk
Wi-Fi connection in every room free of charge.

•SOMERSET

BATH • *B&B*

Marlborough House, Marlborough Lane,
Bath BA1 2NQ
Tel: 01225 318175
www.marlborough-house.net

*Wi-Fi internet access available in all bedrooms,
free of charge.*

EXMOOR • *Self-catering*

West Hollowcombe Self-Catering Cottages,
Hawkridge, Near Dulverton TA22 9QL
Tel: 01398 341 400
e-mail: info@westhollowcombe.co.uk
website: www.westhollowcombe.co.uk.

*Internet access via BT Broadband Open Zone.
Normally available within each cottage, but
depends on atmospheric conditions. A
separate room for communal use provides
guaranteed availability at no charge.*

NORTH PERROTT • *Self-catering*

Wood Dairy, Wood Lane, North Perrott TA18
7TA   Tel: 01935 891532
e-mail: liz@acountryretreat.co.uk
website: www.acountryretreat.co.uk
*Wi-Fi connection at no charge (please bring own
laptop).*

•EAST SUSSEX

RYE • *Hotel*

Rye Lodge Hotel, Hilders Cliff, Rye TN31 7LD
Tel: 01797 223838
e-mail: info@ryelodge.co.uk.
website: www.ryelodge.co.uk

Wi-Fi available in all rooms free of charge.

•NORTH YORKSHIRE

SKIPTON • *Self-catering*

Holiday Cottages (Yorkshire) Ltd, Water
Street, Skipton BD23 1PB Tel: 01756 700510
e-mail: info@holidaycotts.co.uk.
website: www.holidaycotts.co.uk

*Several cottages have Wi-Fi connection
(search facility on website). Mostly free, but
some may charge extra.*

HELMSLEY • *Self-catering*

Valley View Farm, Old Byland, Helmsley,
York YO62 5LG
Tel: 01439 798221
e-mail: sally@valleyviewfarm.com
website: www.valleyviewfarm.com

Wi-Fi connection in all cottages, free of charge.

•ARGYLL & BUTE

ISLE OF SEIL • *Self-catering*

Kilbride Croft, Balvicar, Isle of Seil PA34 4RD
Tel: 01852 300475.
e-mail: kilbridecroft@aol.com
website: www.kilbridecroft.co.uk
Wi-Fi available in Croft Cottage.

•HIGHLANDS

KINCRAIG • *Self-catering*

Alvie Holiday Cottages, Kincraig, Kingussie
PH21 1NE
Tel: 01540 651255.
e-mail: info@alvie-estate.co.uk.
website: www.alvie-estate.co.uk.

BT Wi-Fi router in holiday properties. Free of charge.

•PERTH & KINROSS

PERTH • *Self-catering*

Cloag Farm Cottages, Methven, Perth PH1
3RR
Tel: 01738 840239
e-mail: info@cloagfarm.co.uk
website: www.cloagfarm.co.uk
Wireless broadband available.

www.holidayguides.com

Typeset by FHG Guides Ltd, Paisley.
Printed and bound in China by Imago.

Distribution. Book Trade: ORCA Book Services, Stanley House,
3 Fleets Lane, Poole, Dorset BH15 3AJ
(Tel: 01202 665432; Fax: 01202 666219)
e-mail: mail@orcabookservices.co.uk
Published by FHG Guides Ltd., Abbey Mill Business Centre,
Seedhill, Paisley PA1 ITJ (Tel: 0141-887 0428 Fax: 0141-889 7204).
e-mail: admin@fhguides.co.uk

800 Great Places to Stay in Britain is published by FHG Guides Ltd,
part of Kuperard Group.

Cover design: FHG Guides
Cover Picture: with thanks to
Cutkive Wood Holiday Lodges, St Ive, Liskeard, Cornwall PL14 3ND (see p219)
The Long Cross Hotel & Victorian Gardens, Port Isaac, Cornwall PL29 3TF (see p16)

symbols 🐕 🎠 SB ♿ 🍷 Wi-Fi

🐕	*Pets Welcome*	🎠	*Children Welcome*
SB	*Short Breaks*	♿	*Suitable for Disabled Guests*
🍷	*Licensed*	**Wi-Fi**	*Wi-Fi available*